H·O·M·E
VIDEO
MAKER'S
H·A·N·D·B·O·O·K
ROLAND LEWIS

The

H·O·M·E
VIDEO
MAKER'S
H·A·N·D·B·O·O·K

ROLAND LEWIS

CROWN PUBLISHERS, INC.
New York

A Marshall Edition
The Home Video Maker's Handbook
was conceived, edited and designed by
Marshall Editions Limited
170 Piccadilly
London W1V 9DD

Published in the United States in 1987
by Crown Publishers, Inc.
225 Park Avenue South
New York, New York 10003

**Library of Congress
Cataloging-in-Publication Data**
Lewis, Roland.
    The home video maker's handbook.

    1. Video tape recorders and recording—
Amateurs' manuals.   I. Title.
TK9961.L49   1987   621.388'332   87–15558
ISBN 0–517–56642–7

EDITOR	Carole Devaney
ART EDITOR	Peter Bridgewater
PICTURE EDITOR	Zilda Tandy
MANAGING EDITOR	Ruth Binney
ART DIRECTOR	John Bigg
ASSISTANT EDITOR	Anne Kilborn
ILLUSTRATIONS	Rob Shone
	Annie Ellis
	Ivan Hissey
	Steve Wheele
PRODUCTION	Janice Storr

We would like to thank the following
for their valuable assistance in the
making of this book:

John Creedy
Researcher and text contributor.
Eugene Trundle
Technical contributor.
Barry Fox
Technical consultant.

We would also like to thank all the film
makers who have kindly contributed to
the 'Tips from the Top' featured
throughout the book.

Printed and bound in Belgium

First American Edition

10 9 8 7 6 5 4 3 2 1

THE AUTHOR

During twenty years of professional experience in film making, Roland Lewis has been involved in all aspects of production, from writing and editing to direction and camerawork. He has produced both drama and documentary films and has worked on news, educational programmes, commercials and musical films.

Roland Lewis is currently a Senior Lecturer at the Polytechnic of Central London, where he teaches video, film and television to undergraduates. He has also taught video to community groups and school children, written review and feature articles, and acted as a consultant on both books and film production.

CONTENTS

Introduction   8

Using your equipment   10

Camcorder functions   12

Aperture and exposure   16

Depth of field   18

Focusing   20

Panning   22

Tilting   24

The zoom lens   26

Hand-held camerawork   28

Using a tripod   30

Recording sound   32

Colour and contrast   34

Basic lighting   36

Creative techniques   40

Shot sizes and types   42

Composition   44

Visual sense   48

Visual flow   52

Editing in-camera   56

Shooting your first videos   58

Storyboarding   60

Tape-to-tape editing   62

Top topics   64

Children   66

Informal parties   68

Family outings   70

Special occasions   74

Weddings and ceremonies   78

Travel videos   84

Sports and action   92

Nature   100

Adventure activities   106

Effective presentation   108

Adding titles   110

Rostrum techniques   114

Optical effects   116

Using filters   118

Teleciné transfer   120

Creative editing   122

Adding sound   124

Getting sophisticated	*128*	**Drama on tape**	*182*
Creative lighting	*130*	Writing a script	*184*
Multi-camera techniques	*136*	Planning a production	*186*
Electronic effects	*138*	The video director	*188*
Pop videos	*140*		
The moving camera	*144*	**Personal views**	*190*
Computer graphics	*146*	The video letter	*192*
Scratch videos	*148*	Self-analysis	*194*
		Promoting yourself	*196*
Making documentaries	*150*	Home erotica	*198*
The video crew	*152*	In at the birth	*200*
Interviewing	*154*	Video for kids	*202*
Writing a commentary	*158*		
Using archive material	*160*	**Technical references**	*204*
Demonstration videos	*162*	Equipment specifications	*206*
The video portrait	*164*	Trouble-shooting	*208*
Story of a town	*166*	Caring for your equipment	*210*
Promoting a cause	*168*	International standards	*212*
Creating an archive	*170*		
		Glossary	*214*
Presenting your business	*172*	Index	*220*
Selling your home	*174*	Acknowledgments	*224*
Selling your product	*176*		
Business communications	*178*		
Training and safety	*180*		

INTRODUCTION

Video is the family album come to life – television production for a new generation of home enthusiasts. With a modern camcorder, anyone can shoot live action pictures in colour and with full sound, then play them back on their own TV set. There is no processing, no waiting time between production and viewing. And like audio tape, video tape is cheap and can be re-recorded. If you're not happy with what you have shot, you can simply reshoot.

This handbook teaches you the basics of visual literacy – the grammar and syntax of video. It explains the elements of composition, colour and camera movements, exposure, focus and depth of field. It makes clear the significance of editing and shows how you can put shots together to create flow and make visual sense. It introduces you to a range of inventive techniques that will add lustre and more than a touch of professionalism to the material you shoot.

This is a book about how to make videos – it describes the techniques of video making, not the technicalities of video cameras. It is a creative sourcebook, a catalogue of ideas and a ready reference for each new project you tackle. Use the opening chapters to lay the foundations of your video knowledge, then build on this with the progressively more ambitious subjects covered in the following sections. Explore the possibilities of teamwork and see how it widens your scope and, more importantly, your satisfaction.

Making home videos is mostly a matter of learning how to look – and listen. You can easily start improving your visual sense by watching television in a new way. You can observe the basic principles of how shots are put together and how sequences are linked; you can study the style and pace of the editing; and then, you can listen to the way in which music, commentary and sound effects are used to augment the visuals.

For your own video making, you will quickly learn the habit of thinking visually. This book will show you how to train your eyes to spot the visual potential of a scene and work out how best to show a subject, by composing the shot in your mind before you press the record button. You will see how you must consider the purpose of the shot – what you are trying to show or convey to the viewer. Take a few examples. You want to shoot fast-moving fun and games at a child's birthday party – are you wide enough to get in the whole scene? You want to show a grandmother's joy – are you close enough to capture her expression? You want to record a conversation – is the microphone positioned correctly, are you only getting a profile shot of the speakers, have you caught complete sentences or only incoherent snatches?

This book shows you how you can ensure good results through planning and preparation. Take a wedding, the favourite topic of video makers. By planning what to shoot, when and how, you can make a video record of the event that will deserve a place in the family archive. If you don't plan ahead, you can end up with a tape that is inept, boring or missing out on the essential highlights of the all-important day.

But don't keep your camcorder just for special occasions. Use it often, so that your recordings build into a unique notebook or diary of your life and the world around you. Experience the regular thrill of creative video making; experiment, innovate – and have fun.

Roland Lewin

USING YOUR EQUIPMENT

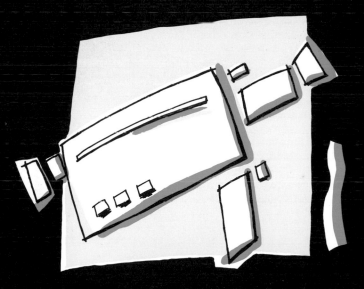

The better you understand your equipment, the better your results will be. The features common to most video equipment and the basic techniques of camerawork are explained in the following pages. Always read instruction manuals carefully and get to know the limitations and potential of your equipment with plenty of test shooting. Use these practice sessions to master the basic skills, to develop the routines that video demands and to increase your self-confidence.

The 'camcorder' is the video maker's main item of equipment. It combines the functions of an electronic camera and video cassette recorder in a single, compact portable machine. It has largely super-seded earlier home video-making equip-ment which consisted of two machines: a camera and a portable video cassette re-corder (VCR). Camcorders can be operated from rechargeable batteries or from a mains source. Many models have an electronic viewfinder that functions as a miniature monitor and enables you to play back the recording immediately and view the results. Simpler record-only types have an optical viewfinder and no play-back facility. There are many different models of camcorder available; the most common functions are illustrated in this stylized model.

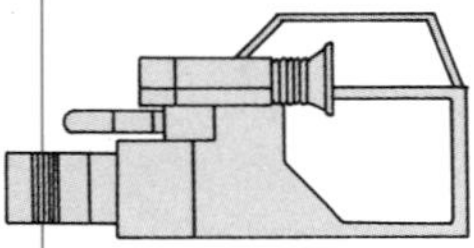

All camcorders have built-in microphones (mics) and record the sound at the same time as the images, on either single or twin tracks. The sound level is adjusted automatically and can be monitored during recording with headphones.

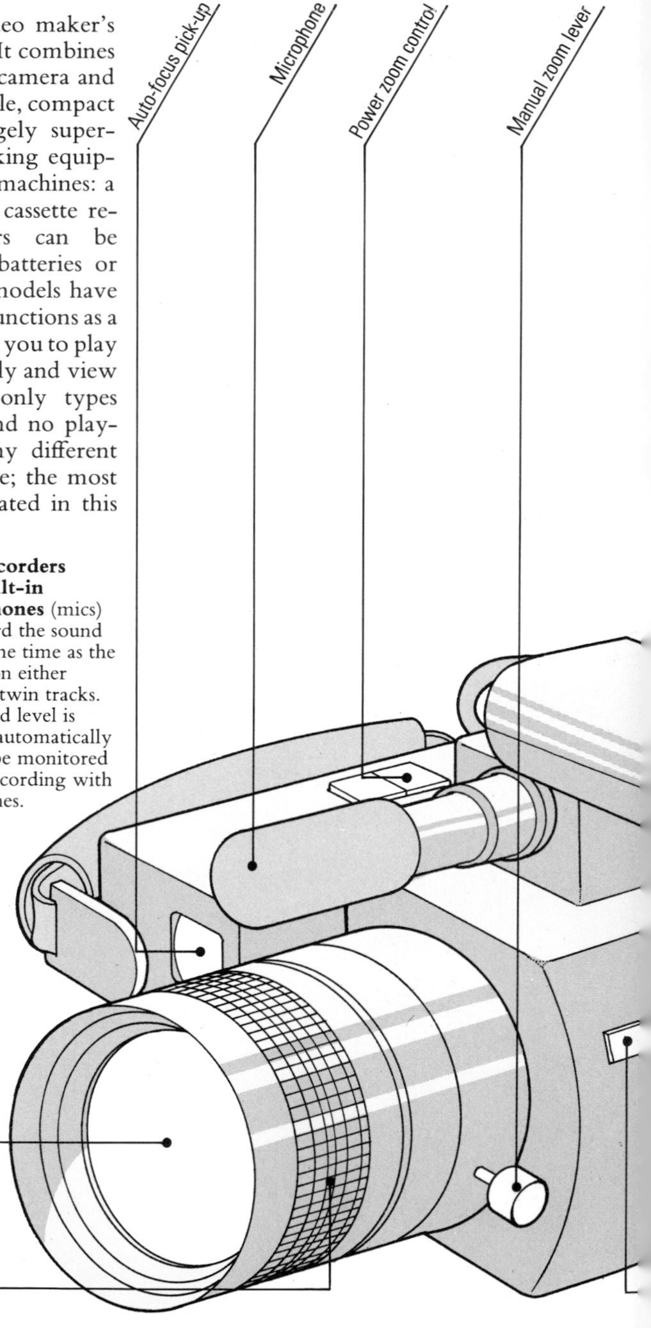

Most camcorders have a zoom lens, which allows you to vary the size of shots while shooting from one camera position and to take zoom shots, in which the subject appears larger or smaller as the shot proceeds. Many models also have a macro setting for shooting details and close-ups of small-scale subjects.

Auto-focus pick-up

Microphone

Power zoom control

Manual zoom lever

Zoom lens

Focus ring

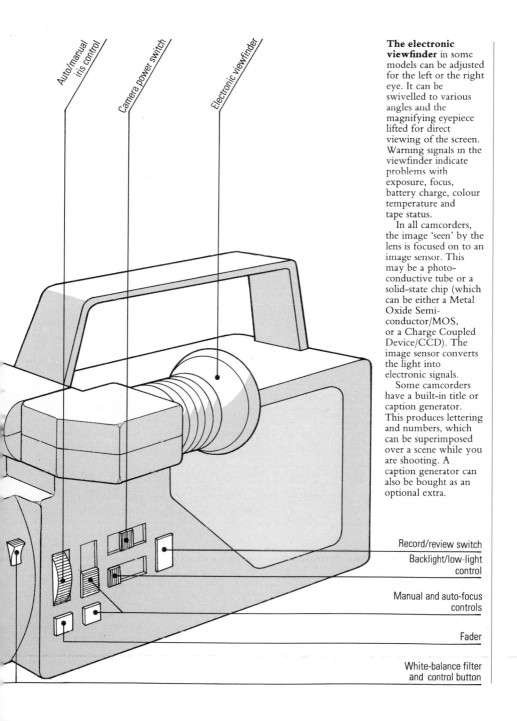

Auto/manual iris control

Camera power switch

Electronic viewfinder

Record/review switch

Backlight/low-light control

Manual and auto-focus controls

Fader

White-balance filter and control button

The electronic viewfinder in some models can be adjusted for the left or the right eye. It can be swivelled to various angles and the magnifying eyepiece lifted for direct viewing of the screen. Warning signals in the viewfinder indicate problems with exposure, focus, battery charge, colour temperature and tape status.

In all camcorders, the image 'seen' by the lens is focused on to an image sensor. This may be a photo-conductive tube or a solid-state chip (which can be either a Metal Oxide Semi-conductor/MOS, or a Charge Coupled Device/CCD). The image sensor converts the light into electronic signals.

Some camcorders have a built-in title or caption generator. This produces lettering and numbers, which can be superimposed over a scene while you are shooting. A caption generator can also be bought as an optional extra.

Knowing your equipment is the basis of good video making. Study these pages and your instruction manual thoroughly to get a clear idea of the purpose and potential of all the camcorder's controls. But no amount of theory will make up for practice, so get out on location and start shooting.

You can record an event at a moment's notice if you know instinctively what to do and where to put your fingers as you prepare to shoot. Once you know how to control the iris, focus and white balance, you can be confident that you will not miss any important action.

Being fluent in your control of the camcorder leaves you free to concentrate on the creative aspects of video making. Know the capabilities of the camcorder's lens so that you will know exactly the type of shot to be got when the lens is set at its widest and narrowest angles. Take time to discover, for example, the kind of shot you will get in the wide angle of a person standing about 2m (6ft) away, or how much of your living room will be covered. Get to know the maximum distance at which a person can still be seen in sufficient detail in the telephoto position, or the minimum distance a subject can be from the lens and remain in sharp focus.

Each time you shoot, the camcorder records sound as well as pictures. Since the built-in microphone is limited in its pickup range, this may determine your shooting position. You can disconnect it and record with a separate microphone.

When shooting outdoors, you will be dependent on batteries as a power source. Be aware that constant or frequent use of certain camera functions (eg pausing the camcorder, rewinding the tape and using the auto focus and zoom motor) will run down the batteries. Get to know the shooting time given by a single battery charge. Always carry spares with you or draw power from a car battery with a special adaptor.

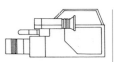

The iris controls the amount of light passing through the lens to the image sensor. It is usually under electronic control and is set automatically. But it can be operated manually in tricky light conditions and for creative control.

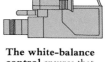

The white-balance control ensures that the colours in a scene are reproduced faithfully, whether lit by daylight or by artificial tungsten light. It can be set either automatically or manually (eg by holding a white card to the lens).

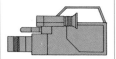

The backlight compensator is used to set the iris when shooting into the light, eg with a person standing indoors in front of a window. The iris adjusts to give correct exposure for the person; the background gets bleached out.

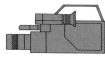

The fader automatically closes the iris, so that a scene fades to black over a period of 2 to 3 seconds. The sound usually fades out at the same time. A new scene can begin with a fade-in. The screen in some models fades to white, rather than black.

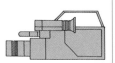

The low-light control is used in poor light conditions to produce a brighter picture by boosting the video signal. However, its use will increase picture 'noise' and produce a grainy-looking image.

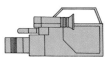

The auto-focus system uses light or infra-red beams to adjust focus automatically as you shoot. Focus tends to be set on the nearest object. You can override the system and focus manually by turning the ring on the barrel of the lens and judging the focus by looking in the viewfinder.

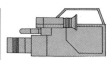

In the record mode, the tape is advanced around the recorder head drum and starts to register the recording. A simple counter keeps a tally of the amount of tape shot.

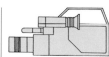

The review facility is a form of picture search and allows the tape to be played back at high speed and viewed in the electronic viewfinder. Some models allow you to check the last few seconds of a recording by auto-playback.

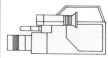

In the pause mode, the tape is halted, but the head drum continues to rotate. Do not keep in pause mode for too long; the tape can get worn and clog the record and playback heads. A still image can be produced on 'pause' during playback.

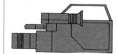

The insert edit facility enables you to add new shots into an existing recording without electronic disturbance at the edit in- and out- points. On most models, only pictures can be added; the original sound continues over the edit points.

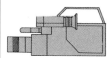

Backspacing is the automatic rewind of a short section of the recorded tape when the machine is paused. When started again, the tape runs forward to the end of the backspace section and the new recording begins. This ensures that the edit points will be free from electronic disturbance.

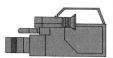

Audio-dub allows you to replace an existing sound track with a new recording while leaving the pictures undisturbed. It is only feasible with formats where the sound is recorded along the edge of the tape, separate to the picture information.

RECORDING FORMATS

Whatever the format of camcorder, the same principles govern recording.

At the heart of the system is a rapidly rotating drum, set at an angle, with recording heads mounted on it. As the tape passes over the drum, the heads convert the electronic video signal from the camcorder's image sensor into magnetic pulses and 'write' the image information on to the tape. Each head provides half the information that makes up one frame of the recording. Because of the angle of the head drum, the video signals are recorded diagonally across the tape in a helical pattern.

Sound is recorded either by a fixed head that records the sound in a linear strip along the tape edge. Or, in hi-fi models, the heads are mounted on the rotating drum and the audio signals are encoded in the picture track.

During recording, a control track of synchronizing pulses is laid down to govern playback speed. When a tape is played back, it is 'scanned' by the rotating heads and the recording process is reversed – magnetic pulses are reconverted into electronic signals to produce images.

Camcorders are available in several cassette formats:
● **VHS** uses $\frac{1}{2}$in tape in a full-size cassette and is the most popular format worldwide for home VCRs.
● **VHS-C** uses a compact cassette; a simple adaptor allows playback on standard VHS machines.
● **Betamax** uses $\frac{1}{2}$in tape.
● **Video 8** is a smaller format, with 8mm-wide tape, and features hi-fi sound recording.
● **4mm** is the latest format development and continues the trend toward smaller lighter camcorders.

APERTURE AND EXPOSURE

The lens on a video camera, like that on a stills or movie camera, is equipped with an iris diaphragm. This metal ring of overlapping leaves controls the aperture and thus determines exposure, or the amount of light that reaches the camera's image sensor. It works just like the iris of the human eye, reducing the size of the aperture in bright light and increasing it in dim light.

Almost all video cameras have an automatic iris, or auto-exposure facility, which adjusts the aperture automatically as you shoot. This is a boon in many video-making situations since it allows you to concentrate on the subjects, their actions and composition.

When the video camera is pointed at an evenly lit subject, the auto iris sets itself to ensure that the brightness of the scene is fully reproduced and the range of colours effectively presented.

The auto iris can cope to some extent with scenes that are unevenly lit. For example, if you take a shot that pans or moves across from a sunlit area to a shady one, the iris adjusts automatically to give proper exposure throughout the pan. But you may find, when the shot is played back, that the result of that automatic adjustment is momentarily visible, as some unevenness in the exposure.

Similarly, shooting someone sitting under the shade of an umbrella on a sunny patio can be difficult with the auto iris, which will adjust itself to the general brightness of the scene and hardly pick up the person in the shade.

The automatic system also has problems when the light is coming from behind the subject ('backlit' subject). A person standing indoors in front of a window, or outdoors with the sun behind them, could appear to be lost in murky shadow or be seen only as a silhouette. The human eye would adjust to compensate for this type of lighting, but the camcorder's auto iris is misled by the surrounding brightness.

Overexposure: With the iris fully open, the scene is too bright, details are bleached out (entire background here is lost), contrast is lacking and colours will be weak.

EXPOSURE WARNINGS

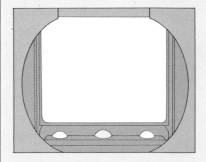

A warning light in the camera's view-finder indicates an exposure problem (usually insufficient light for shooting). This is a useful guide when setting the exposure manually. In some models, the warning appears as a visual display on the screen.

Other lights in the camera warn of different things, such as battery charge, white balance function, auto focus and recorder running.

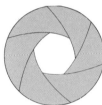

Correct exposure:
With the iris set midway, related to the subject's needs, the whole scene is revealed, with a good range of contrast and sharp detail. Colours will be rendered true.

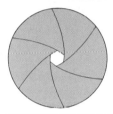

Underexposure:
With the iris closed down, the scene is too dark, shadow detail is lost (the village has disappeared), and colours will be poor. Picture 'noise' starts to intrude.

To cope with this situation, most camcorders have some sort of backlight compensator control. This adjusts the iris (by opening it up) and improves the image quality of the subject, though the background may be too bright or 'burnt out'.

With many camcorders, you can solve these kinds of exposure problems by switching over to 'manual', which gives you control of the iris setting. With an electronic viewfinder, you can assess the exposure and then choose the appropriate aperture.

When setting the exposure manually for a pan shot that moves from a light to a dark area, adjust the iris to suit either the beginning or the end of the shot. If the contrast is too great, it is better to treat the scene as two separate shots and set the exposure appropriate to each.

Most video cameras are equipped with an exposure warning light (*see left*). Some models also have low-light compensators which amplify the video signal electronically to increase image brightness. These allow you to shoot in dim interiors or in fading daylight (*see p. 36*).

KNOW YOUR CAMERA

It is well worth getting familiar with the exposure capabilities of your camcorder.

On most stills and movie cameras, the size of the aperture is measured in *f*-stop numbers, which are shown on the barrel of the lens. On camcorders, usually only the maximum aperture is marked.

Since the electronic viewfinder integral to most camcorders provides only a black and white (monochromatic) image, do plenty of test shooting and play back the results in colour on your TV. Try these exercises:

1 Take a series of shots in a variety of lighting situations to see how the auto iris (and the backlight compensator, if present) responds.

2 Take the same shots adjusting the iris manually and compare results.

3 Shoot a series of shots in various low-light situations.

DEPTH OF FIELD

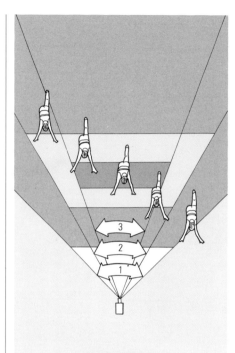

D epth of field is the distance (in depth) between the nearest and farthest subjects in a shot that are in sharp focus at the same time. This principle is important to focusing and some general rules govern it:

● The smaller the aperture, the greater the depth of field. Thus, bright sunlit conditions enhance the depth of field; dimly lit interiors restrict it.

● The greater the focal length of the lens, the smaller the depth of field. As you zoom in, the depth of field is reduced; as you zoom out, it is increased.

● The farther the camera is from the subject, the greater the depth of field.

● Depth of field extends farther behind the focused subject than in front.

The best way to control depth of field, and to use it creatively, is to vary the focal length of the lens and to adjust the distance of the camera from the subject. You may also need to modify the amount of light, by using neutral density filters to reduce depth (*see p. 36*), or additional lighting to increase it (*see p. 38*).

You can easily exploit the rules to advantage. Shallow depth of field can be used to create atmosphere. Shots with out-of-focus trees or flowers in the foreground are classic examples. Similarly, subjects can be separated from their background: try a telephoto shot picking out one face from a crowd. For impact, take deep-focus shots in the wide angle position that show sharp detail from front to back.

VARYING FOCAL LENGTH

With the camera in one position, the depth of field of the shot will change as the focal length of the lens is varied.

With the lens at its shortest focal length (**1**) and the focus set on the centre runner, the depth of field is at its greatest. As the focal length is increased (**2**), the depth of field is reduced. The nearest runner to the camera is no longer in sharp focus. With the lens zoomed in to its longest focal length (**3**), the depth of field will be at its narrowest and only the centre runner is in sharp focus. In all cases, there is about twice the depth of field behind the focused subject than there is in front.

In other words, as the angle of view increases, depth of field increases.

KNOW YOUR CAMERA

1 Line up a wide angle shot of a receding row of bottles on a wall outdoors. Focus on the centre bottle.
2 Compose a second shot in the telephoto position, showing the same number of bottles and with the focus still on the centre bottle.
3 Check the tape back to see the effects on depth of field.

In bright sunlight,
with the lens set at its
widest angle and with
the smallest aperture,
you will get the
greatest depth of field.
Objects will be in
focus from close to the
camera right through
to the far distance.

For creative effect,
use the telephoto
setting to reduce the
depth of field and
produce an out-of-
focus foreground to
the subject. The nearer
the camera to the
foreground, the
greater the out-of-
focus effect.

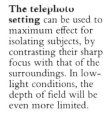

**The telephoto
setting** can be used to
maximum effect for
isolating subjects, by
contrasting their sharp
focus with that of the
surroundings. In low-
light conditions, the
depth of field will be
even more limited.

FOCUSING

On most camcorders, focusing can be controlled either automatically or manually. Whichever method you use, a sharp image of the subject will be produced (seen in the viewfinder) only when the lens is adjusted to ensure that light rays from the subject converge on the camera's image sensor.

Camcorders with auto-focus facilities measure the distance from the subject and set the lens to the correct position. If camera or subject moves, then this is detected and compensated for automatically. However, as the mechanism 'searches' for the new position, momentary changes in focus can be apparent on screen.

Auto-focus systems are not infallible and can misread certain situations. For example, they can be confused by:
● Subjects behind glass, netting or bars.
● Water, falling snow, mist or fog.
● Subjects in continuous motion.

Since the auto focus tends to 'read' the distance from subjects close to the centre of the screen, off-centre compositions and shots with continuous perspective (such as rows of buildings) can also present problems with focusing.

As with aperture setting, you can override the auto-focus system and adjust the focus ring on the lens manually. The procedure for checking focus before each shot is described in the caption below.

With static subjects, manual focusing is easy. Look for any clearly defined subjects, such as straight lines or lettering. With more complicated subjects, use any well-

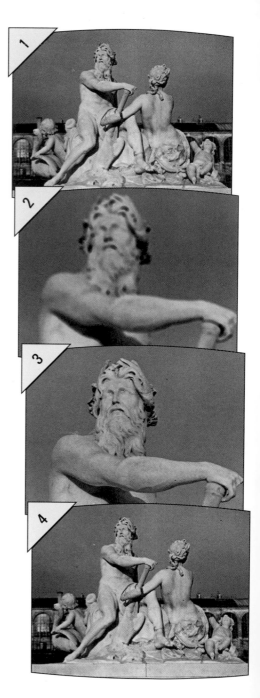

To check focus manually, whether you are zooming or not, follow this basic procedure before each shot (*right*):
1 Set up the shot.
2 Zoom in to a close-up of the subject on which you wish to focus.
3 Adjust the focus until detail is sharp.
4 Zoom out, then compose the final shot.
   This method of pre-focusing the lens ensures that the subject is sharp and remains in focus throughout any subsequent zoom movement.

Throwing focus manually is an effective way to show the relationship between subjects or to introduce a new element into a scene. Here, focus is changed • from the woman in the foreground (**1**) to the stern and staring face of the man behind (**2**). By throwing focus from one face to the other, the sculpture has come to life – a story can unfold.

For such shots, use a tripod and the telephoto setting. Hold the front image for about 3 to 5 secs, then with smooth manual operation, twist the focus ring to bring in the end image and hold for the same time, depending on the action. Vary the focusing speed, to give a sudden shock or a slow revelation.

delineated element for focusing. For close-ups of people, choose the eyes as the ideal point for accurate focusing.

Focusing manually on moving subjects needs practice. For example, you may have to adjust the focus continually as a person walks toward the camera. Retaining focus can be particularly tricky when using the telephoto end of the lens, since this has a restricted depth of field (*see p. 18*).

Similarly, if you move the camera position or alter the focal length of the lens (as in zooming), focus may well have to be changed. And if the depth of field is limited, tilting the camera, say, from the spire of a church down to gravestones in the foreground, may demand a change of focus as the shot proceeds.

Playing around with manual focus can give good creative effects. You could start a shot out of focus and gradually pull it into focus, to reveal the scene. You can also 'throw' focus from one subject to another in a shot. For example, start with a shot of a child looking through the bars of a cage in the zoo, then throw focus beyond to the animals inside.

FOCUSING TIPS

● Use the calibrations, marked in feet or metres, on the focus ring to help judge distances.
● Get to know instinctively which way to turn the focus ring to bring close and distant subjects into focus.
● The 'close focus' distance of a lens is the minimum distance a subject must be from the camera to be in focus. Develop a visual sense for this. At the very closest distances, you will need the 'macro' position (*see p. 100*).

IMPROVE YOUR SKILLS

1 Explore the camera's auto focus to see its uses and limitations. Take shots through glass, of moving water and of reflections in a mirror.
2 Try manually 'throwing' focus, by changing focus from one subject in a shot to another (eg from a person in the foreground to one in the background). Try this at several speeds.

PANNING

The pan (panoramic) shot is a camera movement that is well worth mastering early on. It involves swivelling the camera through a gentle arc, from left to right or vice versa, in one slow, smooth and continuous movement.

In its proper context, panning is an effective, often dramatic, technique. But, if overdone or used arbitrarily, the movement becomes tedious and confusing to the viewer. Panning is best used for:

● Scanning subjects that are too large to get into one shot, eg city skylines, long coastlines, landscapes or large buildings.
● Showing relationships between things, eg panning from a child's face, full of wonder, to the object of her attention.
● Following the action of moving subjects, eg a dog running after a ball.

There are several things to remember when doing a pan shot. First, think the shot through and decide on subjects for the beginning and end of the pan. When hand-holding the camera, start with your body twisted in the opposite direction to the panning movement. As you pan, uncurl and move only from the waist up.

Pan slowly and steadily to allow the viewer to take in the scene. Hold the first and last images for about 3 seconds each, so that the purpose of the shot is clear. Keep any horizontal lines in the picture level. When there are verticals in the shot, keep them upright and where they are close together, slow down the panning speed, otherwise they will blur.

The most effective pan covers an arc of not more than 90°. Panning farther than this can cause camera shake and loss of balance if you are hand-holding the machine; if using a tripod, you could trip over its legs. These are two good reasons for finding a comfortable position and rehearsing the pan before you start.

With moving subjects, panning speeds need to vary with the action to keep the subject sharp. When shooting a child running, for example, the interest is in keeping the child in shot all the time; the background is not so important and can be blurred by camera movement.

Composition is also important with moving subjects. Pan ahead, leaving plenty of 'walking room' in front of the subject so that the viewer's eye is led along with the action (see p. 45).

With a slow-moving subject, such as a fishing boat entering harbour, the pan can also serve to reveal the setting. By using the wide angle position, both boat and harbour can be shown and the action will disguise the panning movement.

Breaking a pan shot down into its clearly illustrates the views covered in the
along a large building component parts different angles and camera movement.

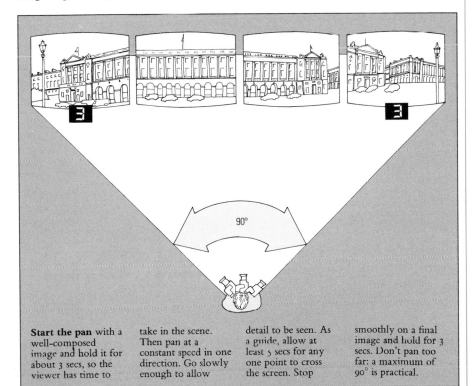

Start the pan with a take in the scene. detail to be seen. As smoothly on a final
well-composed Then pan at a a guide, allow at image and hold for 3
image and hold it for constant speed in one least 5 secs for any secs. Don't pan too
about 3 secs, so the direction. Go slowly one point to cross far: a maximum of
viewer has time to enough to allow the screen. Stop 90° is practical.

TILTING

Tilting is pivoting the camera in a smooth, continuous, vertical movement. In other words, it is a vertical pan.

As with panning, tilting is an effective technique when the subject justifies it. For example, tilting from the bottom to the top of a tall building or mountain emphasizes its height; tilting from the top to the bottom of a volcanic crater reveals its depth. Moving subjects can also be followed, such as an ascending ski lift overhead. Shooting it head-on concentrates the subject, but changing the camera position and combining the tilt shot with a pan reveals the larger scene of the surrounding mountains.

The same rules apply to tilting as to panning:
● Think about what you are trying to show and determine the beginning and end images.
● Rehearse the tilt before shooting.
● Hold the first image for about 3 seconds, then tilt slowly and smoothly, in one direction.
● End by holding the final image for about 3 seconds; do not stop abruptly or tilt past the final spot.
● Do not try tilting up too far or you may lose balance. If you have an adjustable eyepiece on the viewfinder, operate the camera at chest level to get easier tilts.

Exposure can be an important consideration when, for example, you are tilting up a building to include the sky. When there is exposure variation between the start and end of the shot, use the auto exposure which allows the iris to compensate during tilting (see p. 16). Alternatively, set the exposure manually by fixing it for the first or front position and allowing the sky to 'burn out'.

As with the horizontals in panning, keep the verticals upright during tilting. Something slightly off the vertical looks worrying on screen. Remember, also, not to tilt too fast past horizontals, since this will produce a blurred image.

A tall building such as the Eiffel Tower is a perfect subject for a tilt shot. When setting it up, start with an interesting and well-composed frame. Check that any horizontals are level. Decide how far you are going to tilt and compose the final image in the frame. Rehearse the shot, concentrating on a smooth movement throughout and slowing down to end gently on the chosen image.

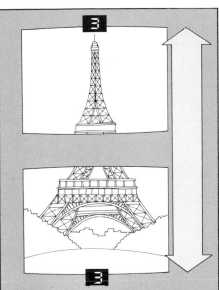

Using a tripod can make tilt shots easier to control. Hold the first and final images for about 3 secs each. Avoid jolting at the beginning or end. Tilt smoothly, and slowly enough to avoid blurs as you pass horizontals. Don't try tilting too far: 90° is the comfortable maximum. If the subject won't fit in the frame, move the camera farther away.

PAN AND TILT TIPS

● Avoid reverse pans or tilts.
● Pan with the action. Panning along a street against the flow of traffic, for example, unless done for specific effect, may disconcert the viewer.
● In the telephoto position, slow down the pan or tilt, since the subject and any movement in the shot will be exaggerated and hard to keep in focus.
● As a rule, do not cut during a pan. But as a technique, a sequence of pans, all in the same direction at the same speed, is an effective way of emphasizing space or distance, eg a scenic tract of countryside.
● A whip or zip pan makes an effective transition between shots by creating a deliberate blurring of the image. Make a rapid pan away at the end of a shot and a rapid pan on, in the same direction, to the start of the next. The briefer the whip pans, the more effective, but ensure both movements are made at the same speed.

IMPROVE YOUR SKILLS

1 Try panning in the wide angle position over a large-scale subject (eg a street of houses) and in the telephoto position over a smaller scale (eg a row of books).
2 To practise with moving subjects, ask a friend to pace between two points a few yards apart. Place the camera at a midway point and pan with them as they move. Keep them in the same part of the frame throughout the shot.
3 Panning and tilting at the same time will inevitably form part of your video making. To practise such combination shots, follow the progress of a jogger running uphill or an aircraft taking off.

THE ZOOM LENS

Camcorder zoom lenses usually cover a range of focal lengths of about 6 to 1, ie the angle of the wide end is 6 times that of the narrow telephoto end.

On most models, the maximum angle of view is not particularly wide (usually about the equivalent of the 'standard' lens on a 35mm stills camera), but perfectly adequate for general purpose shooting. By contrast, the minimum angle offers a strong telephoto effect that is ideal for distant subjects.

It is also possible to get supplementary lenses for most models that screw onto the front of the zoom lens. A tele-converter will increase the telephoto effect by magnifying it by about 40%. The wide-converter will increase the angle of view by a similar amount.

Visual distortion occurs at both ends of the range. With the wide angle, foreground and background appear farther apart, and any movement toward or away from camera is exaggerated. At the telephoto end of the zoom, perspective is flattened, depth appears compressed, and movement toward or away from the camera seems to be slowed down.

These distortions can be used to great effect. For example, wide angle views can exaggerate or dramatize the size and appearance of buildings. Or they can accelerate the speed of, say, runners as they pass close to the camera. At the other end of the range, the compression of perspective produced in the telephoto position can make the runners appear to be very close together and moving only slowly.

Zooming is achieved by movements of the lens which vary its focal length. Zooming in narrows the field of view (and reduces the depth of field); zooming out widens it. The action can be controlled manually or by means of a motor. The motorized zoom control usually has one or two pre-set speeds. On more sophisticated camcorders, a range of speeds is possible by simply varying finger pressure

ZOOMING TIPS

● Get used to using your zoom to vary the focal length of the lens. You will then get your zooms between, not during, shots.
● Avoid 'yo-yo' shots that zoom in and then out again. They have an unsettling effect on the viewer.
● Vary zoom lengths and speeds. Slow zooms tend to concentrate interest; fast manual ones give shock effects.
● Zoom shots can be used creatively for opening and closing sequences. Starting on a detail and zooming out to reveal the whole subject makes an effective introduction. To close a sequence, break the rules with a zoom that deliberately goes out of focus.

on the zoom's rocker switch.

Although the fixed speeds of the zoom motor can limit creativity, they do produce smooth professional results. With practice, different speeds and styles of zooms can be produced manually, by turning the barrel of the lens or by using the zoom lever.

Zoom shots have such a powerful effect that it is tempting to overdo them. Limit their use or your videos will become too 'busy', making them overstated and visually disconcerting.

The zoom shot works best when taken for a good reason – to establish relationships, to reveal, emphasize or dramatize. For example:
● Zoom out from a golfer taking a putt to establish the position of the hole.
● Zoom in slowly on a child's face to emphasize concentration.
● Zoom in quickly on the face of the recipient of a surprise gift to dramatize the moment.

When operating manually, pre-set the focus in the telephoto position (see p. 20).

A good zooming shot entails more than just squeezing the zoom trigger. The final image must be well composed and have a purpose. Simply zooming out from a tight close-up (*left*) to a full frame results in an awkward shot, with too much headroom and an incomplete subject that does not explain the purpose of the shot.

Combining a zoom with a pan or tilt action invariably gives a better composition to a zooming shot. Pulling out from a tight close-up of the subject and tilting down at the same time (*right*) produces a final image that is well composed and that tells the whole story by revealing all of the action.

Start and operate the zoom smoothly, speeding up at the beginning and slowing down at the end to create visual buffers. As with all camera movements, hold the shot at the end so that the viewer can take in the subject (as a general rule for about 3 seconds, or until any action is completed).

To disguise the 'mechanical' effect of the zoom, do as the professionals do, and make other camera movements at the same time. A sweeping pan combined with a pull-out zoom creates a smooth attractive effect. Shots that follow action, such as a horse galloping across a field, may demand such treatment. Here, the action itself also diverts attention from the zoom movement.

IMPROVE YOUR SKILLS

1 As an exercise in zooming manually, have someone walk toward the camera from some distance away. Ease back gently with the zoom lever as they approach, keeping them in full frame all the time. Done properly, this is a most effective shot.
2 Try taking manual zooms at different speeds. You will find the slower ones the most demanding; if the operation is not smooth and controlled, you will end up with a series of jerky movements.

HAND-HELD CAMERAWORK

Lightweight camcorders are designed for hand-held operation. Hand-holding allows you to follow the action freely and to vary both camera angles and shooting heights spontaneously. With the camera on your shoulder, you can tuck yourself into corners, shoot from tricky positions and get novel viewpoints.

Hand-held camera operation needs practice, but the freedom it provides is enormously rewarding and creative. Inevitably, there will be some unsteadiness – even professionals cannot hold a camera completely still.

Camera shake is worst with static subjects, especially in the telephoto position which exaggerates any unsteadiness into a distracting wobble. The easiest way to avoid this is to use the wide angle lens setting, particularly when moving with the camera, and to move closer to subjects rather than relying on zooming.

Camera steadiness improves if you stand securely balanced with feet apart and grip the camera firmly using both hands.

Press the camera against your shoulder or face, and tuck your elbows in for extra control. Remember:
● The lighter the camera, the firmer the grip and pressure required.
● Avoid tight skirts or jackets, and flowing coats that impair mobility.
● Use a camera brace or shoulder support to improve steadiness and distribute the camcorder's weight more evenly.

> ❝ *The professional gets to know the equipment, works with it until all the functions are second nature, until it's no longer necessary to think what to do to zoom out or bring the focus forward. It's mastery of the equipment that frees one to be creative.* ❞

CHARLES STEWART, DIRECTOR/CAMERAMAN
The Police TV series (British Academy Award),
Seeds of Despair (Emmy/US and Peabody/UK awards).

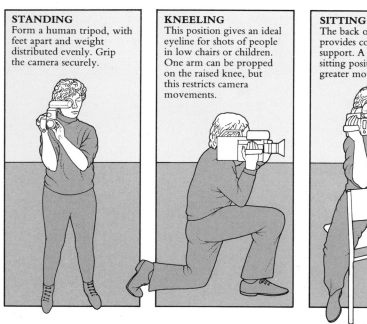

STANDING
Form a human tripod, with feet apart and weight distributed evenly. Grip the camera securely.

KNEELING
This position gives an ideal eyeline for shots of people in low chairs or children. One arm can be propped on the raised knee, but this restricts camera movements.

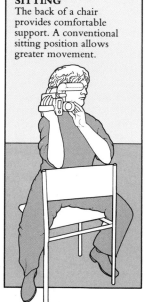

SITTING
The back of a chair provides comfortable support. A conventional sitting position allows greater movement.

WALKING WITH THE CAMERA

Be aware! Make sure there are no obstacles in your way before you begin to crab.

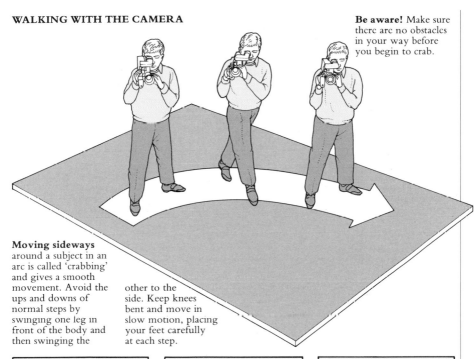

Moving sideways around a subject in an arc is called 'crabbing' and gives a smooth movement. Avoid the ups and downs of normal steps by swinging one leg in front of the body and then swinging the other to the side. Keep knees bent and move in slow motion, placing your feet carefully at each step.

LYING
With your elbows supported by the floor, you get steady shots but limited camera movements. This is an ideal position for getting dramatic angles and for shooting babies and pets at floor level.

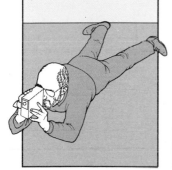

PROPPING
Desks, tables and chairs are good indoor props to improve steadiness. Outdoors, use props like cars or low walls.

SUPPORTING
Use any prop to steady the camera, eg jam yourself up against a doorway or even use a friend's shoulder.

USING A TRIPOD

No matter how good your hand-held camerawork, a tripod specifically designed for video use offers distinct advantages. For example, you can:

● Take steady shots every time, especially in the telephoto position where any camera shake is exaggerated.

● Ensure smooth camera movements.

● Keep the camera level during pan and tilt shots.

● Shoot complex movements more easily, as when following a football game or horse race.

The disadvantages are few by comparison. Carrying a tripod means extra weight and shots may take a little longer to set up initially.

Using a tripod implies a more thoughtful approach to video making, since it involves both handling the equipment and extra planning and preparation. But the additional effort will undoubtedly pay off in improved composition. Furthermore, a tripod is essential for shooting lengthy events, interviews and drama, where hand-held camerawork would not be feasible. Mounting a tripod on a set of wheels to form a moveable stable platform, or dolly, allows you to follow subjects smoothly. You can buy a dolly or make your own (see p. 144).

The correct stance with a tripod is to position yourself comfortably between its legs. Hold the pan handle firmly with one hand, keeping your elbow close to the body. Use the other hand to adjust the camcorder's controls.

When using a tripod for pans and tilts,

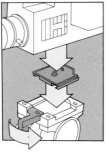

The quick-release mechanism is a plate that attaches to the base of the camcorder. One flick of the release lever disengages the camcorder from the head for hand-held use.

Sturdiness and stability are the keys to a good video tripod. The braces between the legs are essential for steadiness during shooting. The central pedestal column of the tripod can be adjusted by a crank lever to give varying shot heights.

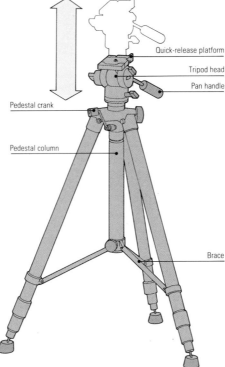

Quick-release platform

Tripod head

Pan handle

Pedestal crank

Pedestal column

Brace

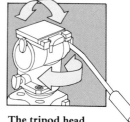

The tripod head allows the camcorder to be pivoted in all directions, using the pan handle. The movement of a friction head should be jerk-free, to allow smooth pans and tilts. A fluid head is ideal, but is more expensive.

Some tripod heads have a spirit level built-in, which allows you to establish the horizontal easily.

make sure it is securely placed. (Some models have spiked feet for steadiness on rough ground.) Control the speed of movement with the pan handle. When tilting, it often helps to hold the camcorder at the same time to steady the movement. Check that the tripod head is pivoting smoothly, so that the shot starts and finishes without a jerk.

With pan shots, arrange the tripod's legs so as to give you a comfortable operating position for stability during the movement. Twist your body from the waist up and lean into the shot, rather than walking around the tripod and risking overbalancing or, worse still, stumbling over its legs.

The central pedestal column of a video tripod is adjustable and allows you to vary the lens height between shots. If the mechanism is smooth enough, you can use it for 'rise-and-fall' shots. For example, a shot of a child playing under a table can 'pedestal up' to reveal the adults dining above.

You can also use a tripod to create trick effects. Set up a shot of a static scene, such as an empty room, and lock off the tripod head. Shoot a few seconds of tape, then pause. When someone moves into the scene, start recording again – they will seem to have appeared magically.

Use this 'stop-start' technique to animate a series of objects or, more humorously, to jump people around different parts of the screen. Make sure there are no other moving elements in the scene; trees waving in the breeze, for example, will appear to jump as their position changes.

A single-stemmed monopod can sometimes be more practical than a tripod. It is light, offers some stability and is easily adjusted to vary shot height. In places where a tripod could be awkward (eg in crowds or following fast-moving events), the monopod can be set up quickly. For extra stability, brace it against the body or press the base against the foot. But since it cannot stand up on its own, camera movements are restricted.

TRIPOD TIPS

● Don't lock off the pan and tilt mechanism during a shot or you will be unable to make minor adjustments to the composition if the action demands it.
● Do lock off after shots, to prevent the camera falling forward on the tripod head.
● Vary the height of your tripod shots as much as possible. Results will be dull if you always shoot from the same height.
● Check the spirit level each time you set up the tripod to ensure it is placed evenly, particularly important when horizontals are involved.

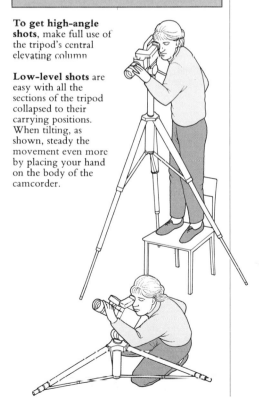

To get high-angle shots, make full use of the tripod's central elevating column

Low-level shots are easy with all the sections of the tripod collapsed to their carrying positions. When tilting, as shown, steady the movement even more by placing your hand on the body of the camcorder.

RECORDING SOUND

Stop reading, close your eyes and listen. After a while, you will become aware of all kinds of sounds – in the room and house, in the street, in the distance. It is these sounds, plus all the others you can record, that make up the other half of video – the part you listen to as you watch.

All camcorders are equipped with built-in microphones for general purpose recording. Some models have the omni-directional type of mic which picks up sound from all around the camera. But, since it is fitted to the camera, it has the disadvantage of also recording the machine's handling and operation sounds, such as those of the focus and zoom motors. In some models, this problem is overcome by extending the mic on a telescopic boom out beyond the front of the camcorder, just off-screen.

Other camcorders have built-in uni-directional mics which gather sound primarily from in front of the camera. Yet other machines have mics that operate in tandem with the zoom lens, so that their area of receptivity varies with the lens.

For the best sound recordings, disconnect the camcorder's own mic and record the sound with an auxiliary mic, plugged into the mic socket. Several types are available (*see box*). This method also means you can involve another person in recording the sound (*see p. 68*).

All camcorders have some form of automatic gain, or level, control (AGC, *see Glossary*), which continually adjusts the recording level to compensate for quiet moments. The result is that any background noise will be picked up.

You can monitor sound as you shoot by wearing headphones. Make sure these are large enough to cover the ears so as to exclude all other sounds. Since you are aware of the sound quality as you record, you can modify the camera position (eg by moving closer to the subject) or the mic position (eg away from some extraneous source) as necessary.

The furnishings and fittings of a room affect quality of sound recording. Hard surfaces (glass, metal, bare walls, tiles) reflect sound and can cause an indistinct recording and reverberation. Conversely, soft materials (carpets, drapes, armchairs, sofas) absorb sound, giving a dull, even a 'dead' response. You can do much to modify a room's acoustics. Drawn drapes, extra rugs and wall hangings will soften sound in a 'hard' room, while sheets of wooden board, glazed pictures and mirrors will sharpen sound in a 'soft' room.

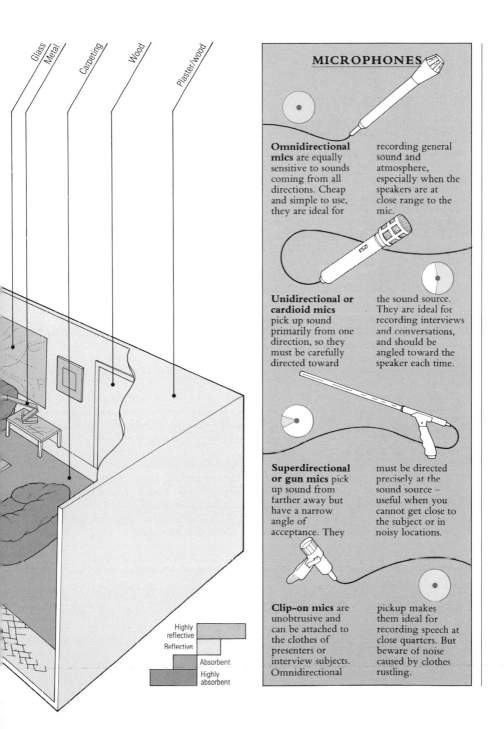

Glass
Metal
Carpeting
Wood
Plaster/wood

Highly
reflective

Reflective

Absorbent

Highly
absorbent

MICROPHONES

Omnidirectional mics are equally sensitive to sounds coming from all directions. Cheap and simple to use, they are ideal for recording general sound and atmosphere, especially when the speakers are at close range to the mic.

Unidirectional or cardioid mics pick up sound primarily from one direction, so they must be carefully directed toward the sound source. They are ideal for recording interviews and conversations, and should be angled toward the speaker each time.

Superdirectional or gun mics pick up sound from farther away but have a narrow angle of acceptance. They must be directed precisely at the sound source – useful when you cannot get close to the subject or in noisy locations.

Clip-on mics are unobtrusive and can be attached to the clothes of presenters or interview subjects. Omnidirectional pickup makes them ideal for recording speech at close quarters. But beware of noise caused by clothes rustling.

COLOUR AND CONTRAST

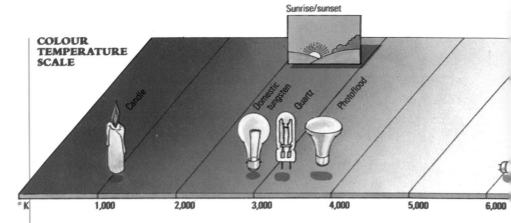

COLOUR TEMPERATURE SCALE

Sunrise/sunset

Candle

Domestic tungsten

Quartz

Photoflood

°K   1,000   2,000   3,000   4,000   5,000   6,000

Even though light appears white, it is made up of all the colours of the spectrum. Different light sources, such as candles, domestic bulbs or daylight, produce different coloured light (*see chart*). But our eyes and brain automatically compensate for these differences and so objects always appear in their correct colours.

The video camera cannot compensate in this way. It has to be adjusted to balance all the colours being received so that the end result the camera 'sees' is pure white, no matter what the source of illumination.

In most camcorders, this 'white balance' is achieved automatically. The camera can be set in the 'daylight' or the 'tungsten' (indoor) mode and this operates a balancing filter. Then a white card or a white lens cap, lit by the prevailing light source, is held up in front of the lens and the white balance button pushed. The colour balance is now set: white objects should be faithfully reproduced and the rest of the spectrum rendered correctly.

Incidentally, the white balance control can be used to create deliberate 'wrong' effects. The bluish tinge produced by using the tungsten setting in daylight can be exploited to give a nighttime effect. Or a cosy dinner-for-two indoors can be made more intimate by using the daylight setting to 'warm-up' the scene.

Because the camcorder's viewfinder reproduces only black and white images, it is

Colour temperature is the temperature to which a material must be heated in order to produce light of a certain colour. This is measured in °Kelvin (°K). The chart shows the range of light sources affecting video and the different colours they produce. The effects are relevant when mixing daylight with any form of artificial source.

easy to forget about white balance. But it is essential to set it every time:
● You turn on the camcorder.
● The light conditions change (eg moving from daylight into artificial light).
● You use supplementary lighting.

The black and white viewfinder also masks the effect of colour casts, which are usually visible to the naked eye. For example, a person standing close to a strongly coloured wall will be tinged with its reflected light. If this effect is not desirable, the subject should be moved to another position.

Compared with photographic film, video has a more limited range of picture contrast. It responds best to relatively low-contrast subjects. A high-contrast shot, containing both brightly lit areas and deep shade, will be difficult to reproduce successfully. It will either be burnt out, with colours bleached, or lost in murky shadow, with all details lost. For this type of shot, it is better to wait until the light conditions are more favourable or to bring in additional lighting to 'fill' the shadows and so reduce the contrast (*see p. 38*).

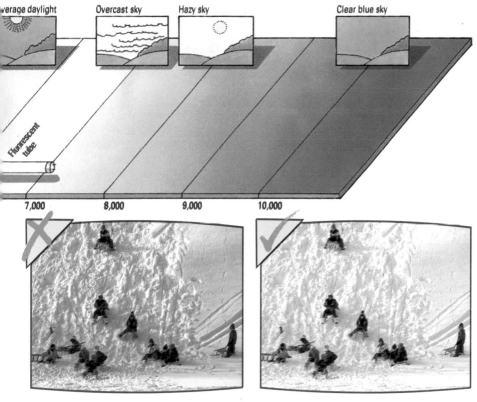

verage daylight   Overcast sky   Hazy sky   Clear blue sky

Fluorescent tube

7,000   8,000   9,000   10,000

Daylight: Incorrect
Using the tungsten filter in daylight gives a mismatch of colour temperatures. Whites are heavily blue-tinged, colours are dull.

Daylight: Correct
With a daylight filter, colours and whites are accurate. Around sunrise and sunset, whites become orange-tinted and in overcast conditions bluish.

Tungsten: Incorrect
When the daylight filter is used in artificial light, whites appear yellowish-orange and colours are unrealistic, producing an overall warm effect.

Tungsten: Correct
The correct indoor filter balances the subject for artificial light. But be careful, since any daylight that creeps in will distort this balance.

BASIC LIGHTING · 1

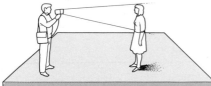

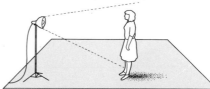

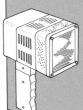

The small video lamp, with low-wattage quartz bulb, is battery-run and can be clipped on to the camcorder. Other models can be hand-held. All produce a flood of hard bright light which falls away rapidly. Colour temperature (3,200°K) is close to domestic tungsten (2,800°K).

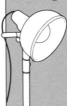

The photoflood lamp is light, cheap and easy to use. It produces a fairly even light over a wide area and softens the edges of shadows. Photoflood bulbs have a colour temperature of 3,400°K, which is higher than domestic tungsten. Bulbs of 275 watts last about 3 hrs, 500 watts up to 6 hrs.

The sharpest, brightest, most lifelike video pictures are taken in bright, evenly lit conditions. A clear sunny day provides ideal light for outdoor shooting. Even on a bright but cloudy day, there is usually enough light around to get proper exposure and good results.

A minimum amount of light is needed before a video camera can record pictures. This amount varies with each model and is determined by the lens aperture (f1.4 in most models) and the sensitivity of the camcorder's image sensor.

The intensity of light given out from a source is measured in lux or foot candles. Candlelight, for example, emits about 10 lux and domestic lighting in an 'average' room at night produces about 100 to 300 lux. The higher the lux, the better the video pictures will be. Although many camcorders can pick up images at as low as 10 lux, the best pictures are taken at over 900 lux, when you have added supplementary lighting.

Daylight in clear sunny conditions outdoors is about 35,000 lux. It can rise to values of 100,000 lux and the video camera cannot cope with such intense light. So, in very bright sunlight or in highly reflective places (such as white sandy beaches or snowfields), it is necessary to use a neutral density filter over the lens, which reduces the amount of light entering the camera to an acceptable level.

Many video cameras have a special low-light compensator control, which boosts image brightness electronically. This allows you to shoot in quite poor light and get 'acceptable' results. Though there will be some loss in picture quality, this is often a secondary consideration when the choice is between capturing precious moments on video or not recording them at all.

The effects of boosting light in this way vary between camcorder models. The colours in the scene may weaken, even change in hue; detail may be less sharp; moving subjects may appear as semi-opaque 'ghosts' against a static background; highlights smear or leave 'tails' as the camera pans; and halos may form around lights. Get to know the capabilities of your camcorder in low-light conditions and decide what results are acceptable. Remember, you can also turn some of these 'problems' to your advantage in creating special effects.

Reasonable pictures can be obtained indoors in a room that receives a lot of daylight, particularly if the walls are pale

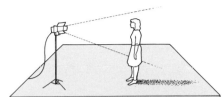

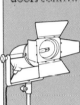

The quartz lamp produces a concentrated and efficient light that can be flooded or spotted. Four hinged barn doors control the beam. The telescopic stand allows the height to be varied. Usually rated at 500 to 1,000 watts each, quartz bulbs give light of 3,200°K, close to domestic tungsten light.

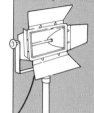

The broad-beamed lamp has a linear, quartz-halogen bulb housed horizontally in front of diffusing reflectors. These powerful lamps (rated at up to 1,250 watts) are more expensive, but produce a flood of diffused light, at 3,200°K, ideal for covering large areas. Bulbs should last for about 15 hrs.

(to reflect light) or you position your subjects near windows. Otherwise, you may need to add supplementary lighting from video lamps (*see p. 38*).

After dark, boost the normal room lighting by improvising with the domestic arrangements. For example:

● Use stronger (higher wattage) bulbs.
● Remove lamp shades.
● Redirect desk lamps and spotlights.
● Bring in more lights from other rooms.
● Open the drapes to take advantage of any street light available.
● Even groups of candles and firelight can increase the illumination level.

Investing in video lighting can improve recordings and extend the range of subjects you can cover. There is a variety of equipment available, from low-voltage, battery-run lamps that clip on to the camcorder to portable, mains-run lamps on stands. Each type of lamp gives a different amount, spread and quality of light (*see illustrations*). The equipment you need will depend on the intended use and the expense of purchase and operation. In addition, the colour temperature of the light produced is different to that of daylight and this will affect the colours of the picture when artificial and natural sources are mixed.

SAFETY FIRST

Using extra lighting in your home can involve some hazards. Sensible precautions will prevent accidents.

● Don't overload your power circuit. In general, 3 or 4 video lamps are about the maximum a domestic circuit will take.
● Turn off a lamp when changing the bulb. When you turn on again, make sure the lamp is pointing away from people – faulty bulbs can explode.
● Never point the camera directly at a lamp – it can burn a spot on the camera's image sensor.
● Lamps get hot, so turn them off when not in use or before moving them. Wear gloves when adjusting the light flaps (called barn doors).
● To prolong life, allow lamps to cool down before dismantling or packing them away.
● Quartz bulbs are susceptible to damp, including sweat. Wear gloves or use a cloth when changing bulbs.
● Coil lighting cables or tape them to the floor or skirting boards, so no one trips over them.

Mixed lighting: Shooting indoors during the day can necessitate the use of supplementary lighting. Even in a well-lit sunny room, there will still be areas of high contrast and subjects near a window will be in shadow on one side.

Increasing lighting levels artificially with video lamps will make the scene brighter and more evenly lit, thereby, lowering contrast between bright and shady areas.

However, when you mix artificial and natural light (ie daylight and domestic tungsten or quartz video lighting), you change the colour balance of the picture.

This is because each source emits light of a different colour temperature and, therefore, a different colour (*see p. 34*).

Mixed lighting plays havoc with the camera's white balance system. When shooting indoors with lights near a window, do you set the camera to 'daylight' or to 'tungsten/indoor'? Whichever choice you make, not all of the colours will be rendered true. The solution is to match the colour temperature of the light sources by using correction filters (*below*).

Using reflectors: Contrast problems can be reduced, and lighting problems avoided, by reflecting light back into, or

Too much contrast: Shooting indoors near a window with daylight as the only source of illumination can pose problems for the video camera. Here, parts of the subject are in heavy shadow. The camera, whether on auto iris or manual, cannot cope with the high contrast. If the aperture is set small, to expose for the brighter areas, foreground shadows will be lost, as here. If the aperture is set wide, to expose for the darker areas, the background will be bleached, or burnt, out.

Colour imbalance: By supplementing daylight with light from a video lamp, you 'fill' the shadows, reduce contrast and increase overall illumination. The contrast problem is now solved, but some of the colours in the scene have changed. With the white balance set to 'daylight'

'filling', areas of shadow. This gives an overall softer, more even light, which is ideal for shooting close-ups or relatively static situations such as interviews.

Special reflector boards can be bought or you can make your own. Heavy white card or polystyrene is ideal, with one side covered in crumpled-up tin foil to scatter the light even more. You can also improvise with white sheets or the open pages of a newspaper. To use a reflector board indoors, prop or hold it near a window, so that the light is angled on to the subject.

This device is so useful that it should become an essential part of your video kit.

Bounced lighting: Another important lighting strategy involves directing lamps at large reflective surfaces (such as pale walls, low ceilings or reflector boards) to bounce light back on to the subject.

Although bouncing light reduces the illumination produced by the lamp, it provides diffused, low-contrast lighting that can be ideal for video. Indirect lighting like this is also less discomforting for people. The intensity of the reflected light will vary according to the distance from the surface being used. But beware of strongly coloured walls, which will cast their colour on nearby subjects.

(which has a bluish cast naturally), the subject has an overall orange/yellow glow. If the 'tungsten' setting (which has a yellow tone) were used, the scene outside the window would have a bluish tinge.

Colour balance: To correct the colours, the temperature of *one* of the light sources must be changed to that of the other. The easiest way is to match the artificial light to daylight, by clipping a blue daylight

correction filter or gel over the lamp. Although this reduces the lamp's output, its colour temperature is raised to that of daylight. With the white balance set to 'daylight', all the colours are now correct.

CREATIVE TECHNIQUES

An interesting entertaining video, and one that you will
want to see and be seen again and again, is one that is not
merely a record of events — it has visual impact and
coherence. Making such creative videos requires advance
planning and an understanding of the basic video
language. This section describes some of the essential
creative techniques that the professionals use and explains
how you can employ them in your own productions.

SHOT SIZES AND TYPES

Varying the subject matter within the frame, by changing its size or angle of view, is what makes a video interesting for the video maker, as well as for the viewer.

A shot is a single recording. It lasts from the moment you press the record button to when you pause or stop. A sequence is simply a series of shots, usually covering a single event or set in a particular location, such as flying kites in the park.

Sequences should be made up of different sized shots to keep visual interest. Professional film and video crews have a language of their own to describe shot sizes. Each serves a specific function in directing attention to the events on screen in a way that will be most rewarding to the viewer. It is useful to be familiar with some of these terms (see box).

A sequence of events to illustrate various shot sizes might be: a general view of a beach, with groups of people; a long shot of a girl digging in the sand; a mid-shot of her concentrating on the job; a close-up of the sand moving; a big close-up of a crab that scuttles out, cut to another big close-up of her surprised face.

Besides different sizes, there are also different types of shot. Once again, each type serves to orientate the viewer and allow easy comprehension of the events.

Although shooting a person at their eye level is the most natural approach, it need not be the only one. Varying the camera height and angle is a good way of showing relationships. For example, shots from high angles clarify spatial relationships, as in the progress of a tennis game or a baby looking up at her mother.

Low-angle shots can be used creatively – to show the baby's point of view, for instance. They also serve to emphasize drama: a high-jumper clearing the bar or a skier racing downhill almost demand low-angle shots.

To get a natural feel to your videos, avoid shooting people looking directly at the camera lens. This looks rehearsed and artificial. Ideally, shots should be taken three-quarters-on or as close to full face as possible. Of course, if two people are talking, you can take an over-the-shoulder shot from behind one of them to the person beyond, whose eyes will be on the face of the person they are talking to, rather than staring into the lens.

Profile shots do not show much facial expression and are best used for scenes of people listening to or looking at something.

SHOT SIZES

Wide shot (WS): Also called the general view or very long shot, it should be included at or near the start of a sequence, to establish the scene and orientate the viewer. Such shots can be static or moving, so long as they reveal the scene generously, in time and space.

Long shot (LS): Closing in on the subject, this shot still retains a wide view and serves to direct attention to the subject by isolating it from what may be a distracting background.

Medium shot (MS): Sometimes called the mid-shot, this draws attention to the subject still further, by eliminating part of it and concentrating on a special feature.

Close-up (CU): One of the most valuable video shots, it shows significant detail or facial expression. Its size is most effective on the TV screen and its frequent use by professionals shows how highly they regard it.

Big close-up (BCU): Framing the subject even tighter gives an exaggerated view and shows further details. It is a shot full of impact and drama, and for these reasons should not be overworked. A BCU of an essential detail is often necessary for a sequence to be fully understood.

Most shot sizes are described in terms of the human figure, as illustrated here:

1 Wide shot (WS): This wide view of the overall scene serves to establish the main subjects and their relationship to each other. The WS is an important shot, to orientate the viewer.

2 Long shot (LS): Closer than the WS, this shot isolates the subject, or subjects, from the general background and focuses attention on the main theme. The entire figure is included, with some space top and bottom of the frame.

3 Medium shot (MS): By eliminating part of the subject, you concentrate the area of interest. Compose the shot from just below the waist upward. A good follow-up shot is the medium close-up, cut off at chest level.

4 Close-up (CU): An ideal shot to show detail or facial expression, it is cut off just below shoulder height, leaving some space above the head.

5 Big close-up (BCU): Visually striking and full of impact, this shot includes most of the forehead down to just above the chin. Use the BCU sparingly, otherwise you limit its dramatic effect.

Picture composition is all to do with arranging the elements of a shot in such a way as to communicate your message effectively, while at the same time achieving a pleasing, well-balanced image.

Unlike stills photography or even painting, where the shape of the frame can be varied, the video frame has fixed proportions. It is 3 parts high to 4 parts wide and whatever the elements of a shot (curves, verticals, horizontals or diagonals), they must be framed within this format.

The more you practise and exercise a critical eye on your results, the better your composition will become. 'Stop and look' is the golden rule. But remember that what the eye sees may be different from what the lens, and hence the viewfinder, shows. The lens distorts – perspective is flattened in the telephoto position, and a wide angle lens can cause distortion at the edges of the frame. Light and colour are also important considerations in any picture, but remember that colour will not be seen in the monochromatic viewfinder.

Therefore, every time you set up a shot, juggle with the compositional elements, by moving the lens or the camera position, so as to frame the subjects most effectively. Make it a habit to scan every part of the scene in the viewfinder. Pay particular attention to the edges where unwanted elements may be lurking, such as half a person or part of a building.

Constantly remind yourself why you are taking the shot – what you are trying to convey and what impact you hope to achieve. Exclude anything irrelevant to the scene. For example, a shot of a bride and groom exchanging marriage vows needs to be framed tightly enough to capture the intimacy of the moment; to include the best man and bridesmaids at this time would detract from the effect.

Framing must also be considered in relation to potential movements of the subject. If the frame is too wide, extraneous matter may distract from the

Looking space: When composing a shot of a person looking off-screen, either in profile or three-quarters-on view, always leave more space in front of them than behind (*top*). This principle is called leaving 'looking space'. Besides creating a natural balance within the frame, it also reinforces the sense of direction. With the subject jammed up against one side of the frame (*left*), the shot looks uncomfortable.

RULE OF THIRDS

A useful guide to good composition is the 'rule of thirds'. Imagine the area of the viewfinder as a grid, divided into thirds both across and down (*above*). Balance the key elements of the shot along the lines or where they cross. This is helpful when composing scenic shots by ensuring that horizons and vertical elements look balanced.

Framing faces: When composing a medium close-up or close-up shot, arrange for the eyes to be positioned about one-third of the way down the screen (*top*). This gives a comfortable feel within the frame. If the eyes were placed higher, the top of the head would be cut off; if they are too low (*left*), there is too much headroom and you are in danger of showing a disembodied head, with the chin resting on the bottom of the frame.

Walking room: When panning with a subject moving across screen, always compose the shot so that there is plenty of 'walking room' ahead of the subject (*top*). This creates a comfortable balance within the frame and also makes visual sense by reinforcing screen direction. With the subject too far to one side of the screen (*left*), he looks as though he is pushing the frame along. So remember, always pan ahead of a moving subject.

subject; if the frame is too tight, changes in movement or position may be difficult to contain within the frame.

A shot that looks well composed at the start may end up looking awkward once a subject moves. For example, when interviewing someone, always anticipate changes in their position. If you are shooting in close-up and the subject unexpectedly leans forward in the chair, your shot will be ruined if you are not ready to adjust framing, by easing out slightly on the zoom. Be ready to tighten up again when the subject sits back.

A shot of a horse jumping must be wide enough to show the fence and its height (but not so wide that other objects intrude), and framed loosely enough to show the horse and rider clearing the bars.

There are special compositional 'rules' to consider when panning with moving subjects or taking shots of people looking or pointing off-screen (*above*).

> ❝ *To the layman, the word sounds mysterious and its rules difficult, whereas in fact everyone possesses an innate sense of composition. It is one of the distinctive characteristics of the human being, like the gift of speech or a feeling for rhythm. The capacity for composition could be described simply as a sense of arrangement. Anyone who organizes objects on a desktop ... harmonizes the furniture, carpets, curtains is displaying a sense of spatial composition.* ❞

NESTOR ALMENDROS, CINEMATOGRAPHER
Sophie's Choice, Kramer vs. Kramer, Days of Heaven (Oscar)

COMPOSITION · 2

Create a new shape within the fixed TV format by shooting through a window, as from the back of a car. This novel view draws attention to the subject.

Shooting in mirrors breaks up the frame to give a distinctive composition, offering a scene within a scene. This shot can be used to create visual confusion.

COMPOSITION DOs

● Do keep horizontals level, especially when panning. Keep verticals upright when tilting.

● Do keep important elements away from the edges of the frame.

● Do search every part of the viewfinder before taking the shot to make sure there are no unwanted elements.

● Do decide in advance on the first and final images when panning, tilting and/or zooming. Compose them in your mind; better still, rehearse them first.

● Do be ready to adjust the framing, or recompose if necessary, when shooting moving subjects.

● Do leave some space between the top of people's heads and the frame.

● Do remember to leave 'looking space' and 'walking room' in front of your subject, to reinforce the sense of direction on screen.

● Do rely on your eyes for perceiving colour; the viewfinder shows only black and white.

● Do create depth in your shots by experimenting with foregrounds, focus and lighting.

Because of the two-dimensional nature of the TV screen, it is up to the video maker to create the illusion of a third dimension by composing shots which have visual depth.

There are several ways of doing this. Movement is probably the most obvious means. People moving toward or away from camera immediately create a sense of space and depth.

With static subjects, the angle of the shot can give an instant appreciation of perspective. For example, shooting a line of trees or buildings from three-quarterson shows depth. Similarly, a group of people strung out across the screen in a straight line is flat; give the scene depth by shooting from the side, or above, so that variations in height can be comfortably arranged and the receding scale emphasized.

Use the foreground to suggest depth. Framing a scenic view with the branches of a tree in the foreground is effective. A shot of one person with the shoulder and head of another in the foreground also serves to add depth, as does including a tray of drinks in the front of a shot at a crowded party.

Focus differentials can also create depth. Using out-of-focus features helps to sug-

The 'Dutch tilt' shot is taken with the camcorder set at a deliberate and strong angle to the horizon, to give a dynamic, often disconcerting, view of the subject.

Diagonal framing is an effective way to vary shots and a pleasing alternative to head-on composition. It can also be used to reinforce direction of movement on screen.

gest different planes. For example, showing a subject close to the camera out of focus, or having the background of the main subject defocused, uses separation to hint at the third dimension.

Variations in lighting, too, suggest depth. The contrast between a bright area and a shaded one in a shot immediately gives perspective to the scene and is particularly effective when reinforcing foreground and background relationships.

Composition can be varied within the fixed proportions of the frame to get interesting shots. For example, creating a new shape within the frame can produce a striking image – composing shots framed through doorways, windows or arches adds a new dimension to the scene.

Altering the screen shape also makes for interesting composition. For example, blacking out some of the scene, by shooting with the lens partly obscured by the edge of a wall or pressed up against a hole in a fence, produces a distinctive shape and concentrates the subject in the frame.

Composing diagonals, framing with mirrors and the 'Dutch tilt' shot are used for a specific purpose and their compositional balance reinforces that purpose (*above*). They should be used with discretion so as not to abuse their impact.

COMPOSITION DON'Ts

● Don't cut people off at the joints, eg at the neck in close-up or at the ankles in long shot.

● Don't always move the camera with the subject. Compose some shots in which the action is contained by a static camera.

● Don't have distracting objects 'growing' out of people's heads, eg telephone lines coming out of their ears or leaves springing from their hair. Remember, the telephoto setting compresses space and you can easily miss such details.

● Don't shoot, say, a green subject against a green background. It will disappear!

● Don't always centre subjects. Displace them and balance with other elements.

● Don't always arrange subjects in a straight line across the screen. Use diagonal composition to include them all and create visual depth.

● Don't always follow the rules. Take an analytical look at TV shows and see how the professionals bend the rules.

A

B

As an exercise in continuity, tape a 5-minute live action sequence and replay, freeze-framing if necessary, to analyze the 'rules' in practice. Note how action is continuous from shot to shot, observe how screen direction and speed of movement are maintained across cuts, and look out for neutral shots which allow the screen direction to be changed.

When watching any action sequence in a TV show, you will become aware that it is made up of a number of individual shots. These shots have been assembled or edited together in such a way that the result is immediately understandable to the viewer.

Consider a car chase, for example. In a professionally made film, the viewer knows exactly who is chasing whom and can follow the action, even at high speeds. The whole scene makes visual sense. But the film's production team have worked hard to get this sense, by employing a logical form of visual language to convey meaning to the viewer.

As a video maker, you should be aware of some of the basic rules of this visual language, in order to avoid visual jolts in your own work. Although these rules apply to constructed events, like a chase scene in a drama (ie building a sequence around one subject in continuous action), they are relevant to all forms of video making. Sooner or later, you will come up against these visual principles, so it is best to be aware of them first.

Continuity of action: A fundamental rule when showing continuous action of the same subject is to be consistent in the general direction of movement on screen.

Consider a shot of a bride and her father leaving home in a limousine. They drive off, exiting screen-right. The next shot of the limousine must show it entering screen-left, ie moving in the same direction as seen in the last shot. If it entered screen-right, it would look as if the bride had changed her mind and returned home. If, indeed, she has done this, then the car's change in direction needs to be shown.

As well as consistency in direction, there also needs to be consistency in speed and position of the same subject from shot to shot. For example, a shot of a skier speeding past the camera should *not* be followed by a shot of the same skier coming to a halt. The change in speed and the skier's position (from bent knees to upright stance) gives a visual jolt on screen which will be confusing to the viewer.

You should, therefore, aim to show a complete action in any one shot (ie the skier slowing down *and* coming to a stop) or you can insert a cut-away (*see p. 52*) to bridge the change in speed and position.

Line of action and the 180° rule: To avoid visual discontinuity of action subjects, imagine a line drawn through the scene representing the direction of action. In general, successive shots should be taken from one side of this line only.

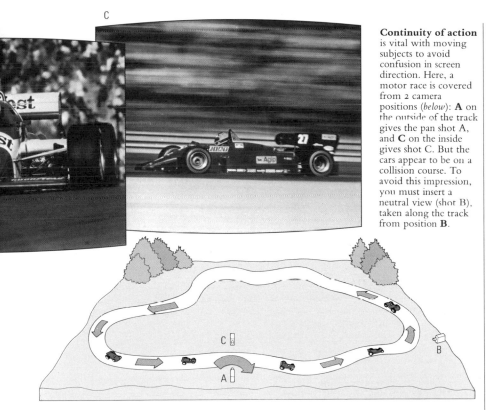

Consider a sequence of runners on a track and think of the track itself as the line of action. Choosing a camera position on the outside of the track will always give shots of the runners passing in the same direction. If you then move the camera to the other side of the track, you have crossed the line of action and shots will show the runners moving in the opposite direction.

This sort of visual disruption in the flow of action will be disconcerting for the viewers. They may think you have moved on to cover another race. This is avoided by staying on one side of the line and taking successive shots from anywhere within a 180° arc (hence the name of this rule).

Sometimes, you will want to cross the line of action to get shots from other vantage points. To do this without interrupting visual continuity, you can take a 'neutral' shot which has no evident screen direction, such as a shot straight along the track or line of action showing the runners moving toward or away from camera. Such a shot will act as a visual buffer to change the direction of movement. The following shots, taken from inside the track, can then quite naturally show the runners going in another direction.

A more elaborate way to change screen direction during a sequence is to keep shooting as you cross the line of action, so that the runners are seen approaching, passing and then departing during the one shot. This reversal of direction prepares the viewer for the following shots taken from the opposite side of the track.

The same rules that apply to continuous action sequences, such as runners racing around a track, also apply to less active subjects. Continuity of screen direction and the 180° rule (*see p. 48*) are important considerations in, say, a sequence showing two people playing cards at a table.

Continuity of eyelines: Like the line-of-action rule, establishing and retaining an 'eyeline' between two people is an important concept. It should be applied whenever you want to cut between successive shots of people relating to each other, whether they are talking, listening, looking or playing. Look at any interview or dialogue scene on TV to see this in practice.

Taking the example of two people at a card table, the first shot of such a sequence should be a long shot. This establishes their relative positions with, say, a man on the left of the table and a woman on the right. When you take closer shots, to show facial expressions or hands dealing cards, these positions must be retained so that the sequence makes visual sense to the viewer.

Imagine an eyeline between the two people which, like the line of action, should not be crossed between consecutive shots. If you follow the long shot with a close-up of the man (seated on the left and thus looking to the right) and then cut to a complementary reverse angle shot of the woman (seated on the right, looking to the left), all will be well with screen direction and continuity.

If, however, you took the shot of the man from one side of the table and then moved to the other side to take a shot of the woman, she will now appear to be sitting on the left and looking in the same direction as the man. Thus, by moving the camera position, you have crossed the eyeline and caused visual confusion for the viewers, who may begin to wonder whether they are watching a game of cards or musical chairs.

As with the line of action, you *can* cross the eyeline – by cutting to a neutral shot,

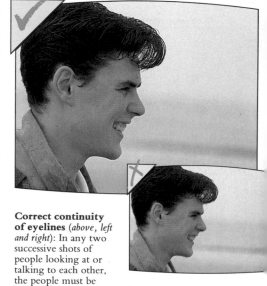

Correct continuity of eyelines (*above, left and right*): In any two successive shots of people looking at or talking to each other, the people must be looking in opposite directions, and appear to be facing each other, to make visual sense. Here, one is looking right, the other left. Their matching eyelines confirm the spatial relationship.

with no evident screen direction, such as a view of one player from directly behind and above the other. Or you can reverse the eyeline direction by shooting as you move around the table. A classic shot is from directly above the table.

The eyeline rule also applies to inanimate objects. For example, two shots of pictures hanging on opposite walls in a room need to be shot from one side of an imaginary line drawn between them, so that their relationship will be understood.

People and objects should be treated in a similar manner. For example, when a close-up of someone looking off-screen is followed by a shot of the object of their attention, then this second shot must be taken from the same side of their gaze. It will then be clear exactly where the object is in relation to the person.

Eyelines can also be confirmed by camera angles. For example, a shot taken

Incorrect continuity of eyelines (*above*): Given a dialogue scene, these two consecutive shots make no sense. Both people are looking in the same direction; the viewer could be misled into assuming that they are looking at a third person, not yet seen. This common continuity error occurs when shots are taken from different sides of the eyeline.

from a high angle down on a child looking up at a clown's face needs to be matched by a shot from a low angle looking up at the clown.

The conventions of eyelines can sometimes be used to good creative effect. Say a shot of an excited spectator at a baseball game is followed by a shot of a player making a home run, taken from a matching eyeline, the audience will assume that the spectator is reacting to the runner. In fact, the spectator shot could have been taken much earlier or even at a different game. But, by intercutting these two shots with matching eyelines and similar backgrounds, the audience is fooled into thinking that the two events are related.

You can exploit this type of audience assumption still further by intercutting shots, taken at quite different times, to get an exciting sequence of, say, a child seen to be stalking a lion in the African bush.

Continuity of appearances: The general and detailed appearance of a subject should remain consistent from shot to shot and throughout a sequence.

This is rarely a problem when you are shooting events as they happen. But if you are recording drama, for example, which may involve shooting on different days with the same people in several locations, then you need to be aware of potential gaffes that can occur in continuity.

● Lighting and exposure must remain consistent throughout a sequence. Working indoors, this is usually easy to control. But with outdoor work, you have to contend with changes in weather from day to day. On occasion, this may mean being patient and waiting for similar shooting conditions to match your earlier takes.

● Action and positions need to be consistent from shot to shot. For example, if a long shot of a waiter serving at table is followed by a closer shot, the waiter should still be serving the same customer.

● Details of the background should be the same throughout a sequence. For example, if the drapes in a room are closed at the start of shooting, they should remain so for all subsequent shots (unless, of course, you show someone opening them).

● Clothes, make-up and props should not change, without explanation, during a sequence.

For example, a woman who appears wearing a red dress, dark glasses and a hat should be wearing all these items in the next shot, unless you have inserted a shot of some or all of them being removed. Sequences that show people smoking, drinking or eating also present tricky situations. The length of a cigarette needs to diminish from shot to shot, and the level of drink in a glass must not increase miraculously between successive shots, unless the glass is seen to be topped up.

If there are changes between shots and you cannot reshoot, then you will have to edit accordingly, to restore continuity.

VISUAL FLOW • 1

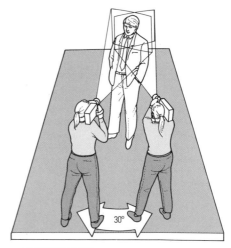

Establish the scene and develop the theme. This applies to any video, whatever the subject you have chosen – marriage ceremony, sports event, summer vacation. Aim to break the subject or event down into a series of shots, or sequences, that flow together naturally, so that the viewer experiences the sense or feeling of the event.

Sequences should be made up of different sized shots, for visual interest (see p. 42). But when you change or cut between two successive shots, the size of the second, and ideally its angle, must be sufficiently different to allow a smooth transition. If both shots are of the same size, or taken from the same angle, the subject will appear to 'jump' on screen.

For example, consider a sequence of a baby being spoon-fed. You may shoot a close-up of the baby eating, then pause the recording (eg while the spoon is being refilled) and start again in close-up. The result will be a distracting jump between the first and second shots, since the baby is bound to have changed position and expression during the pause.

To avoid such a 'jump cut', you can change the second shot size to, say, a medium shot of both baby *and* parent. Or, you can change the shot angle, starting with a three-quarters-on view of the baby, followed by a profile shot. Both methods have the additional advantage of disguising any minor changes in position of the subject. Combining both a change in size *and* a change in angle is what you should aim for.

Anticipating what the viewer might expect to see next helps to give a natural flow to events. Taking shots of complementary subjects aids this flow. 'Reverse angles' are valuable continuity shots (see box). So are 'point-of-view' shots where, for example, a shot of people looking or pointing at the sky is followed by a shot, taken from their point of view, of what they see – an aircraft, Superman ...

Change camera angles between 2 shots of the same size to avoid the subject 'jumping' on screen.

The left camera angle gives a full-face view. By moving at least 30° right, cut to a three-quarters-on shot.

Shooting a long event in its entirety may not be feasible or even desirable. Showing highlights is much more interesting. Linking them is the challenge. An obvious and easy way is to use the fade-in/out facility available on most camcorders. But there are other, more creative ways.

'Cut-aways' and 'cut-ins' are examples of linking shots that bridge the gap between actions or positions, or cover time lapses. Take a shot of a ferry coming slowly into harbour, then cut away to people waiting on the quayside, then cut back to the ferry tying up at its mooring. This last position will seem natural because the cut-away shot has served to cover the boat's passage in time.

The sequence might continue as follows: cut away to the expectant face of a girl in the crowd; cut back to long shot of

Changing shot size between 2 shots from the same angle also avoids the subject 'jumping'. Here, a medium shot can be cut to a close-up, by moving the camera or by changing the focal length of the lens.

REVERSE ANGLE SHOTS

One method of achieving continuity of flow is to use reverse angle shots. These are frequently seen in dialogue scenes on TV, where a shot of the speaker is followed by a shot of the listener. The second shot, the reverse angle (*below*), is the complementary sequel to the first shot and the two together make a natural pair. Both shots should be of the same size, to reinforce the relationship between the subjects.

Of course, you can take reverse angle shots involving subjects other than people. An owner's view of a cat might be followed by the cat's view of the owner (*bottom*). Or a shot of a car racing toward camera can be followed by the matching reverse angle of it speeding away.

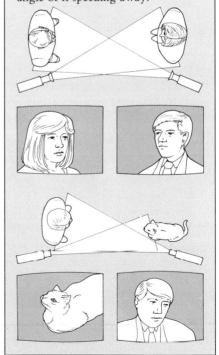

the passengers disembarking; then, cut in to a detail, say a close-up of one passenger's smiling face, followed by a zoom out to show the girl waiting by the gangway.

Here, the cut-away and cut-in shots have served to direct attention to the next event without disorientating the viewer — and, incidentally, given you time to change the camera angles. An event that may take up to an hour in reality has been summed up in 6 easy shots, with subtle transitions between events in time and place. To be convincing, such linking shots need to be held long enough for the viewer to take in the scene (a minimum of 3 seconds) or to cover any action.

There are many ways to link changing scenes. One approach might be to show a person in close-up, followed by a shot of them seen from a different angle, then a zoom out to reveal the new setting.

VISUAL FLOW • 2

Making a successful video involves mastering all the aspects of visual sense, such as screen direction and eyelines. It also involves creating a visual flow of interlinking images by, for example, using various shot sizes, reverse angles and linking shots such as cut-aways.

The key is to think visually – not in terms of single attractive shots, but in sequences of effective images that progress the sense or feeling of the subject. With practice, this 'visual literacy' will become second nature. The sequence illustrated here is one way of achieving such visual flow.

A dramatic low angle opens the sequence and establishes the fairground theme ☞

A mid-shot focuses attention on the activity that will form the storyline ☞

A matching reverse angle continues the action, which can now be expanded ☞

A reaction shot, taken from a low angle, dramatizes the moment of success ☞

A cut-in detail, of the prizes on a shelf, acts as an effective link shot ☞

A wide shot reveals the location and   introduces the two main characters ☞

A long shot, panning ahead of the subjects,   confirms screen direction ☞

A close-up serves to concentrate interest   and leads the viewer to the next shot ☞

A reverse angle, taken as a point-of-view   shot, develops the action ☞

A change of height adds variety to the   shots and helps direct attention ☞

A reverse angle shot with matching eyelines   concludes the sequence.

EDITING IN-CAMERA

Editing a video tape allows you to determine the way in which you show events, the length of individual shots and sequences, and the overall length of the programme.

Video can be edited in two ways. Tape-to-tape editing involves copying sections of the recorded tape on to a second, blank tape and putting the material in order as you go (*see p. 62*). The other method is editing in-camera. This means that you decide on the sequence, the order and the length of shots *as you shoot*. The tape will therefore be a 'live' show, compiled exactly as you recorded events.

Editing in-camera requires advance planning and some quick decision-making on the spot, since you will be making edits as shooting proceeds. But it is a discipline worth mastering because it forces you to anticipate events and consider the visual flow of the whole programme. Jotting down a list of shots beforehand will pay dividends at the time of shooting.

How long should a programme be? Always remember you are making a video for an audience, not just for yourself. Tapes run between 30 minutes and 4 hours. However, even relatives with a personal involvement will pale at the prospect of watching a 3-hour tape of your daughter's marriage. So, leave your viewers wanting more, not less. As a rule, aim for an edited in-camera video of about 20 to 30 minutes long.

How long should an individual shot be? This, of course, depends on the subject matter and whether it is static or moving. For static subjects, there are some general guidelines:

● Hold a static subject on screen for an average of 7 seconds. However, the length of general views, long, medium and close-up shots will vary with the subject (*see photographs*). A long shot of a new location may need a 10-second hold, while a close-up of a subject already seen in wider view may only need 5 seconds or less.

7 Hold static general views of new subjects long enough for the viewer to take in the scene. Allow at least 7 secs and, if there is detail in the shot, allow 10 secs.

● How long you hold close-ups of people will vary with the action. Allow a minimum of 3 seconds. Don't hold so long that people become self-conscious, or so short that you fail to register their expression.
● With pan, tilt and zoom shots, hold the front and end images for about 3 seconds each (although you don't always need to hold the front image of a zoom-out).
● Shots of written material (eg street signs, plaques) should be held long enough to be read. As a guide, read the words to yourself and then allow half as much again for slow readers.

With moving subjects, consider these general points:
● Aim to include a complete action in any one shot before cutting.
● When there is a lot of action (eg skiers or windsurfers) or a lot of interest and detail (eg a street parade), allow the shot to run until there is a natural break.
● But remember, too many lengthy shots become tedious, while too many quick cuts are irritating.
● Let the subject dictate the overall pace, eg coverage of a lively party benefits from quicker cutting than a tranquil scene of a potter or glassblower at work.

5 **Cutting to a closer shot** of the same subject need only be held for 5 to 7 secs. Hold for longer if there is any action or a street sign or plaque to be read.

3 **A detailed close-up** of a subject already seen can be briefer still, as little as 3 secs. If your shot is timed for *Big Ben's* chimes, hold for the time you want sound.

● Don't cut while the camera is still moving (as in a pan, tilt or zoom) since the result will be an abrupt edit.

Sound is another consideration that may determine shot length. Remember that when you pause the camera, you also pause the sound. So, for example, when recording the best man's joke at a wedding reception, don't cut the shot until he has delivered the punchline. Sound will also dictate the camera's position if you are relying on the built-in microphone; to record a guide's speech, for example, you will need to be close enough to catch the words. Of course, you can always add or replace the original sound with your own commentary or music later (*see p. 124*).

Cameras with electronic viewfinders allow you to review the tape at any stage – an invaluable facility when editing in-camera. You can check back on the recording to date and, if unhappy, simply retake the scene.

Some camcorders allow you to insert new shots into sequences already taken. Titles can be added later or close-ups of details missed can be inserted while you are still on location. This technique, however, requires some precision (*see p. 122*).

IN-CAMERA CUTTING POINTS

Camcorders operate on a 'backspacing' principle to produce 'clean' edits between shots (ie edits free from electronic disturbance). Each time you pause the recording, the tape is automatically wound back over the last second or so of the shot. When you start shooting again, the tape runs forward (while the electronics lock on to the control track of this short section) and the new recording starts. As a result of this backspacing, you lose a fraction at the start of each shot. The amount varies with each model, so it is important to get to know how your machine operates.

Backspacing is only a problem when trying to capture quick moments of activity. You must compensate for this loss when timing shot lengths or by anticipating the action slightly at the start of a shot, eg with someone diving into a pool, start recording the action *just before* they dive, not *as* they dive.

Choose a good subject and you are halfway toward making a good video. Colour, activity, variety, detail and an outdoor setting will all help to ensure that your first videos are interesting to make, not too demanding to shoot and great fun to watch.

Choose subjects that are accessible and easy to record, such as children riding bikes in the park, a picnic in the woods, a local market or an outdoor show. Before you go shooting, check the following:

Equipment checklist
● Check the camcorder's battery is fully charged. Take at least one charged spare.
● Put a tape in the camcorder and carry a spare for extra shooting.
● Check the camcorder's functions and clean the lens with photographic tissue.
● Consider whether you will need a tripod, portable video light (fully charged and with spare bulb) and an auxiliary microphone.
● Always take headphones when recording live sound vital to the programme, which, if missed, cannot be repeated.
● Take a pure white card for setting colour balance on location.

Location checklist
● Set the white balance for the prevailing light conditions.
● Set the iris and focus to auto or manual, as required.
● Do a test shoot to check that picture and sound are recording successfully.
● Review the recording from time to time, and at the end of the shoot.
● If you take a break during shooting, always replace the lens cap and be careful where you put the camcorder down.

After you've viewed your efforts at home on the TV, get some audience reaction. This is *the* test because, after all, you are making videos for other people to enjoy. Don't be defensive! Learn from their comments, then apply this knowledge to your next video. Soon you will be your own most sensitive critic.

A visit to a farm is an ideal subject. This is a good establishing shot to set the scene; including people in the foreground creates visual interest and a sense of depth.

When following action, leave 'walking room' in front of the subject. In this pan shot, the horse is too far to the right.

A potentially good shot is spoiled by excluding part of the subject. Tilt up for a more pleasing composition.

Galloping horses make an excellent action subject. But with this sort of panning shot, it can be difficult to keep the horizon level without using a tripod.

Children watching the geese could make a good cameo, but this shot is taken too far away to show any detail. Move closer or zoom in for a tighter view.

The value of the close-up – by framing to include the horse in the foreground, you create visual interest in the composition.

Another successful close-up, well worth the wait. Tight framing directs attention to the gentle moment.

It is easy to forget about lighting when busy shooting. Here, the child is underexposed due to strong backlight.

A simple long shot gives a natural end, carefully framed to include the figures in a good diagonal composition.

STORYBOARDING

> *Kleiser [Director, Grease and The Blue Lagoon] was a master at using the storyboard ... Every morning he would sketch out each shot one after the other like comic strips, and this made it easy to discuss the camera angles for the day's work, since we had concrete examples.*

NESTOR ALMENDROS, CINEMATOGRAPHER
Sophie's Choice, Kramer vs. Kramer, Days of Heaven (Oscar).

7. Close-up. Girl points off right. Both look angry.

18. Po long puttir Drive

21. Travelling shot of children (take from back of car). Girl's cap flies off (1st clue for rescue party).

22. long in fore Childre right an stream

Many of the videos you shoot will be documentaries, where you have simply documented, or made a record of, events over which you had little control. At a wedding or birthday party, for example, the event is not yours to direct and so you must record scenes as they happen.

Making up your own story, and getting family and friends to enact it, will give you complete control over the event. Keep the plot or storyline simple for your first efforts. Include a lot of action scenes, especially when children make up the cast, and limit the amount of dialogue so the 'actors' will not get tongue-tied during shooting. Let the pictures tell the story.

Once you have devised the general storyline, work out the details by drawing up a storyboard, where each shot is visualized on paper (*right*). This may sound complicated, but you don't have to be an artist or an ace-director to do it. Simple sketches of stick-people will suffice, with the bare outlines of other features and background drawn in. Number each sketch or frame, and write a summary below, describing the action and type of shot planned.

Compiling a storyboard, no matter how basic, in advance of shooting is a useful technique for several reasons.

● It forces you to think about what you are shooting and why. You can concentrate on getting a natural logic or flow to events and anticipate likely linking shots.
● It helps you to pre-plan the details of continuity of action and appearance.
● Visualizing individual shots on paper makes you think about composition.

int-of view,
shot of villains,
g loot in car.
off at speed.

19. Medium shot.
Children rush in from
left, grab bikes and
exit right.

20. Low angle
(Dutch tilt) from
roadside as car races
past. Children in pursuit.

shot. Stream
ground.
arrive, look
go toward

23. High angle, through
branches. Children
crossing water on tree
trunk.

24. Low angle, medium
shot of children
crossing. Boy snags
sweater (2nd clue).

● When editing in-camera, the story-board acts as the master plan for ordering your shots or sequences as you shoot.
● When editing tape-to-tape, the story-board gives you a basic plan against which you can order your shots later.

Professionals rely on storyboards when making films, commercials and pop videos.

A section of a storyboard shows the shots planned for an action sequence of two children chasing thieves. Each shot is visualized and planned for content, camera angle and shot size. Highlight key shooting points as reminders. Once on location, details may change but the overall sequence will be shot according to this plan. Drawings can be much simpler than these. Each person will have their own visual shorthand.

TAPE-TO-TAPE EDITING

You will probably want to keep most of your edited-in-camera videos intact. But there will be occasions when you want to reorder the recorded material and edit it into another form.

Editing a video is very different from editing film or an audio tape, where the material is cut and spliced into the desired order. To edit a video, the chosen sections of the recorded tape are copied onto a second, blank tape.

This process is called tape-to-tape editing and it has several advantages. By distilling the best of your recorded material, you can make a programme of ideal viewing length with good pace and visual flow. You can eliminate unwanted material; change the length of individual shots and reorder them; take in parts from other, previously recorded tapes; and add titles and other graphics (see p. 110).

However, since tape-to-tape editing involves a copying process, there is bound to be some reduction in quality. The images lose a little of their definition, there is evidence of picture 'noise' and colours are slightly degraded. The sound track tends to deteriorate a little and pick up hiss. And all these problems will be accentuated on copies made from the edited tape. However, using a high-grade tape and a good quality VCR (video cassette recorder) will minimize these defects.

The easiest and most accessible tape-to-tape method for home use is called assemble editing (see box). Any combination of tape format can be used, so copying from 8mm to VHS or Betamax is straightforward. The only technical concern is that the VCR being used as the edit recorder should be able to make 'clean' edits.

Assemble editing is simple but not very accurate; however, with practice, you can get well-timed edits between shots, especially if during shooting you make full allowance for backspacing at the start of shots (see box, p. 57). For more accurate work use an edit controller (see p. 122).

HOW TO ASSEMBLE EDIT

Connect the camcorder to the VCR (via audio and video links) and the VCR to the TV (below).

Before editing, 'log' your tape: make a list of the shots you want, the order you want them in and note their numbers from the camcorder's counter. Then, proceed as follows:

1 Insert a blank tape in VCR, wind it forward for about 30 secs, then set machine to record-pause.

2 On your recorded tape, find the start of the shot, or 'edit', then rewind the tape for a few seconds.

3 Run the tape on the camcorder. Just before you reach the beginning of the edit or 'in-point', release pause on VCR.

4 Continue recording until you are a few seconds past the end of the shot, then pause VCR and stop camcorder.

5 Play back the edit to check your timing is accurate. Let the tape run and just as you reach the end or 'outpoint', press pause on VCR. Repeat steps 2 to 5 for the next edit.

Some VCRs allow you to insert edit, ie add new material into an already edited tape (see p. 122).

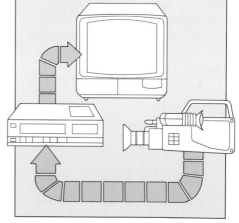

Editing shots to give visual flow to a sequence clarifies the situation for the viewer. Compare the unedited version (*top*) with the edited one (*above*). The unedited shots are puzzling. What are the children looking at in the first 3 shots? What is the

relationship of the squirrel to the children in the next 3?

By simply putting these 6 shots in a different order, using the tape-to-tape editing method, the sequence makes sense and the story unfolds. By alternating shots of the children with those of the

animal, a sequence of natural reverse angles is built up.

Tape-to-tape editing allows you to shoot in a more convenient order, to take longer shots for cutting back later and to concentrate on one subject at a time, taking it from several angles.

TOP TOPICS

There are several topics universally popular with video makers. 'Top Topics' tells you the creative approach appropriate to each and gives ideas on how to tackle the variety of challenges you are likely to encounter. Each of these popular subjects will have a set of requirements that needs to be met if you are to get the best video record. There will be variations, for example, in the time spent on pre-planning and preparation, the equipment needed and the creative techniques to be used.

CHILDREN

Video offers the perfect medium for making a record of children as they grow up. A series of tapes, capturing key episodes in their development, will become a permanent treasure for both adults and children.

You will probably build up a lot of material over the years, so it is a good idea to date the sequences as you shoot them, by using the camcorder's caption generator. Or a more interesting way is to take cut-away shots of newspaper headlines at the time of shooting. Then, if you make a composite tape later, these cut-aways can be insert edited to link sequences and remind you of other events going on when you shot the tapes.

Very young children, taking their first steps or playing with a favourite toy, are good subjects for a simple visual approach.
● Allow for long takes, so that the action can develop naturally.
● Keep the camcorder at the child's level as much as possible. Use a tripod with the legs splayed. Or, if hand-holding the camera, take up a comfortable position sitting with your back against a wall or tree trunk, and knees raised as props for the elbows to help camera steadiness.
● Use the zoom lens to follow action, as with a toddler crawling toward camera.
● Take frequent close-ups, to capture the variety of facial expressions. Remember also to get close-up reaction shots of parents and others to use as cut-aways.
● Don't forget the sound. Children's speech, laughter and exploratory noises can be delightful. Use an auxiliary mic to get the best recordings.
● When shooting indoors with extra lighting, make sure the light is gentle to avoid the child reacting to glare. Bounced or diffused lighting is ideal (see p. 38).

As children get older, they can become camera-conscious. Capture youngsters at their most natural when they are un-awares, concentrating on something or involved in an activity. Another approach

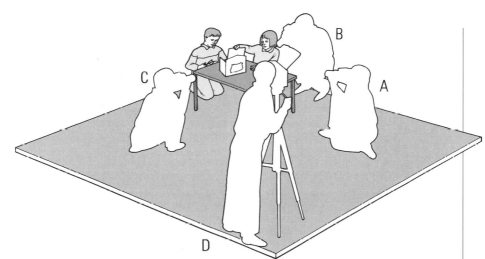

Children are best recorded when they are concentrating on some activity. This sequence (*left*) shows one way of telling a story in a few shots, taken from 4 camera positions (*above*).

Kneeling in position **A** gives you shot A, a low-level close shot of the boy. By crouching in position **B**/shot B, you get a big close-up that forms a natural bridge to the third shot. Kneeling in position **C** gives a matching reverse angle of shot A. Standing up and moving to the tripod in position **D** gives the final frame of the sequence, a long shot which reveals the whole scene.

Such a sequence would work equally well by starting with the long shot D or even the big close-up B. Cut-aways of adults watching the play would make good linking shots.

SHOOTING BLIND

A discreet way to record children un-awares is to 'shoot blind', without holding the camera to your eye. Use the wide angle setting and, with practice, you will get to know exactly the angle of view covered. Take up a well-balanced stance and simply hold the camcorder steady at your side, aiming it in the right direction. If the subjects move, adjust the camera position.

is to shoot surreptitiously – take telephoto shots in mirrors or from hidden vantage points, such as from an upstairs window or behind a hedge. And, with practice, you can 'shoot blind' (*see box*).

If children become self-conscious and start playing up to the camera, don't worry too much; simply record their pranks and funny faces peering into the lens and then rewind the tape if you don't want the shots. Once children get used to the camera being around, they will relax and get on with their own interests.

Children are natural performers, so take advantage of their desire to show off or display their skills in front of the camera by making a record of their achievements. Their collaboration will ensure you get the best camera positions and sound. An audience always helps in such situations, so marshal a few appreciative relatives and record their applause to end the sequence.

INFORMAL PARTIES

A party may be informal, but your video record of it should be structured to give sense, atmosphere and visual flow to the event. The aim throughout will be to use a 'candid camera' approach and to concentrate on capturing sound as well as pictures.

This will mean hand-holding the camera most of the time so that you can move about freely. To avoid being obtrusive, use the telephoto setting. Be prepared to adjust your position by moving the camera or easing the zoom wider to accommodate people's movements. Lean against any support to improve camera steadiness: walls, doorways, chairs, even people's shoulders will do.

Pre-plan as much of the shooting as possible. Work out a variety of camera angles. Look for positions that give general views to establish large groups of people – high-angle shots are ideal. Plan for low-angle shots also, to get people sitting on sofas and chairs. If you know in advance where the food and drinks will be, set up a shot with these in the foreground, to add visual depth to the scene.

Getting good sound recording at a party can be difficult with the camcorder's built-in microphone. Only the general murmur of chatter will be picked up, not individual voices. It is therefore best to use a separate, unidirectional or cardioid mic (*see p. 33*).

Ideally, the mic should be handled by a second person working with you as part of a team. They should behave like an informal interviewer, moving among the guests and prompting them to talk. The mic should be held at chest height, placed equidistant between the 'interviewer' and the subject, and angled toward the speaker each time.

Follow the mic, with the camcorder on pause, and wait for the right moment to start shooting. Once conversations are established, you can then capture real off-the-cuff material. When working like this, always wear a good pair of headphones so

Conversational groups (*above*) can be recorded at a party by having a friend walk around with a hand-held microphone, picking up real conversations. If the group is small, stay wide to include all the people. In low light, direct a battery lamp on the group.

An outdoor party, such as a family barbecue (*right*), is a good opportunity to get some high-angle establishing shots of the whole group from an elevated position, such as an upstairs window. Be aware of contrast problems around midday when there are deep shadows.

that *you* can follow the talk as well and therefore avoid cutting the shot at the vital part of a story or joke.

● To start with, keep your shots fairly wide, to include all the people in the conversational group.

● As you move in for closer shots, look and listen for who is going to speak next. Such anticipation of action allows you to adjust your position in advance.

● Try to keep *both* eyes open, one trained on the image in the viewfinder and the other watching the action around you.

● In general, concentrate your shooting on the speaker. But it is also interesting to see the listener's reactions, especially when a story or joke is being told. If you are editing in-camera, you will lose the sound each time you cut to a reverse angle shot of the speaker/listener. To avoid this, pan gently from one to the other and then back

A party video should tell a story. The beginning and middle are easy; finding a good ending is more elusive. An obvious way to end by showing the guests waving goodbye. But a more imaginative way could be to invite guests to watch shots of themselves as they arrived at the party. When they are watching, you record their reactions on a separate tape. Then edit these onto the party tape later.

again. Or take a wider shot to include both of them.

● If you are going to edit the tape, concentrate on the speaker and take cut-away shots later of the various listeners.

● Don't forget composition. Balance the shots so there is natural 'looking space' (*see p. 44*) in front of people.

● Other link shots can imply the passing of time, such as cut-aways of ever-diminishing supplies of food and drink. Or return occasionally to a single establishing shot of the party to show its progress. Such a recurring shot should be taken from the same position each time.

● Shooting indoors in confined spaces is a good opportunity to try out a screw-on, supplementary wide angle lens (*see p. 26*).

Background music can pose problems when recording sound. The music will, of course, change each time you pause and restart the camera. If possible, get the music turned down, or even off, when you are trying to capture conversational pieces.

Sequences of people dancing are fun to do. Vary shot height and angle, cutting quickly from one to the next. But remember that cutting the picture means cutting the sound, so you will have to dub an appropriate sound track on afterward. For this to work, all your shots will have to be of people dancing to the same tempo.

Supplementary lighting will probably be needed when shooting indoors (*see p. 74*). Lighting should be indirect to avoid high contrast. One way is to diffuse light by bouncing it off walls and ceilings. Colour gels can be placed over the lights to create a warm party atmosphere. When you are moving around, involve a third person on your team to hold a battery-operated video lamp for extra light.

A day trip to an historic site, a national park, a stately home, in fact any interesting location, provides an ideal subject for a video record. Try to create sequences that capture the atmosphere of the place as well as its physical features.

Doing some preliminary research is always useful to give you an idea of what to look for. Photographs in guide books will have been taken from the best positions, so watch out for these when on location. Making up a storyline and mental shot list is also worthwhile; once there, you may well adapt these.

Introductory shot, to intrigue viewer ☛

View of castle from different angle ☛

Linking shot of family exploring grounds ☛

Close-up of boy pointing upward ☛

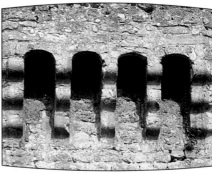

Point-of-view shot of detail from below ☛

Tilt up to wide shot, to establish theme ☞

Reverse angle, to introduce family ☞

Head-on shot of family approaching ☞

Low-angle view of castle and family ☞

Long shot of receding figures ☞

Concluding shot, to echo opening image.

An edited in-camera sequence of a family's visit to a special place might consist of the kinds of shots illustrated on the previous page and further explained here. Although planning a storyline and mental shot list will help, much of your location shooting will involve 'thinking on the feet' and reacting to opportunities as they occur. To create visual coherence, take cut-aways, cut-ins and reverse angles to link members of the family and the sights they see. The final video should reflect the pace of the visit.

The opening shot of a sequence does not have to show the main subject. An attractive composition, setting the atmosphere and pace of the programme, will arouse interest and lead the viewer into the subject.

Tilt up and zoom out slowly to reveal the main subject, using the swan's movement as a cue. Or you can treat these images as 2 separate shots; they will cut together well with the strong visual link of water and daffodils.

Frame the people in an attractive composition within the archway. Hold long enough for them to pass close to camera and out of shot. This neutral view, with no strong screen direction, allows you to cut from the last scene.

A low-angle shot from behind serves three purposes: the figures in the foreground add depth to the shot, the angle of view accentuates the impressiveness of the castle and the composition shows the family's viewpoint.

Close-ups are an important part of any sequence to register facial expressions. Wait for an interesting composition, such as the boy pointing upward which can then be followed naturally by a shot of what he sees.

Pace, atmosphere and natural flow of events are important to retain in your video recording of a family outing. A relaxed stroll through beautiful gardens should convey a feeling of unhurried calm to the viewer; a flurry of bargaining at a flea market should also feel authentic.

The opening shot of any sequence is clearly important because it sets the scene. A general view or establishing shot should be shown near the start, to orientate the viewer, but it need not necessarily be the first shot. A new subject or location can be introduced as a visual discovery to build audience interest. For example, a shot that starts looking along a path can then tilt up gently to reveal a house or a person. Shots that start out of focus and are then gradually pulled into focus make intriguing introductions, as do zoom shots that start on a detail and then pull out to reveal the whole subject.

Establishing shots can be used to lead into the action. After a general view of a waterfall, for example, zoom back slowly to get a shot of a person gazing at the scene. Then cut to a reverse angle shot of another person standing talking to them. The

Cut to a reverse angle, medium shot to introduce the family, who are seen looking and pointing off-screen. Hold this shot long enough to record any comments. Also, cut in to get close-ups of expressions and reactions.

A natural follow-up, this wide shot shows what the family are looking at. The castle is seen from another angle, with depth and scale in the scene. You could hold this shot until the group moves out of frame.

Leapfrog ahead of the action to record the family's reactions as they approach. By starting close on the blossom and zooming back to reveal the family, this shot acts as an effective bridge from the last location.

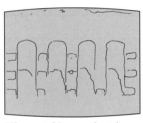

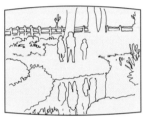

The matching angle, taken from the boy's point of view, reveals the object of his interest. Having cut to this shot, you can then develop the theme with a sequence showing other details of the castle's fortifications.

Look for some natural shots to close the sequence, such as a view of the family walking away from camera. This shot could start on the reflections of the figures, then tilt up to reveal them strolling along the bank.

Finding the final image for a sequence can be a challenge. Here, the grebe on its nest is not only a pleasing image in itself, but also reflects the opening shot of the sequence and could symbolize the idea of 'going home'.

setting and characters are now revealed; the 'plot' can begin.

For key shots, such as the family arriving at a new location, it is best to go ahead of them and set up the shot in advance. By 'leapfrogging' ahead of the action in this way, you can capture spontaneous reactions to events as they happen.

Shooting a series of views or details of the place you are visiting makes a good montage sequence of impressions. This is often a neat way of visually rounding off the video. Leave such shots until toward the end of your visit, when you will be familiar with the features of the location.

Live sound is not always wanted on a video – you can add your own sound later (*see p. 124*). But you may want to record a guide's commentary on the place you are visiting. In this case, get as close to the guide as possible if you are using the camcorder's built-in mic. Better still, get one of the family to hold a separate directional mic. If editing later, keep a note of the guide's main points so you can shoot these subjects while still on location and insert edit them later (*see p. 122*) at the relevant parts of the commentary.

SPECIAL OCCASIONS • 1

One of the joys of video is that you can make a full and permanent record of special family occasions. These happy memories will form part of the family archive, to be viewed for years to come.

You will need some control over the event in order to get the best possible camera positions, lighting and sound arrangements. You will also need to be 'in the know' about any surprises planned (presentation of gifts, entry of the birthday cake, arrival of a 'special' guest) so that you are in the right place at the right time.

For evening events, lighting is a prime consideration. Think about the following:
● Work out a simple lighting plan and test it before the event. Aim for a plan that needs minimum adjustment.
● In small or crowded rooms, place lamps well back near walls and keep cables coiled or taped to the floor.
● Place lamps in an arc on the camera side, so that there is no danger of shooting into or against a light.
● A single 'key' light, above a table or at the centre of a room, is important. You will also need some 'fill' light to avoid heavy shadows, unflattering to the eyes.
● Candlelight alone will not provide enough light for shooting. But as an extra source, it is most effective when close to a subject. A star filter enhances the effect.
● Coloured filters on the camera add warmth to the scene, as do colour gels on lamps.

A few more shooting tips for indoor occasions might be:
● The voices around the table are as important as the faces, so use a separate microphone to that of the camcorder. Place it centrally and do a sound test, speaking as you move round the table.
● Use mains power for indoor work. You can shoot plenty of material without worrying about charging batteries.
● Don't forget to include yourself in the video. Brief someone in advance, hand over the camera and relax!

Work out a lighting plan well in advance of shooting.

When using fill light, remember that it can be either diffused or reflected. Pale coloured walls, such as those in the room illustrated, are ideal for bouncing light, to give an overall soft effect.

Microphones should be hidden from view as far as possible. Reduce the problems of unwanted noise by placing the mic upright on a simple desk stand or isolating it with a pad of foam.

The backlight is set off-screen left. Its function is to help separate the subjects from the background and add extra modelling and visual interest.

Beware of excessive highlights on bald patches or blonde hair. Try moving or diffusing the light, or applying powder make-up to the skin.

A fill light, from near and slightly above the camera position, softens the shadows created by the key light and reduces contrast.

Spectacles produce reflections and cause lighting problems that are difficult to solve. Minimize trouble by avoiding lights at the same level as the spectacles.

The key light, shining from above the centre of the table, provides the main illumination for the scene. On its own, it would produce deep shadows and strong highlights, especially on pale clothes and fair skin. The fill and back lights soften these contrasts.

An omnidirectional microphone, hidden among the table decorations, is ideal for recording conversation around a table. But beware of picking up excessive noise from crockery or from people stretching across or kicking the table.

Creative preparations for a video of a special occasion are as important as the technical preparations taken to ensure good light and sound.

Plan your shooting by getting a breakdown of the main events from your hosts. Arrange for enough time to set up the camera for each activity, especially the little 'surprises' of the party. Move the furniture about to suit your purposes (within reason, of course) and to ensure your camera path is clear. Place flowers or foliage to make attractive compositions for your shots. Use drapes to soften the appearance of the room and decorations to break up large areas of blank wall. All this may sound a little 'bossy', but your audience will thank you for it later.

Most special occasions have a progressive logic of their own, so continuity is not a problem. Start with a sequence that helps set up the event, such as guests arriving or the decorated table.

Once people are seated, take a 'master' shot to establish their positions at table and then use your various camera positions for mid-shots and close-ups of people. Look for shots that will convey the feeling of the occasion – a mid-shot of a boy seated between his grandparents, a gentle pan over faces deep in conversation, a close-up of an excited child blowing out candles. These are the moments to record.

Fading out between sequences is a useful way of indicating time passing. But explore other ways, such as starting a sequence with a close-up of discarded wrapping paper or an empty wine glass. Another way is to return at intervals to the same shot, say of a candle; as the evening goes on, so the candle burns down. Remember to take this recurring shot from the same position each time, so it is recalled by the viewer.

Look out for a neat way to conclude the tape, such as a final chorus of 'Happy Birthday' or the hosts waving goodbye to their guests at the door.

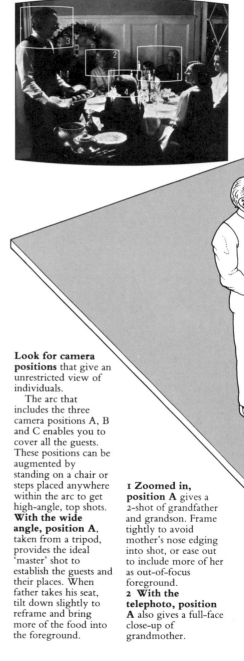

Look for camera positions that give an unrestricted view of individuals.

The arc that includes the three camera positions A, B and C enables you to cover all the guests. These positions can be augmented by standing on a chair or steps placed anywhere within the arc to get high-angle, top shots.

With the wide angle, position A, taken from a tripod, provides the ideal 'master' shot to establish the guests and their places. When father takes his seat, tilt down slightly to reframe and bring more of the food into the foreground.

1 Zoomed in, position A gives a 2-shot of grandfather and grandson. Frame tightly to avoid mother's nose edging into shot, or ease out to include more of her as out-of-focus foreground.

2 With the telephoto, position A also gives a full-face close-up of grandmother.

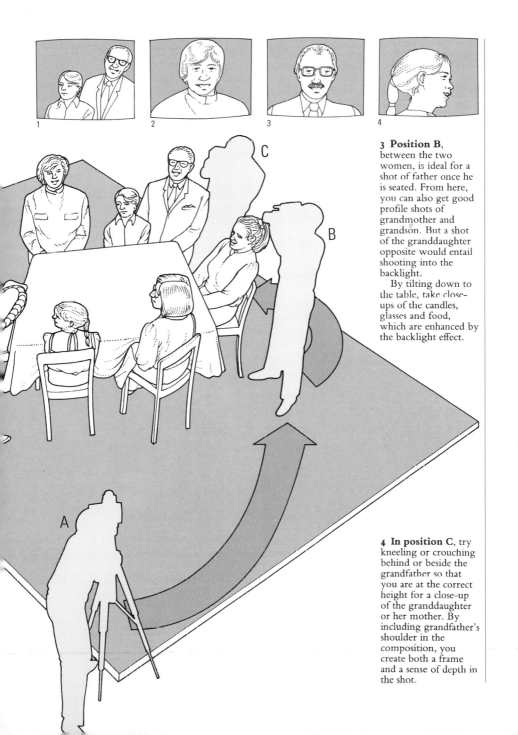

3 Position B, between the two women, is ideal for a shot of father once he is seated. From here, you can also get good profile shots of grandmother and grandson. But a shot of the granddaughter opposite would entail shooting into the backlight.

By tilting down to the table, take close-ups of the candles, glasses and food, which are enhanced by the backlight effect.

4 In position C, try kneeling or crouching behind or beside the grandfather so that you are at the correct height for a close-up of the granddaughter or her mother. By including grandfather's shoulder in the composition, you create both a frame and a sense of depth in the shot.

Video provides an excellent means of recording ceremonies and other big occasions – not just weddings, but also prize-givings, christenings, Bar Mitzvahs, retirement presentations and celebratory dinners. Because these are all 'one off' events, over which you will have little or no control, you must take steps to ensure that your record of the event is as complete as possible. Remember, too, that the tape will be an important personal record, valued by family and friends. Keeping them in mind throughout will help you decide what to shoot.

Planning is the key to a successful wedding video. Whatever the location, you should make a thorough check of all technical aspects of the shoot before the day. If the wedding will include a religious ceremony, start by checking whether you can shoot in the church itself. This will mean getting the cooperation of the minister; he may ask you to restrict your shooting to a single camera position.

Check that there is sufficient lighting by shooting a test tape. Work out the direction of sunlight and where it may fall during the ceremony and take account of its effects.

If you need more light, ask if you can use a battery lamp on the camcorder or bring in additional quartz lamps on stands. Concentrate any additional lighting on one area (eg near the altar) and choose broad-beamed, soft lights that will not dazzle the participants or create harsh unflattering shadows.

Church acoustics are often reverberant, so you will need to get the microphone close to the subjects to get good results, particularly when vows are being exchanged. Ideally, use a cardioid mic set between the couple and the minister. Alternatively, use a directional mic attached to the camcorder or held by an assistant. If the church has its own mics and amplification system, you may be able to take a direct audio line to feed into the camcorder's sound input.

Later, at the wedding reception, adopt a more 'candid camera' approach. Capture, without intruding, a special moment with the newly weds (*right*). Shoot in the telephoto position and get cut-aways of individual guests and their reactions during the speeches. Young children make great subjects and are rarely camera-conscious.

A wedding video requires advance planning and preparation to ensure that you capture all the key moments in the 'big day'. Work out a shooting plan so that you are always in the right place at the right time. Remember, you will only get one take of each stage of the event.

Capture the build-up to the ceremony. Record the bride having her hair done (*left*) or someone fixing her veil. Get to the church in good time to cover the bride's arrival (*below*). Take a low-angle shot (with door open to avoid reflections) to show off the dress.

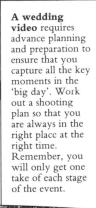

Even if you cannot shoot in the church, you may be allowed to make a sound recording which can be dubbed over shots taken outside the church. Or you could dub the sound on to a video tape compiled from the photographs of the wedding, shot with a rostrum camera.

The best camera positions are likely to be near the door and close to the altar (*see p. 80*). Look around for any other good angles or positions, for example, from a balcony, organ loft or the head of the aisle. If you plan to shoot from more than one position, work out how to move between them without creating a disturbance.

There is usually a wedding rehearsal, so use this to test your positions and to make sure you know the order of the service. Plan your main coverage with a story-board or shot list. This will make shooting decisions easier.

To create a more complete video of the 'big day', shoot some material of the build-up to the ceremony itself. You could start with photos from the family albums, showing the couple growing up, and move on to a close-up of the wedding invitation. Follow these with well-composed shots of the church that set the scene, then cut to a sequence showing preparations for the reception. Next, try to include an informal sequence of the bride and bridesmaids preparing themselves, but be careful that you don't add unduly to their nervousness. After this, be sure that you get to the church in good time to tape the arrival of the guests.

Find a position where you can pan with each group as they walk toward the church door; this will create a natural sequence of shots that edit together smoothly. Include shots of the bridesmaids waiting and the groom and best man chatting or checking their watches; ask them to display the ring for a good close-up. Conclude this build-up sequence with a shot of the church clock showing the appointed time.

Getting the best coverage of church weddings is a matter of preplanning and working out your camera positions in advance. Ideally, the event is best covered by a small team, using 2 or more camcorders, and editing the material together later (*see p. 136*). But you can get good results shooting with one camcorder, so long as you plan your coverage and get into position quickly.

Start by setting up outside the church to show the bridal car approaching. Shoot in the telephoto position and pull back to the wide angle as the vehicle approaches. Cut away quickly to any onlookers, then move around to show the bride stepping out.

You will then need to move quickly ahead to set up near the church door and pan with the bride as she enters. Conclude this shot by fading out picture and sound.

If you are able to record the ceremony, shoot from a tripod, with its legs fully extended, from a position at the front almost parallel with the minister. From here, you can get a three-quarters-on shot of bride and groom, a profile of the minister and a clear view of the congregation. Arrange beforehand for the bride's father and best man to stand slightly back, so that they do not obscure or distract from the bride and groom.

Set the white balance and you are ready to record. Start by fading into a wide shot of the congregation as the first hymn is sung. Then tighten in on individuals in the front row. During the early part of the service, you can alternate between close-ups of the bride and groom, and shots of the congregation. Try panning slowly from face to face along a pew and include shots of bridesmaids and pageboys. For these individual shots, the sound will be non-continuous but, by making a separate audio recording of the whole service, you can dub sound on later.

Record the exchange of vows as one continuous shot. Pan and zoom with the action and make sure you are framed

A position near the path can be used for a series of panning shots to show the guests entering and the bride arriving. A second position opposite the door is ideal for shots of the newly weds as they leave.

A position close to the door is ideal for covering the bride's arrival. When the ceremony is over, move to the end of the centre aisle and record the couple as they lead the congregation out.

Take advantage of the official stills photographer organizing people into groups. Get shots of the families as they pose for the pictures and take reverse angle cut-aways of the photographer and of the guests looking on.

The key position for covering the wedding ceremony is to one side of the altar, almost parallel to the minister. You can get close shots of the minister, bride and groom, and a clear view of the congregation. Set the camcorder on a tripod, with legs fully extended.

tightly on the bride and groom as they speak. Tilt down to show the ring being placed on the bride's finger, then widen as the couple kneels. Finish by panning to show the congregation's reactions after the newly weds have kissed.

If you want to cover the signing of the register in the vestry, remove the camcorder from the tripod and use it hand-held for speed; clip on a battery lamp if necessary. While this is happening, have a friend move your tripod back to the church door so you are ready to cover the bride and groom as they walk down the aisle. Start this shot with a fade-in as the processional music begins and zoom out slowly as the couple moves toward you. Hold the shot as they pass by and then keep shooting as the congregation follows them out of the church. An alternative strategy is to set up outside the church to show the couple emerging.

Most weddings are covered by an official stills photographer and this can be a great help to the video maker. While the official photographs are being set up outside the church, you can shoot more informally; record a sequence of the various groups preparing for their photos and use reverse angles of the stills photographer to link the shots.

This is often a time for lively banter between family and friends, so try to get in close with a directional mic to capture the sound. Also, use the telephoto setting to get informal shots of the guests, both individually or in groups, while they are relaxed and enjoying the spirit of the occasion.

End the sequence around the church with the newly weds being driven off to the reception. Again, you will need to be in position to show them getting into the car. Conclude with a static low-angle view of the car driving away, then fade out.

If you are the only person covering the event, you will now need to move fast and get in position for the reception.

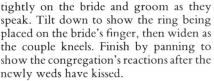

The wedding reception contains key elements for which you can plan in advance, including the receiving of the guests, toasts, speeches and cake-cutting.

For an indoor reception, check the existing lighting, socket positions and room layout in advance. You are unlikely to be able to illuminate large areas, so concentrate on where the main events will take place. Two or three 500-watt quartz or photoflood lamps should be adequate.

Have the camcorder set up on a tripod ready to cover the guests being greeted. Frame the receiving line as a diagonal composition, with the bride and groom in the foreground and everyone visible. Vary your shots by including close-ups of individuals, then pulling back to show the whole group. Move behind the bride and groom, to frame shots from between their shoulders. Use the bride's veil as a natural soft-focus foreground.

For recording speeches, toasts and cake-cutting, proceed as follows:
● Set the camcorder on a tripod at 45° to the speakers and guests. Use an auxiliary cardioid mic on a stand close to the speakers or have a friend direct a gun mic.
● Start with a close shot of the best man as he starts to talk, then pull out to include the bride and groom. Pan across to show the guests' reactions, then cut back to catch the start of the groom's reply.
● By making a separate sound recording of the speeches and toasts, you are free to shoot cut-aways of the guests in groups.
● For the cake-cutting ceremony, set up a backlight above head-height to add vibrancy to the appearance of the cake and a halo effect to the bride's veil. Get in close for impact, using the wide angle setting. Shoot from a low position as the cake is cut, but make sure you are not shooting into the backlight. Then, rise gently to show the couple kiss.
● Use the rest of the reception for informal candid shooting. Start on a tripod in the telephoto setting and pick out faces

When recording a religious ceremony, such as a Bar Mitzvah, camerawork should be restrained, to remain seemly. Use discreet zooms and pans; take cut-aways of religous features beforehand to edit in later.

and interesting incidents happening around you, such as children lost in the mêlée or playing games. Then, move about, hand-holding the camera in the wide angle setting, to capture groups of people in conversation. A battery light can be useful and a directional mic to catch snippets of talk and laughter. Use this opportunity to conduct informal interviews and record news about distant relatives and friends.

When the newly weds leave for their honeymoon, shoot the sequence hand-holding the camera, so that you are free to react to the situation (eg following the bouquet as it is thrown) and intercut between wellwishers and the couple. Move back to the tripod (set up in advance) for a final low-angle shot of the car.

As with weddings, other formal ceremonies demand thoughtful preparation before shooting, although your exact approach will depend on the event. For religious ceremonies, such as baptisms and

Cover a graduation ceremony from one position and pan with the recipients as they collect their degrees.

Hold the shot on stage, let the person walk out of frame, then cut to the next subject approaching.

At a baptism, position yourself close to the font and opposite the minister. Use a tripod for

camera steadiness, with its legs extended to give a high-angle view of the infant. Use soft or reflected light.

Bar Mitzvahs, your freedom in the use of camera positions may be limited, but acoustic and lighting plans will be similar to those of a wedding.

At a baptism, you will need to be near the subject. Use a wide angle to pan and tilt with the action. Remember to tighten in for close-ups of reactions and smiling faces. For best sound, have one of the group hold an auxiliary cardioid mic just above waist-level and out of shot. Use bounced or diffused lighting to avoid dazzling the baby.

For a confirmation or Bar Mitzvah, try to find an elevated position that will give you a clear view of the participants and the congregation. To get a continuous record of the sound, you will need to shoot long takes, stopping only when there is a break in the event.

Anniversaries, retirements and award ceremonies are all natural subjects for a video record. Plan and shoot as follows:
● Find out the arrangements in advance,

so that you can record only sections of long speeches and be ready to line up shots of surprise award winners.
● Set up in an elevated position at about 60° to the main participants, so that you can swivel around to get separate reaction shots of the audience.
● Set lights high on their stands at about 45° on either side of the subject to give even illumination. In big halls, quartz lamps of 750 watts or more, possibly in pairs, may well be necessary.
● Turn the lamps toward the front rows when shooting reverse angles.
● Place a cardioid mic on a stand in front of the speakers and, if you are using a mixer, an omnidirectional mic at the front of the audience.
● Start with carefully composed shots of awards or prizes laid out.
● Pan with each winner as they come up to receive a prize and hold the shot, letting the person walk out of frame. Then cut to the next recipient approaching the stage.

Whether you are travelling at home or abroad, vacations provide great opportunities for video making. Not only do you have new subjects to stimulate creativity, you also have the time to concentrate on technique.

Most of your shooting will be done outdoors and you will soon discover that daylight has several different qualities. Time of day, weather conditions, direction of light, reflective surfaces (such as sand, water or whitewashed walls), passing clouds – all these will change the nature of light and therefore affect exposure, depth of field, colour balance and picture composition.

Strong direct sunlight, for example, will produce intense colours and hard outlines. In such light, scenic views are best shot with the sun behind you or slightly to the side. Be aware of your shadow and avoid including it in the scene. With close-ups of people, direct sunlight is best avoided since it will make them screw up their eyes or shield them behind dark glasses.

Strong sunlight also means high contrast and heavy shadows, which can affect the exposure especially when using the auto iris (*see p. 16*). Adjusting the iris manually will help, but may result in highlights being overexposed. Alternative approaches are to move closer to the subject to exclude the overbright area, or rearrange the shot so that the sun slants into the picture, reducing the contrast.

Cloudy but bright conditions produce low contrast and are therefore ideal for video work. Since the light is diffused, shadows are softened and people's skin tones are shown off to best effect. Shooting when the sun is weak or the light failing can also be effective with close-ups of people. On dull days, however, there will

PROTECTING EQUIPMENT

● Protect the camcorder from extreme heat and humidity. Never leave it in a hot car or direct sun.
● Condensation is caused by extreme changes in temperature, so avoid moving the camcorder from, say, the ski slopes into a heated interior. Most models have a dew-warning system.
● Prevent sand or water getting into the camcorder at all costs. When necessary, enclose it loosely in a plastic bag, with a hole cut out for the lens, but only do this for a few minutes at a time since heat or condensation can build up.
● Protect the camcorder from shocks and vibrations while travelling by keeping it in an equipment case or cushioned in your lap.
● Protect the lens with an ultraviolet (UV) filter and always replace the lens cap when shooting is finished.

Passing clouds that suddenly obscure the sun will affect exposure and contrast. An easy way of keeping a check on this, without straining your eyes, is to hold a pair of sunglasses horizontally and watch the cloud movements reflected in the glass.

Bright but cloudy days are ideal for video work and give a great depth of field, particularly useful for scenic shots.

be so little contrast that a scene will look flat and colours will appear muted.

Exposure should also be geared to the subject. With shots of dramatic skies, for example, it does not matter if other parts of the shot are dark or underexposed. With backlit subjects, you have to decide on the effect you want. You could treat a shot of an angler, with the light coming from behind him, as an atmospheric silhouette. Or, by using the camcorder's backlight compensator, you will register more detail in close-up.

The brighter the light, the greater the depth of field. In strong sunlight with the lens at the wide angle setting, anything more than a few feet away will be in sharp focus, even if it is moving. Exploit this depth of field in good light by taking striking deep-focus shots from a low angle of, say, a fast-moving stream or runners coming round the curve of a track.

A polarizing filter eliminates reflections, enabling you to see through glass or below the surface of water. It also darkens the sky and whitens clouds. These effects are evident above: transparent water, intense sky. Polarizing sunglasses give the same effect when held in front of the lens.

A neutral density filter is essential in very bright conditions to prevent overexposure. Here, the filter effectively cuts out the intense light from the sun and reflective surface of the sea. Another effect of this filter is to reduce depth of field (already shallow in this telephoto shot), so that the windsurfer really stands out sharply from the background.

Contrast may be too high for the video camera on clear sunny days. But natural reflective surfaces, such as white sand, reduce the contrast by scattering the light and reflecting it back to 'fill' the shadows.

Remember to use an ultraviolet filter when shooting on beaches to protect the lens against sand and salt water. It also has the effect of cutting out blue haze, to give clear sea and landscapes.

A strong visual subject, such as California's Disneyland, is a gift to the video maker. Capture the variety of the place, its atmosphere, the visitors and their reactions. Shoot your impressions and edit the shots later with a lively sound track.

Give full rein to your creativity when making travel videos. Take plenty of material, using various shot sizes and angles, and edit it later at your leisure.

With scenic landscapes, you could include an interesting feature and relate it to the surroundings. For example, pan with the movement of a walker to reveal the scenery behind. Sounds recorded on location (such as bird song or flowing water) can be mixed in later with music and/or a commentary.

With activity vacations, record events in sequence so as to give visual sense and continuity. Make full use of establishing, medium and close-up shots to tell the stages of a story, whether it is putting up a tent, preparing for scuba diving or setting out on a fishing trip. Think ahead in the shooting and aim to show only the highlights of each activity, linking them with cut-away shots of the participants.

Live sound is likely to be more important in these situations to give atmosphere

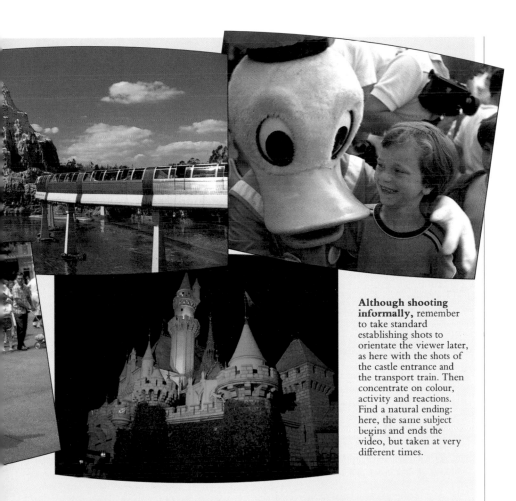

Although shooting informally, remember to take standard establishing shots to orientate the viewer later, as here with the shots of the castle entrance and the transport train. Then concentrate on colour, activity and reactions. Find a natural ending: here, the same subject begins and ends the video, but taken at very different times.

and authenticity. Use a separate mic to ensure a good recording of, say, people shouting instructions or the reeling-in of a fishing line.

The aware video maker is always on the alert for potentially humorous situations. A serious task, like putting up a tent for example, can develop into an hilarious scene. You can also contrive entertaining sequences by quick linking of contrasting shots; for example, cutting from shots of energetic children racing about to shots of

their parents dozing peacefully in the sun. The humour of such sequences can be underlined by editing the shots later to the lyrics of some popular song.

A visit to a fairground or theme park will provide an abundance of images. Take an informal approach here, shooting impressionistic shots and linking them with regular, cut-away close-ups of your family's expressions and reactions. Again, editing the images later and adding a lively sound track creates a memorable record.

HOME TRIPS

Before setting out on your travels:

● Check that the camcorder, tripod and other equipment are working, by shooting a short picture-and-sound test and playing it back.

● Pack a blower brush and a good photographic cloth or tissues for cleaning the lens.

● Check batteries are undamaged and fully charged. Take at least one spare. A battery belt is ideal for giving extended recording time.

● Take the battery charger. An adaptor for recharging from a car is also useful.

● Include a small video light, with fully charged battery, spare bulbs and charger. A reflector board will also be useful.

● Pack an auxiliary microphone, extension lead and headphones.

● A lightweight cassette recorder can be useful for taping extra sounds.

● Take your mains adaptor and RF connection leads – you may be able to check your tapes on a hotel TV.

● Always carry spare tapes – your format may not always be available.

● Pack a selection of filters. Neutral density, ultraviolet and polarizing filters are the most useful to bring with you when travelling.

Shooting parts of a subject and then revealing the whole is often a more interesting way of showing a static subject than simply taking a single long shot (*above left*). Instead, a series of 4 intriguing details keeps the viewer guessing until the final shot, which reveals the full character of the statue. Do the same with buildings or machines.

Preparation is the key to returning from your travels with successful videos, whether you are touring around your own country or in foreign lands.

Before leaving home, do some basic research; study maps and guide books to get an idea of the possibilities for shooting. Since you will probably be taping a lot of material on a variety of subjects, decide in advance on a 'shoot to edit' policy, which will save you worrying about the exact order of your shooting at the time. Take plenty of linking shots and order the sequences later at your leisure, by tape-to-tape editing (*see p. 62*).

If you have worked out a structure for your video record in advance, then editing in-camera (ordering the shots as you shoot) will be more feasible. So that the viewer can follow the story easily, you will need to signpost the way, sometimes literally by linking sequences with shots of route markers, posters or even maps to introduce new locations.

Travelling shots, taken from trains, coaches or boats, are also a good way to

convey changing scenes. Adding titles, using a caption generator, provides a good linking device. And you can add a full commentary and/or music later.

Each place you visit will have its own distinctive features. In composing a video portrait of a town, for example, develop a running theme in the story, such as its architecture. General views from elevated positions, perhaps from a church tower or nearby hilltop, will set the scene for later coverage at street level.

Shooting buildings, statues and plazas may be an important part of your record. Wait for the right time of day to shoot. Buildings, for example, are best seen when the sun is either directly on or slanting across them. Avoid shooting when the sun is directly overhead, which produces deep areas of shadow, or in hazy light. Use a polarizing filter to strengthen sky colour and cloud formations (*see p. 85*).

Vary your approach when shooting buildings. Starting with a general view and moving in on details is an obvious way. Doing the reverse is often more interesting: start on a detail, such as some ornate stonework, and then cut to a wide angle of the whole façade. Or you can start with a close-up of someone coming out of the main door and then zoom back to reveal the building. Create interest, depth and scale in your shots by including foliage in the foreground or people seated or walking nearby.

GOING ABROAD

You will have to be more selective about the additional equipment you take when travelling abroad. Besides weight and space considerations, remember the following:

● Insure your equipment, including third party cover.

● Customs officials can be suspicious of video gear. So take all purchase receipts with you to produce on re-entry to your own country. Check ahead on any formalities or restrictions that may apply in the countries you are visiting.

● Airport X-ray checks are *not* harmful to video tapes, but beware of electromagnetic checking devices. If in doubt, ask for your tapes to be hand-searched.

● Always carry your camcorder as hand-luggage. Even the sturdiest of cases will not protect against rough handling at airports or docks.

● For recharging batteries, you will need a voltage transformer for converting to mains power if the national grid is different.

● You may also need an adaptor for plugging into local mains sockets.

● Differing international standards may prevent you from playing back tapes on a local TV (*see p. 212*).

A good travel video should make your audience feel that they were with you on location. Parades, markets, city scenes and night life are some of the subjects that offer the essential ingredients – colour, movement, people and sound.

Street markets make lively sequences. Find an elevated view to show the whole scene and then concentrate on the trans-actions going on at one or two stalls. Position yourself at one side of the stall so you can get shots of both the customers and the vendor. Make full use of the telephoto position and the zoom to get cut-away shots of the merchandise, tight close-ups of people's expressions and cut-ins of money changing hands.

Using the camcorder may go virtually unnoticed in the flurry of a market square.

But in other situations, you should take measures to be unobtrusive. To shoot café or street life, for example, an observ-ational, 'candid camera' approach is needed for discreet shooting.

The best way to do this is to become part of the scene. Settle yourself at a table with a drink and relax. Set the camcorder's functions to automatic, the lens to tele-photo and leave it on 'pause'. Be patient, wait for events to happen. When you spot a likely subject in the distance, start shoot-ing, supporting the camcorder with your elbows on the table.

With nearby subjects, shooting blind is a discreet method. Place the camcorder at the edge of the table and set it to wide angle, aimed toward the subject. You may not get perfect composition, but you will

A parade or procession is a lively subject. Turn up early and find a good spot from which to shoot your key sequences. An elevated position is ideal, to get high-angle shots of the action; tightly composed, as here, the pattern of movement is accentuated to good effect. When cutting between shots, be consistent in screen direction: if the parade passes out screen-left, make sure it enters again screen-right in the following shot.

A fireworks display makes a spectacular subject, with all the attendant effects of flashing coloured lights and atmospheric sound. Use a tripod to compose a wide shot of sky and ground. When setting the iris, it is important to include another illuminated area in the shot, as here with

get some magic moments. Camcorders with an adjustable viewfinder are invaluable in this situation, because you can glance down to check composition first.

When shooting a local festivity, such as a parade, find a key position to get maximum coverage as the parade approaches. A street corner or balcony is ideal. Also, try to get in front of the parade and shoot from a low angle as it passes.

With a continuous action subject like this, shots will have to run longer than usual, especially when recording live sound such as a brass band. Keep shooting until a convenient break occurs.

To make such an event really come alive for the viewers, take plenty of cut-away linking shots of the crowd watching – children on their parents' shoulders or observers looking down from windows.

Many places are at their liveliest during the evenings. Night life can be a good subject if there is sufficient light for shooting – floodlit buildings, plazas or torchlit processions can all give satisfactory exposure. The light from shops, cafés and street lamps can also allow recording of general activity. A fireworks display, though a little tricky to take, makes a wonderful subject (*below*).

Live sound will greatly enhance your travel videos. To record sound only, you can use a separate lightweight cassette recorder. Or the camcorder itself can act solely as a sound recorder, in which case leave the lens cap on and use an auxiliary mic for the best results. Music and personal commentary can be added later.

the floodlit building. The exposure should then be able to cope with the intermittent bursts of light as the fireworks explode.

Street markets offer scenes of great activity, colour and sound. Take up a position at the side of a stall where you can get medium shots and close-ups of both the buyer and the seller, as well as cut-aways of the goods. From a position behind the stall, you can take full-face shots of customers inspecting the merchandise, shots of the passing crowds and the stalls opposite.

There are any number of outdoor action subjects you can video, with plenty of movement and excitement. Although the subjects may differ, all events will have certain features in common that you should aim to cover.

● Find out the details of the programme well in advance from the organizers, so that you know the timing and order of events and can therefore plan to be in the right place at the right time.

● Take an exploratory walk around the course or venue beforehand. Look for likely camera positions that will give visual variety and a clear view of the action, as well as catching the most exciting moments, such as at difficult parts of the course or near the finishing line.

● Rehearsing shots before the real action begins will pay dividends. Use time trials or practice sessions to concentrate, for example, on getting the correct panning speed and focusing on fast-moving subjects in the telephoto position.

● Begin your coverage with wide shots, from an elevated position if possible, to set the scene and show the layout of the venue. Then, get closer to the action and use a variety of shot sizes and angles.

● A tripod is essential for steady camerawork, especially with fast action, long takes and panning shots.

● Shoot the highlights of an event or take longer, continuous action shots. For visual coherence, concentrate on a few subjects by taking long shots and close-ups to establish characteristic features which your audience can identify later.

● Take plenty of cut-away shots of off-course activities, the spectators and their reactions. These can be edited into the final tape to link action sequences and give continuity to your coverage.

● Enlist the help of another person to handle the sound. They should get as close as possible to the subject, using a separate unidirectional mic on an extension lead. A gun mic picks up sound even better, but

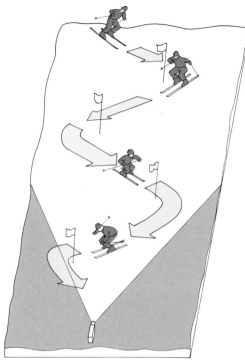

Downhill racers on a ski slalom can be covered from a single camera position at the bottom of the slope, opposite the centre line. From here, with the lens in the wide angle, the skier's zig-zag pattern of descent can be shown in full. Take static low-angle shots, or record continuous action, starting in telephoto and zooming back.

must be aimed carefully at the source. Work closely together so that you are covering the same subject at the same time, to ensure sound and pictures match.

With some events that involve a pre-determined course or track (such as motor rallying, tobogganing or horse racing), you will see the subjects only intermittently. So, for the sake of continuity, an ideal camera position would be on a bend, a little way back from the course (*see diagram, p. 93*), from where you can cover 3 different views of the action – a head-on approach, a panning shot around the bend and a retreat shot.

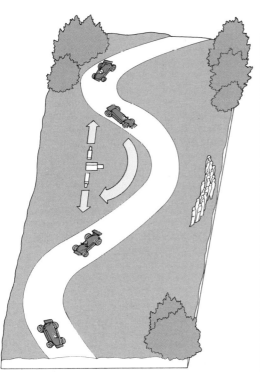

Shooting from a bend is an ideal position for covering fast-moving subjects on a course or track. From this spot, you can get 3 types of shot: a telephoto view as the subjects approach and slow down coming into the bend; a 90° pan as they round the bend; and a static shot as they accelerate away. Intercut these 3 to create continuity.

When shooting from a bend, the subjects will be out of view at first, so it is important to set up a signalling system with a friend. By being forewarned of the approach, you can start recording in good time and not lose any of the action at the start of the shot due to the backspace editing inherent in camcorders (*see p. 57*).

Your helper should be positioned farther up the course, ahead of you, and as soon as the subjects are in sight, should signal (by waving, rather than shouting which would, of course, be heard on the sound track). Your helper should be out of shot when you start recording.

SNOW TIPS

When shooting in the snow, dress sensibly. Wear loose natural fabrics that allow you to move and sweat easily: thermal underwear, a wool shirt with pockets, water/windproof overtrousers (which can be taken off without removing boots), headgear that allows you to wear headphones, heavy-duty gaiters to keep snow out of boots and sturdy hiking boots with cleated soles for good grip. Choose a duvet anorak with deep pockets (for carrying tapes, filters, lens tissues) with non-slip shoulder pads to help steady the camcorder and a wired visor hood for wind protection. Mittens with pop-out fingers are handy for operating camera controls. Wear a battery belt under the anorak to keep the batteries warm (they lose power in sub-zero conditions).

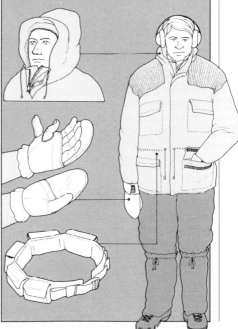

LOW-ANGLE SHOTS

Certain action subjects, such as downhill skiing, long jumping and pole vaulting, are ideal for low-angle shooting. Highlight the drama of the moment by placing the camcorder almost at ground level; with the lens set to wide angle, speed is accentuated.

Visual impact is further enhanced by live sound. With the help of a friend, record sound with a separate directional mic placed close to, and aimed directly at, the subject. They should wear headphones to monitor the sound.

With high-speed subjects, manual focusing is often best. Before shooting, pre-focus on that part of the scene where the subject will enter (*see p. 20*). In situations where you cannot see the subject's approach (such as ski jumping), set up a signal system with a friend so that you will be recording in good time, and in perfect focus, as the subject bursts into view.

When shooting in snow conditions, take sensible precautions – dress warmly and protect the camcorder (*see box, p. 93*). Since snow is bright and a powerful reflector, be prepared to adjust the iris manually or use the backlight compensator to get correct exposure of the subject, especially when shooting into the light as with low-angle shots. A neutral density filter is an essential part of your video snow kit, as is a battery belt as a power source and a groundsheet for comfortable camerawork.

COMPRESSED ACTION

Shooting fast-moving subjects head-on in the telephoto position produces spectacular compressed action shots, in which perspective is flattened and movement appears unnaturally slow. By adding a tele-converter to the camcorder's zoom lens, this effect is accentuated. The limited depth of field in such shots can also be exploited to isolate part of the action.

Likely subjects include racing cars, motorbikes, cyclists, powerboats – the faster the action, the more impressive the shot.

Camera shake is always more exaggerated in the telephoto position, so a tripod is essential for compressed action shots. The steadiness it provides also emphasizes the feeling of movement within the frame.

Pre-focus such shots manually, by focusing on a chosen area and then letting the subject come into focus with the action. Or try the 'follow focus' technique, where focus is continually adjusted as the subject comes closer. The front and end focus positions (ie first and last) should be determined in advance and the shot rehearsed several times to ensure smooth focus changes (*see p. 145*).

Patterns of action can also be revealed dramatically by telephoto shots. For example, a head-on view along the bends of a toboggan run will show the toboggan swinging, apparently slowly, in and out of frame as it progresses downhill toward the camera.

CONTINUOUS ACTION

Display events, such as show jumping, rodeos or dressage, involve a subject in continuous action within a confined space. Such events are best covered from an elevated position. Following the action will involve long takes, so get comfortable and use a tripod. Smooth, steady camera movements are important since many of your shots will consist of panning and tilting at the same time.

Start your coverage with wide shots, framed loosely so as to accommodate changes in action. When you are accustomed to the pattern of movement, you can become more confident in your shooting. Begin to tighten up on the composition, to give visual variety and concentrate interest. But keep your finger on the zoom control and be prepared to ease out with the action. Don't overdo pans and/or tilts; remember, a wide static shot can contain the action just as effectively.

Focusing on continuous motion may be difficult, particularly when you are operating manually. Staying wide eases the problem. Use the event's warm-up sessions to practice adjusting focus while panning, tilting or zooming. Telephoto shots are demanding and need rehearsal.

For sound, get a friend to hold a separate directional mic and point it at the subject for the best recordings; if working on your own, attach the mic to the camcorder's accessory shoe.

FAST PANNING

High-speed action is complemented by high-speed panning, with the subject in sharp focus all the time and the background blurred by camera movement.

Fast pans are best done from a position that gives a clear view and is set well back from the track so you can cover an arc of 60° to 90°. Shooting subjects as they round a shallow bend, for example, is ideal, since they will be at about the same focusing distance from the camera throughout the panning movement (*see diagram, p. 93*).

Get a friend to give you a visual signal of the forthcoming action. In the meantime, you should keep one eye on the approach track and the other on the viewfinder.

The timing of the pan is important. For wide angle pans, start the movement just as the subjects come into shot. Pan slightly ahead to give lead space and emphasize screen direction.

Panning in the telephoto position can be tricky, but gives more dynamic results. Start panning *before* the subjects come into shot so that you are up to their speed once they are in shot. This way, you avoid a jerky start and a shot that is continually trying to catch up with the action.

Fast panning certainly needs rehearsal. The backspace editing that happens with all camcorders at the start of shots is particularly relevant here and knowing how your model works will save a lot of frustration later (*see p. 57*).

The kind of sports coverage seen on TV is difficult for an individual video maker to emulate simply because the professionals use multi-camera coverage and slow-motion action replays to enhance their productions.

However, you can get excellent results with a few well-chosen camera positions and an objective or plan of action. Do you want to make a record of entire sections of the event, or simply give a general impression of the sport? Or do you want to use the tape to scrutinize and evaluate (see p. 98) certain performances afterward?

Each sport will have its own approach, but some general comments apply:

● Light should not be a problem for outdoor daytime events. For night recordings, most stadia are floodlit with lamps balanced for TV coverage, thus presenting no problem for the video maker. Similarly, indoor venues, for such sports as basketball, bowling, squash and gymnastics, are also adequately lit for video recording.

● A caption generator with a stopwatch function that shows up on screen can be used most effectively during track events. Press the button as the starting pistols fires. Another professional touch is to punch out captions in advance, with the names of competitors and their events, and bring the words up on screen at the start of each performance.

● Don't run out of tape during an important part of the action. Better to change cassettes with some tape to spare than be caught out. Take several blanks with you and also some spare batteries.

Team games: A simple record of games, such as football and hockey, can be covered from a single, elevated camera position in the stands, ideally near the halfway line. Record continuous action shots by panning and zooming with the play, which will be useful for later analysis, especially of team strategy.

Of more general interest would be a record of the occasion itself, not just the

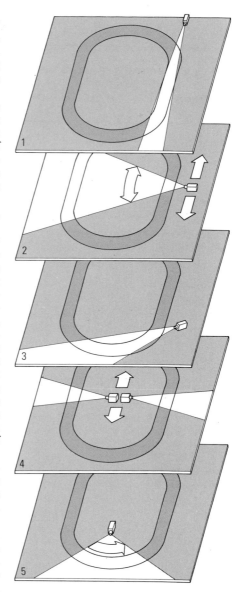

Track events can be shot from several camera positions. To retain continuity of direction, shoot from one side of the 'line of action' only (**2**, **3**). If you cross the line to shoot from inside the track (**4**, **5**), take a neutral shot (**1**), with no evident direction.

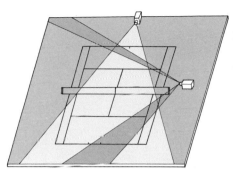

Tennis is best covered from an elevated position along the centreline, from the end of the court that avoids shooting into the sun. Frame some shots tightly, pulling out just as the ball is hit. From a position at the side of the court, get good coverage of individual players (don't try to pan between them) and also cut-aways of the crowd's heads following the action.

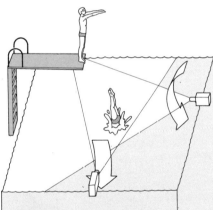

Highboard diving, in deep diving pools, is best seen in profile from an elevated position, or head-on. Both positions allow you to tilt down with the action. With longer pools, use the telephoto to frame the diver tightly, zooming out just before the dive. If there are underwater observation windows, get dramatic shots of divers plunging below the surface.

game. Shoot this in a more impressionistic way, recording the highlights from several positions. With a football game, for example, start with shots of the crowd arriving and the players coming onto the pitch. From the elevated position, get long shots and telephoto coverage of the action.

Moving down to ground level, take action shots from the side of the pitch, but remember to shoot from one side only or you will reverse the direction of play and destroy continuity (see p. 48). By positioning yourself near the goal where you anticipate most action will be, get dramatic coverage of goals or touchdowns.

Give coherence to your coverage by picking out a particular player and following his progress during the game. Take cut-aways of the crowd, scoreboard and referees to link action sequences. Add a professional, and fun, touch by having a friendly expert with you to give a running commentary of the game into a hand mic.
Track events: For short races run over a straight track, such as the 100 metres, capture the whole event as continuous action. An elevated position, ideally near the finishing line, will give good coverage of the athletes. Start with a telephoto shot as they spring into action, then widen the lens angle as the race proceeds.

Longer-distance track events give you an opportunity of moving the camera to get a variety of shots (see diagram, p. 96).
Field events: These can be covered as continuous action from a single camera position facing the athlete. High jumps or pole vaults are made more dramatic by a low-angle shot of the run-up, followed by a continuous tilt of the jump itself. Don't compose the shot too tightly or the tilts will become exaggerated.

Cover a long jump at a short distance from the end of the sand pit. Hold a low-angle shot to show the subject's approach and jump, then stand up smoothly to record a top shot of the jumper's traces — the footmarks in the sand.

Analyze your own performance in the privacy of your home by turning the camera on yourself. Yoga, keep-fit, dance exercises – any of these will benefit from self-analysis.

The set-up is simple: with the camcorder on a tripod, frame the area where you will perform. Set the lens in a wide enough angle to cover all the movements. To make sure your position is correct, get someone to stand in for you. Alternatively, connect the camcorder to the TV and judge the position from the screen. Choose a plain background to show up every action. Any video lamps being used should provide soft, even lighting that comes primarily from the front. For instant assessment of your performance, playback the tape on the TV and take the necessary steps to correct your movements.

Video offers a uniquely accessible medium for analyzing individual sports performances or reviewing entire events. The ease of recording material and the immediate playback facilities provide a useful instruction tool for both coaches and sports enthusiasts.

Most VCRs are equipped with a pause button that allows you to freeze a particular frame for detailed examination. More sophisticated machines offer playback in fast and slow motion. The fast playback can be useful for analyzing team strategies and individual placements throughout a game. The slow playback gives you time to examine the action.

Even closer analysis is possible with frame-advance VCRs, which enable you to inspect the tape frame by frame. Video cameras with high-speed shutters make this form of slow-motion and freeze-frame analysis even more effective by ensuring a blur-free recording of each frame. This is ideal for checking actions, such as a golfer's swing, a gymnast's movements or a tennis player's serve.

Making a video record for later analysis of a performance (whether it be a sport, dance or aerobics) is not necessarily a creative exercise. It is a functional recording, made for a specific purpose. But it still deserves all the care and attention you would give to other subjects. Bear in mind these points before and during shooting:

● Get the advice of a coach or instructor on the sort of material that will be most useful to record for the purpose of analyzing the activity in question.

● Always use a tripod for camera steadiness and limit the number of camera movements, such as pans and tilts, which may prove distracting on later playback.

● Make sure the subject is well lit from the front in order to get clear, bright, well-focused pictures you can examine later. Also, avoid distracting backgrounds behind the subject.

● Make good use of the wide angle for full-length views to record continuous action of the whole movement.

● With a portable monitor on location, you can playback results immediately, so allowing the subject to take corrective action to improve technique on the spot.

● Use a high-grade video tape for the recording, which will give consistently good reproduction on the repeated playbacks that you intend.

Tennis and golf are ideal subjects for analysis by slow–motion, freeze-frame playback. Position the camera in front of the player, with the lens set wide enough to include the whole stroke or swing.

Subjects should be front-lit and set against an unfussy background, so as not to distract from the action. Closer shots can be taken of specific details of play, such as the tennis player's foot position or the golfer's arm swing and club grip. Use the telephoto setting to avoid distracting the player's attention.

Create a simple storyline about the activities or daily routine of a pet animal. Since you know your pet's habits and can predict its behaviour to an extent, you will have some control over the recording.

With a little patience, you can get good behavioural shots of animals exploring their territory outdoors. If you know their routine and favourite areas, you can set up shots in advance, shooting in the telephoto position from ground level. Reinforce the 'wild' effect by excluding people from the scene. Catch a dog burying its bone, unaware of your presence. Show cats stalking through long grass or shrubs, running along a wall, sharpening their claws on trees, meeting neighbouring cats or poised in readiness to jump or pounce. Remember to retain continuity of action and appearance from shot to shot (*see pp. 48–51*), to give visual coherence.

Kittens and puppies can easily be induced to play with any small moving object. Get someone to dangle a soft toy on a string so that you can take striking low-angle shots of a cat standing on its hindlegs stretching upward. Allow such shots to run and edit them later.

The movements of a puppy chasing a ball around a room or two kittens playing with each other are usually too fast to capture. But if you can confine the action to a small area (by, for example, tying a toy to the leg of a chair or penning the kittens into a space), you can follow the action, and retain focus, more easily.

You can also set up action shots, such as a cat leaping between two tables, racing upstairs or jumping down from a wall, by using food or milk as a reward. You may even be able to cajole your pet into repeating the action several times for the benefit of the recording.

Compose these types of shot in advance and pre-focus the lens. Make sure you are recording before you call the animal, so that none of the action is lost (due to

LOW-LEVEL SHOTS

When recording pets, get down to their level as much as possible to show their perspective on the world. For this type of low-level shooting, lie on the floor propped up on your elbows, or shoot with the camera cradled in your lap, or even with it placed directly on the floor in front of you, as illustrated.

Use a collapsed tripod, with its legs fully spread, for steady, low-level close-ups of an animal when it is stationary (such as a cat lapping up milk or a rabbit munching a lettuce leaf). A tripod also allows smooth, low-level pans and tilts when following action, such as a dog retrieving a stick.

Shots taken from a low angle also emphasize the impressive appearance of some dogs, such as Dobermans or Wolfhounds. Low-level shooting can be used to dramatize animal behaviour, too, such as a cat bristling or getting ready to pounce.

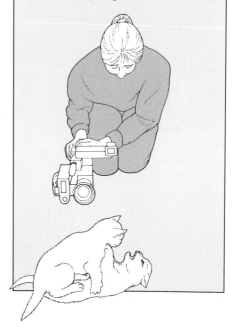

MACRO SHOOTING

The zoom lens of most camcorders has a 'macro' setting, beyond the wide angle position, that allows you to focus on subjects at very close quarters, in fact almost right up to the front of the lens. You can fill the screen with small subjects or with details of large subjects. Nature studies are particularly striking – small beetles pollinating a flower head (*right*), drops of dew on a blade of grass, a caterpillar feeding on a leaf.

When you use the macro, the zoom and auto-focus functions are disengaged. Focus manually, by moving the zoom lever or by changing the distance between the lens and the subject. The depth of field is very shallow, so accurate focusing and steady shots from a tripod are vital. Any movement, such as petals stirring in a breeze, can upset

the focus. Shoot in controlled conditions if possible, such as in a conservatory. Since the lens casts its shadow over the subject, arrange for the lighting to come from the back or from the side.

backspace editing, *see p. 57*) when it comes into view.

The time to get close-ups is when pets are feeding or grooming themselves. Get down to their level for the best shots (*see left*). This is also an opportunity to get close-up sounds (purring, lapping or licking) with the mic held just out of shot.

Be aware that black or dark fur absorbs light and this will affect exposure. You may have to adjust the aperture manually or even use the backlight compensator to boost image brightness when shooting against light backgrounds. If you do need extra lighting (with rabbits in a hutch, or gerbils or budgies in a cage), think of the animals – make sure the light is indirect and not too hot or so close as to make them uncomfortable or scared.

Dogs are often easier to record than cats, since they are usually more controllable and willing to repeat actions, such as retrieving a stick. In this case, position yourself near the owner and, with the lens set to wide angle, pan with the action. When the dog returns, tighten up the lens angle to get close-ups of the stick being placed in the owner's hand or at the feet. Finish with a shot of the dog being stroked.

Action shots of a dog jumping over a wall are best captured from a low angle, panning as the dog runs forward, and then holding for the actual jump. For a really dramatic view, get the dog to jump over *you* – lie on the ground and take the shot as the dog approaches and jumps, out of frame. Pre-focus on the spot where it will take off.

Birds or wild animals attracted to your back garden by food can be recorded discreetly from an open window, with the camcorder on a tripod and the lens set to telephoto. Add a tele-converter to get big close-ups of the action. Restrict camera movements; simply frame the feeding area and wait for the subjects to come into shot. Another approach is to use a remote control unit (*see p. 102*).

NATURE • 2

Patience, silence and stillness – these are essential rules to observe when making wildlife videos. Reading about your subjects in advance, to gain a knowledge of their general habits and behaviour, can save valuable time while on location. But, since animals are unpredictable, you must be prepared to respond quickly and instinctively to opportunities as they occur.

Most of the time, you will be shooting from a distance, with the lens set to telephoto. Accurate focusing is therefore vital due to the reduced depth of field. It becomes even more critical when you add a supplementary tele-converter to the lens.

In some locations, there will already be hides available from which you can record animals at quite close range. You can also make your own hide, from a simple portable 'tent' that can be camouflaged. It should be large enough to accommodate you, a tripod and a fold-up seat for the time spent waiting. Only the lens of the camera should protrude from the hide.

Another approach is to use a remote control unit, which allows you to operate all the main camera functions at a distance from the subject. Leave the camcorder/tripod set up near a place you know the animals frequent (such as an otter's run down to the river or a wolf's trail back to its den). Conceal yourself downwind as far away as the portable monitor's lead will permit and view the shot on screen. Pick up sound effects with an auxiliary microphone placed near the trail.

Aim to build up simple sequences showing particular animals and their activities. Sometimes, you can tempt them into view by putting down food. Vary your coverage and make it more comprehensive by returning to the location on different days to record other events in the animals' daily routine.

Wildlife expeditions or safaris offer great opportunities for the video maker.
● Follow the advice of a local wildlife guide when choosing locations.

WILDLIFE EXPEDITIONS

● Bring a sturdy tripod, ideally with a fluid head for smooth pans and tilts, and with spiked feet for setting up on rough ground. A monopod is lighter but not so versatile.

● Use a tele-converter to extend the focal length of the lens for shooting distant subjects. The depth of field is even shallower than in the telephoto position, so focusing becomes critical, especially with moving subjects.

● A remote control unit, with a battery-operated video monitor, can be useful for situations where your presence could disturb activity, such as recording nest-building birds.

● Bring a protective groundsheet or airbed for comfortable low-angle shots, and a lightweight collapsible seat, such as an angler's canvas stool, for the time spent waiting.

● Pack a large umbrella to shade both you and your equipment in exposed conditions.

● **Reminders:** Never leave equipment in hot vehicles and protect it against dust and dirt. Take extra tapes and power supplies, such as a battery belt. Keep an ultraviolet filter on the lens for protection and for shooting in heat haze.

● The best time for shooting is usually in the early morning or late evening, when the animals are at their most active.

● Set your equipment up near a much-frequented place, such as a water hole or river bank, to get rewarding coverage of a variety of animals.

● Keep your fingers on the zoom and focus controls in readiness for action. Keep the tripod head unlocked and be ready to pan and tilt at a moment's notice.

● It is almost impossible to shoot successfully from a moving vehicle on rough

With a tele-converter on the lens, you can get super-telephoto shots from a great (and safe) distance. Focus is critical, especially with moving subjects, such as a running lion. Close-ups are even closer with this lens; you can almost count the ground squirrel's whiskers. Foreground is sharp, background blurred.

terrain. But when you stop, try shooting from the roof, which not only gives an elevated viewpoint but also offers a secure and flat base for setting up the tripod.

● If, for safety reasons, you must shoot from inside the vehicle, put the lens as close to the glass as possible to cut out reflections. Brace yourself and support elbows on knees, to steady the camcorder.

● Be on your guard at all times and be prepared to abandon the shoot if danger threatens. Don't be stubborn – your safety is worth more than a good shot.

66 *Treat nature with respect, patience and understanding. Try to learn as much as possible about the subjects before you start. Gain experience on simple projects in your garden ... I always regard the filming of wildlife as a privilege.* 99

MAURICE R. TIBBLES,
WILDLIFE FILM-MAKER, CAMERAMAN
for *The Voyages of Charles Darwin*
(British Academy Award).

behaviour is unpredictable, you may have to shoot a lot of material and edit it later. But you should still aim to construct coherent sequences and get appropriate linking shots at the time.

Animals, even in zoos, have their own routines. Many become active just before feeding, so it is worthwhile finding out these times and getting in a good position before the crowds gather.

Animals also have patterns of behaviour and, although individuals vary, knowing the general pattern will help you to decide on a creative approach for each group.

When the big cats, bears or wolves are active, they often pace to and fro in regular predictable fashion. Frame an area and let the animal walk into it, then pan slowly with its even pacing, but be ready to ease out to accommodate changes. Create flowing sequences by alternating coverage between animals in an enclosure. Even when stationary, you can capture action details, such as a lion yawning or swishing its tail.

Herd animals, such as zebras and deer, can be quite nervous. By observing the leader of the group, you can often anticipate when action is going to occur. Keep to a wide angle setting for general movements, cutting in to closer shots when the animals are grazing peacefully.

Active primates, such as chimps, gibbons and lemurs, are much more unpredictable in their movements, especially the young ones. Don't attempt to keep up with them by panning, tilting or zooming. Instead, concentrate on one area and record the action there; frame a regularly used part of the enclosure, a platform, branch or plaything, and simply let the animals move in and out of shot. Vary the height of the camera and lens angle to include as much of the action as possible.

Aim to be there when the monkeys are fed because their behaviour at this time can be particularly easy to follow. Individuals will collect food from the communal tray and move off to eat it alone. This is an ideal

Action shots of dolphins (*top*) or seals are best taken from an elevated position to show the whole of the pool. Watch the show through once and rehearse camera movements. To capture a dolphin's jump, set the lens to a wide enough angle to catch all the action. Zoom in for a close-up of the reward.

Children's reactions to animals (*above*) are ideal cut-aways, or they can make a good theme on their own.

Wildlife parks and zoos provide an ideal opportunity to video a great variety of wild animals under controlled conditions. Since modern zoos provide maximum vantage points for visitors, you will have little trouble in finding good camera positions.

Be aware that when shooting through glass or wire mesh, the auto focus can be misled by the surface and may not focus beyond (*see box*). In such situations, rely on manual focusing.

Take a good look around the zoo before you start shooting, to find likely subjects and plan your coverage. Since animal

WIRE SHOTS

Auto focus is misled by netting, glass and mesh. But, even when focusing manually, the pattern of wire mesh will appear in your pictures (*left*) if you are shooting too close to the cage and in the wide angle (which gives the greatest depth of field). Where permissible, shoot right up against the wire or through one of the holes. Better still, move farther away and focus on the subject in the telephoto setting so that the mesh is out of focus (*right*).

When shooting through glass, as in an aquarium, stand at an angle to avoid reflections or use a polarizing filter. Focus manually and use the low-light control if necessary.

time to get close-ups. Grooming activity also provides a good opportunity to compose static shots, with the animals intent on their task.

Rhinos, giraffes, elephants, hippos and camels – these larger animals tend to move about slowly and often stand in one place. Others, such as pandas, orang-utans and gorillas, spend a lot of time just sitting. Such inactivity gives you time to concentrate on creative camerawork. Construct portraits of individual animals with a series of well-composed shots, maybe starting on a close-up detail (a gorilla's eyes or hands, for example), then zooming out to reveal more of the body. Or, try pulling focus or panning gently from one animal to another in the group, to compare their behaviour or appearance. At feeding time, reverse angle shots between the keepers and their charges, with cut-aways of the crowd's reactions, make lively sequences.

Remember that dark fur or skin can give contrast problems and affect expo-

sure. Thus, for example, wait for a gorilla or elephant to come into the sunlight for a more even exposure, or use the backlight compensator control when shooting a low-angle shot of a giraffe's head against the sky.

People looking at animals are almost as fascinating to record as the animals themselves. Position yourself at the side of the enclosure, facing away from the animals, and compose a shot. Start recording just before people move into frame; this way you will capture their first reactions.

Editing shots later can produce amusing behavioural sequences, such as shots of a female chimp grooming her young intercut with shots of a mother wiping candy floss off her child's face.

Many animals are very vocal. The roar of a lion or the hoot of a gibbon is loud enough to be picked up by the camcorder's microphone, but for quieter sounds and more specific pickup, use a directional mic pointed at the subject.

ADVENTURE ACTIVITIES

If you are already an expert in some adventure activity, such as scuba diving or parachuting, share the thrill and excitement with others by making underwater or aerial videos. But be sure of your capabilities before taking on the extra responsibility of handling video equipment in such situations.

Water activities: Sailing, canoeing, rowing, water skiing, windsurfing, as well as shooting on beaches and around pools – recording all these activities is possible with the camcorder protected in a simple splashproof housing (*see box*).

You can take dramatic sequences of canoeists shooting the rapids, or a yacht or powerboat race, from one of the competing craft. Get all-action shots of waterskiers from the towing boat and high-speed close-ups of windsurfers from a nearby boat. Low-level shots from the shore or shallows will capture head-on the essence of surfboarding.

A completely waterproof housing (*see box*) opens up a whole new world to the video maker – the world of underwater life, whether in the open sea or in lakes. Although the housing is heavy and bulky on land, it becomes light and easy to handle underwater.

There is no need to descend to great depths in the sea to get great pictures. The best light, and often the most abundant marine life, is in the top 10m (30ft), which is accessible to competent snorklers. Even lying face-down on the surface with the camera beneath the water can give good pictures. Light will be reflected off a pale sandy seabed in shallow waters.

Of course, all the wonders of marine life are revealed to the scuba diver, equipped with proper subaqua gear and a video lamp attached to the camcorder.

● *Never dive alone.* Video is an absorbing occupation and you can easily forget everything else in trying to get the best shots. Always dive with a buddy and keep them in sight at all times.

IN THE WET

Protecting the camcorder inside a special housing allows safe shooting of water activities. Sony's waterproof housing (*above*) enables you to shoot underwater to depths of 40m (132ft). The lens is of fixed focal length; focusing and white balance are pre-set. There is a microphone at the front and a full-frame viewfinder on top to square up shots. A video lamp, attached to the housing, is essential to bring out the true colours underwater. The only operating functions are the on/off switches of the camcorder and lamp.

The Sony camcorder (*below left*) is also fully automatic once in its splashproof housing (*below right*) and allows you to shoot action water sports at close quarters.

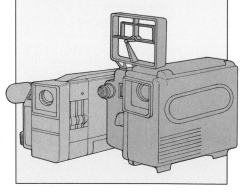

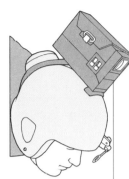

A compact camcorder, fixed to a helmet, allows you to take spectacular shots while sky-diving, parachuting or hang-gliding. The eyesight at the front of the helmet is used to line up shots.

● Keep camerawork simple and avoid elaborate movements.

● Swim at an even pace to take long drifting shots that can be edited together smoothly later.

● Underwater camcorders do not have a zoom lens, so you must move in for close-up details of subjects.

● Light is absorbed rapidly in the sea, different wavelengths being eliminated with depth. The red end of the spectrum is the first to go, but a video lamp directed on the subject will restore true colours. Without a lamp, shots will have a bluish/green tinge.

Aerial shooting: Exciting 'in-flight' videos can be taken from an aircraft or helicopter. Noise will make communications difficult, so discuss with the pilot in advance what you want to record and where. The best time to shoot is during the 2 hours after sunrise or the 2 hours before sunset, when long shadows on the land bring out the contours. Around midday, the craft's shadow can creep into shot.

When shooting from an aircraft, find a comfortable position with a clear view; avoid having the wings in shot. Hold the camcorder firmly against your shoulder or cheek to prevent vibration. Keep the lens at its widest angle and use the aircraft's movements to give you sweeping views of the landscape, all of which can be edited together later into a smooth sequence. Take care with exposure when including varying amounts of sky in shot, and beware of shooting directly into the sun or light – on auto iris, your shots will be heavily underexposed. Use a polarizing filter to cut down on reflected light and an ultraviolet filter to reduce haze.

A slower, smoother and quieter flight is got in a hot-air balloon and you can take shots much closer to the ground. If on safari, record herds of animals such as gnus or zebras from the air. You can also vary your shots much more; shoot toward the horizon or directly down to the ground, zooming in on details.

Spectacular aerial sequences can be taken when you are hang-gliding, parachuting or sky-diving (*above*). This is strictly a 'no hands' operation – rely totally on the camcorder's automated functions. Record a bird's-eye view by panning and tilting with your head.

EFFECTIVE PRESENTATION

Devote creative effort to the post-production stage of video making and you will add gloss and entertainment value to your programmes. 'Effective Presentation' covers a range of useful techniques that will make your videos more professional. These include how to add titles and how to create interesting audio and visual effects. The possibilities for creative editing of material on video, even incorporating old ciné films, expands the scope of home video productions enormously.

Well-designed titles, credits or captions will add a professional touch to your video productions. They should be attractive, legible and held long enough on screen to be read easily. The choice of typography, background and layout should all reflect the tone of the subject.

The easiest way to produce lettering on screen is with the use of a caption generator (*opposite*). Most camcorders either have this facility built in or it is an optional extra. With it, you can key in instant titles, using the electronics of the camcorder itself; these can be displayed alone on screen or superimposed over an appropriate background.

Besides titles at the beginning and credits at the end, you can also generate captions during the course of the programme – to introduce a new sequence (eg identifying athletes and events at a school sports day) or to indicate a change of date and location (eg compiling a video diary of your travels) or time (eg countdown to the events of a particular day, such as your daughter's wedding day).

If you are editing in-camera, you must create and shoot the titles at the exact point you want them on the tape. Alternatively, you can fit them into a predetermined position in the tape later, using the insert edit facility.

A basic caption generator produces lettering of different sizes and colours, which can be positioned in up to 5 lines anywhere on screen. More sophisticated models allow you to 'scroll' titles up or down the screen, or even zoom them up to full size.

Always do a rough layout of the title in advance, to determine if the words will fit and where best to position them. Draw up a grid on paper, with the lines and spaces available; then fill in the squares with the letters of your title.

Following some elementary design rules should enable you to produce pleasing results. The illustrations on pp. 111–13 demonstrate a few simple techniques.

When superimposing a caption-generated title on a picture (*above*), make sure the words fit comfortably against the background. The positions of 3 of the titles (*right*) work well on the sky, but the last line of the 4-line title is obscured by the horizon. Avoid fussy backgrounds and use a contrasting colour for the letters so they will stand out.

One-line titles look best centred on screen and placed just below the mid-line.

Centre 2- or 3-line titles if the words balance each other or form a neat block.

Titles can be aligned to the left, but avoid too many short words and indentations.

Align the title to the right to make 2 longer lines, placed about mid-screen.

With rub-down lettering (*left*), choose the typeface carefully. The best are often the modern typefaces, plain, bold and with clean strong lines. The styles illustrated show what will and will not work.

Because of the TV's problems of picture definition and horizontal scanning lines, some typefaces will be illegible. Avoid fine lines, which may break up; condensed type, which will fill in; fancy scripts, such as copperplate, which are hard to read; and styles with outlines whose features will disappear.

Instead of using the caption generator to create titles (which only provides one typeface, though in various sizes), you can produce your own artwork. Obviously, this approach offers much greater freedom of style and design. Main titles, in particular, are important in establishing the character of a programme at the start.

The artwork you produce can be shot using a rostrum camera (*see p. 114*) and inserted as part of the editing process.

Lettering: There are several methods you can use to make attractive titles:

● The simplest, 'no fuss' way is to hand-write a title directly on to pale coloured card (white card can produce excessive glare and contrast). Use a thick felt-tipped pen, paint brush or calligraphic pen to print clear bold letters.

● Use a stencil set or plastic 3-D letters, as used for display or noticeboards.

● Rub-down lettering is versatile and gives a professional finish. Capital letters, a little over 1cm ($\frac{1}{2}$in) high, are ideal. Laying down letters is a visual thing – your eyes will tell you if you've got it right, whether the letters are crooked, too close together or too far apart. It will become easier with practice, but a few guidelines might be: line up the letters on a coloured card along lightly drawn rules, which you can erase later. Keep the spacing between the lines to less than the capital height and then judge the distance to leave between letters by eye. When centring words, start with the middle letter and work outward. Allow the width of a capital 'M' between words.

● A list of credits can be appropriately typed directly on to coloured paper. But since the letters are small, you will need to shoot with a close-up lens, which will show any imperfections in the lettering.

● Lettering machines produce strips of lettering that can be laid down on card – a cheap alternative to typeset titles.

● Black lettering is best done on coloured card. White lettering on black card or dark colours can look effective.

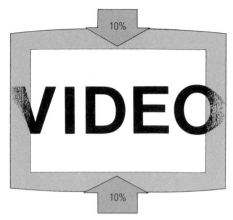

Position the title so it is not cut off at the edges of the TV screen. For safety sake, allow for a 10% cut-off all round. Visual distortion also occurs at the edges of the screen, making the letters unreadable.

When you lay out the lettering, check that it is not too close by measuring the area carefully; looking in the viewfinder can be deceptive since it tends to show slightly more than the TV screen will accommodate.

● Rub-down lettering can be put on sheets of acetate, which can then be laid over a textured background, photograph or specially drawn picture.

● A novel way to superimpose a title is to rub lettering down on a sheet of glass. Prop this up close to the lens and in front of the opening scene of your video. In the telephoto position, focus beyond the glass on to the scene and then throw focus to reveal the title.

Layout and design: When preparing titles for video use, there are a number of important factors to be considered:

● Although TV screens differ in size, they are all the same shape, with a ratio of 3 (vertical) to 4 (horizontal). Title cards can be made of any convenient size so long as they conform to this ratio; professionals favour 22.5 × 30cm (9 × 12in) format.

● Always allow a safety margin around the edge of the artwork (*above*).

● You can use coloured cards to split the screen, either horizontally or vertically.

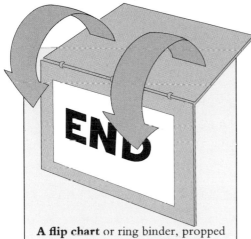

A flip chart or ring binder, propped up on an easel or table with the title or caption cards bound inside, is a simple way to shoot titles. Record the cards as they are flipped down in succession to introduce movement into the sequence. Use similar lettering and layouts for each card to avoid the titles 'jumping' on screen.

● Titles should be simple, bold and clean, and make good use of the area. Some sample layouts are shown on p. 111.

● Choose your typeface with care since several styles will not reproduce successfully (*see p. 110*).

● Unless scrolling up a list, limit the number of credit lines. Seven is the maximum; more, and the letters will be too small to read. With a lot of text, separate it on to several cards.

● Make sure the letters or lines are not too close; problems with picture definition will made them illegible.

● Main titles can be made up of capital letters. When there are many credits, use upper and lower case letters for ease of reading.

● Avoid mixing type styles – it looks messy and can be illegible. Vary the appearance by mixing the type sizes.

● Cast and credit lists look neatest in blocks, with the 'roles' ranged left and the 'names' ranged right.

Make titles special by shooting them on location and editing in-camera. A vacation in Hawaii, for example, can be introduced by drawing the word in the sand or by using pebbles or shells to form the letters. Setting your title near the water's edge can even give you a natural 'wipe' effect! Use anything relevant to your theme. Try making titles with coins, buttons or matches, displayed on coloured card. For nature subjects, make up the words from twigs, flowers or leaves. Announce a birthday party with the person's name spelt out in candles. Children's drawings and lettering make ideal opening titles for videos of family subjects.

ROSTRUM TECHNIQUES

A rostrum set-up allows you to shoot a great variety of stills material for inclusion in your videos. You can take shots of artwork, such as captions and titles, and add variety to 'live' material by including photographs, paintings, newspaper cuttings, maps, old documents and magazine pictures.

These shots can be insert edited anywhere in a prerecorded tape. Or you can compile a complete video of such stills material based, for example, on the family photo album and other memorabilia, brought to life with a commentary, an interview as voice-over, or music.

The ideal rostrum set-up is illustrated (right). Lamps on stands are not always necessary. If the daylight is good enough, you can shoot from a tripod with the material fixed in position, either horizontally or vertically. Check that the subject is evenly lit and not overshadowed by the camcorder.

In low-light conditions, boost illumination with a small, battery-operated video lamp, clipped to the camcorder's accessory shoe and directed on to the subject. Check that there are no reflections or 'hot spots' of bright light on the subject.

To make sure the subject's position is correct, connect the camcorder to the TV and check on screen that it is aligned properly, centred and level, and that the composition of the shot is satisfactory.

Different subjects demand special considerations:

Artworks of captions, titles and credits:

● Before shooting, work out how long each shot should be held on screen. Time captions, by reading them aloud, then allow half that time again for slow readers. With main titles, allow more – 3 times your reading speed.

● Alignment is vital when you want words or images to appear in the same place on screen each time or stepped down the screen in successive shots.

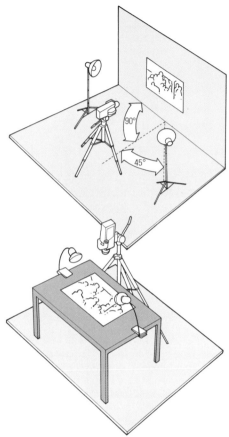

The ideal rostrum set-up for shooting stills material is to fix the subject to a wall (*top*) or lay it flat on a table (*above*). With the camera on a tripod, set at a convenient operating height, position it at 90° to the subject, either directly in front or above, depending on the set-up. Two matching lamps, set either side at an angle of 45° to the subject, will ensure a flood of even lighting. To check this, hold a pencil at 90° from the centre of the subject; the shadows on either side should be of equal intensity. Use video lamps on stands, such as photofloods, or clip-on desk lamps fitted with photoflood bulbs. Rostrum set-ups allow steady camera movements to be made over small subjects, to extract shots of various sizes, as shown for the painting opposite. Take particular care over focus and use a supplementary close-up lens for greater detail.

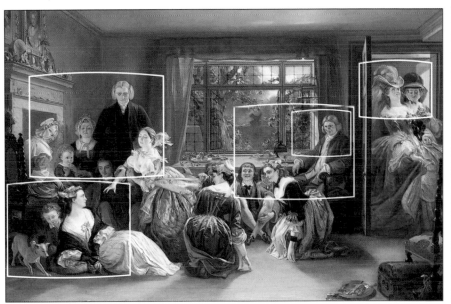

Bring a narrative painting to life by treating it as live action and creating a sequence of various shot sizes. Using the rostrum set-up, shoot within the frame. Pan, tilt and zoom as you would with live subjects, but because of the small scale, rehearse these camera movements carefully.

A shot sequence for this painting could be: a close-up of man by window; pull out to reveal group; cut to people by fireplace; tilt down to lady looking right; cut away to ladies entering; cut to long shot of room.

Photographs and paintings:
● You will need to eliminate any reflections, of yourself and the camera, from the shiny surfaces of glossy photographs or glazed paintings. Try tilting the subject slightly, so that its surface is not parallel to the camera. Or use a polarizing lens filter. Or mask the camera with a square of black card or cloth, with a hole cut for the lens to poke through.
● When choosing subjects, remember the fixed proportions of the video frame (3 parts high to 4 parts wide).
● Some subjects will be the 'wrong' shape, such as narrow or upright photographs. You can simply acknowledge a frame or outline and include it in the shot. But make it presentable first – by mounting on a coloured card or some other surround to act as background.

● Another solution with subjects that are the wrong shape is to shoot only *within* the frame. You can compile highly original videos in this way, by editing together a series of details from old photographs or paintings (*above*), then adding a suitable sound track.

Entertaining videos for children can be made using a series of illustrations, perhaps drawn by the children themselves. Cut the images together and accompany them with a recording of your own story.

Newspapers, documents and maps:
● Documentaries or travel videos often call for detailed shots of maps, photos or documents. Use a supplementary close-up lens, which allows you to zoom in tightly on the subject for minute details.
● Panning over headlines is effective, but don't go too fast or the letters will blur.

OPTICAL EFFECTS

Increase the creative impact of your video making by exploiting a range of optical effects. Attractive and original results can be produced in-camera, several of them achieved by simply improvising with a piece of black card.

Experiment, by all means, but don't be tempted to use effects that are out of keeping with the style and theme of your video. Optical effects should enhance the subject, not distract from its contents.

Fades: An automatic fader facility is built into most camcorders and allows you to fade out the picture and sound at the end of a shot and fade in to the next.

With a fade-out, the image becomes progressively darker until the screen goes black. This is known as a 'fade to black'. (A 'fade to white' is available with some camcorder models, where the image gets increasingly brighter until the screen is a solid white.) A fade-in is the opposite to a fade-out; the screen is black to start with and the image is gradually lightened until it reaches its proper exposure level.

Fades are simple to do and create a most useful device for:
● Making transitions between live action sequences.
● Changing a series of main titles at the beginning of a tape or credits at the end.
● Indicating the passage of time (useful for lengthy events) or changes of location (ideal for travel videos).

You should plan a fade-out in advance, by determining the closing shot of a sequence. Remember, when setting up the next scene, that you may need a fade-in at the start. However, it is not always necessary to follow a fade-out with a fade-in. On occasion, it is effective to fade out a scene, then cut to a bright new scene, fully exposed. This gives the cut to the new shot particular impact.

Automatic fades will all be at the same speed. If you want to vary the length of fades, you can override the auto system and adjust the iris manually. This is usually only possible when shooting in relatively low light, when the aperture is already set wide. By turning the aperture ring, you can make the picture gradually fade to black. Keep checking the image in the viewfinder to ensure that all parts of the picture disappear, including the brighter areas. Remember, when on manual, that only the picture fades, not the sound, so at the end of the fade, pause the recording.

In situations where you are shooting in bright conditions and the lens is stopped down (ie small aperture), use this same approach to produce a fade to white, by gradually opening up the iris.

Wipes: Another way to create transitions in time or location is to use a simple 'wipe' effect. Set the camcorder to manual and use a tripod to get a steady effect. At the point where you want to cut a scene, slide a square piece of black card smoothly across the front of the lens to cover it. The result is a blacked-out screen.

A wipe is most effective when done rapidly, so that the viewer is less aware of the effect and simply reads it as a change of image. Precise timing is needed, especially when editing in-camera. If editing later, you can adjust the timing between a wipe-out and a wipe-in.

Wipes can be made in a variety of ways to get particular effects.
● Slide a card across the screen from one side to give the impression of a curtain closing.
● Blot out a scene by a wipe-out to black down the screen and follow this with a wipe-in rising up the screen. A filter holder (see diagram) is useful for guiding the card in both directions.
● Move two cards in from opposite sides of the screen at the same time and speed, so they meet to black out the scene. Reveal the next location by drawing the cards apart.
● Combine a wipe with a fade. For example, end a sequence with a fade to black, then start the next with a black wipe that reveals the new location.

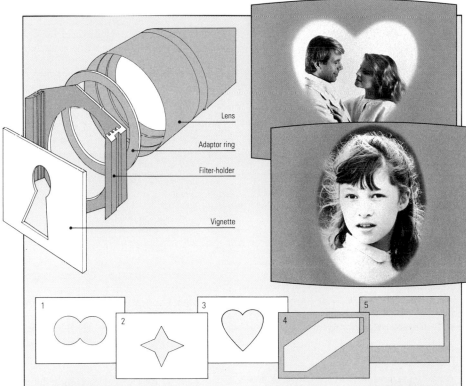

Lens

Adaptor ring

Filter-holder

Vignette

VIGNETTE EFFECTS

By mounting a black card with a cut-out shape on a standard filter holder (*top*), you can produce new screen shapes within the fixed 4 × 3 format. The picture contained within the cut-out shape is called a vignette.

Standard shapes are available or you can make your own original designs (*above*).

Because the vignette effect is visually strong, use it with discretion. Shots must be carefully composed so that the subject or action is centred within the space. Since the card is positioned close to the lens, the edge of the cut-out will appear soft. It will be sharpest in bright light at the wide angle due to increased depth of field.

A vignette cut-out mounted in a filter holder can reinforce a romantic scene (heart shape) or spotlight a subject (oval). Besides standard shapes (1–3), you can make your own, for example, to give a diagonal emphasis (4) or a wide-screen effect (5).

● Combine a vignette cut-out with lettering from a caption generator for title sequences, eg with the cut-out shape in the upper part of the screen and the lower part blacked out, use the solid area for superimposing caption-generated titles.

● Combine a black wipe with a vignette cut-out in the same holder. Use the wipe to reveal the vignette at the appropriate moment.

● With an oval or circular cut-out, zoom in on the subject until it is neatly framed within the central space.

USING FILTERS

Photographic filters are used to correct or modify the behaviour of light and to create special effects. There is a wide range available. Some are optical glass discs that screw on to the lens, while others are squares of glass, plastic or gelatin that slot into a filter holder mounted on the lens (*see diagram, p. 117*). Several filters can be used in combination to get multiple effects (*see box*).

Corrective filters: Three filters in particular are useful accessories for shooting in various light conditions.

● An ultraviolet (UV) filter, of clear glass, absorbs scattered UV light and eliminates blue haze on outdoor shots, to give clear aerial, land and sea views.

● A neutral density (ND) filter, of an overall grey colour, reduces the amount of light reaching the camcorder's image sensors, which is essential in excessively bright conditions (*see p. 85*). Another important effect is to reduce depth of field.

● A polarizing filter, of light grey, eliminates reflections so you can shoot clear images through water and glass, and reduces glare from shiny surfaces. Rotate the filter to determine the amount of reflection to be removed and, for maximum effect, position the lens at an angle of 35° to

the surface. A polarizer also deepens colours and creates contrasts, particularly between sky and clouds (*see p. 85*).

Colour-balancing filters: By filtering out particular wavelengths, these filters correct colours in certain light conditions or modify light to get specific effects, but they reduce the amount of light entering the lens.

● An amber filter takes out the bluish tones in overcast cloudy conditions and in shadow areas, creating a warm effect and darkening light skin tones.

● A blue filter reduces the reddish tones of late evening or early morning light and makes scenes appear cooler.

● A violet filter can eliminate the bluish-green cast of certain fluorescent lights.

Special effects: A range of specific filters changes the appearance of the subject, rather than the light itself. Like all visual 'tricks', such effects should be used with discretion and only where appropriate.

● A single, deep-colour filter adds drama and atmosphere to a scene (*photo 1, above*). Light areas pick up the colour best.

● A sepia filter gives an 'antique' look, particularly effective with old black and white photographs and period subjects.

● A graduated filter, half clear and half

Special effects are created by specific filters: (*above, left to right*) a coloured filter (red), a graduated filter, a diffusion filter and a star filter.

coloured, can dramatize skylines (*photo 2*), simulate sunsets and intensify colours. A graduated ND filter is ideal for scenes with overbright skies. Line up the filter carefully along the horizon to disguise the change of colour; the wider the aperture, the more indistinct the edge line.

● A diffusion filter, with a slightly rippled or dimpled surface, softens the image and causes highlights to flare and diffuse (*photo 3*). It can be used to reinforce romantic, dreamlike or glamorous shots.

● A fog filter creates a soft misty effect, producing halos around lights. The effect is increased as the aperture is widened.

● A star filter, with a grid of parallel lines etched on its surface, creates a number of rays radiating out from any strong point of light, such as street lamps or neon signs (*photo 4*). The filter can be rotated during the shot to change the pattern of stars.

● A multi-image filter breaks up the subject into several images that blend with one another. Best results are obtained with a wide aperture and dark background.

TIPS ON FILTERS

● Handle filters with care. Avoid finger marks on gelatin filters.

● Create some unusual effects. Try combining a diffusion or a fog filter with a star filter, or a coloured filter with a multi-image filter.

● To improvise a soft-focus effect, smear a little Vaseline on a piece of clear glass and hold it in front of the lens. An old Hollywood trick is to stretch fine-mesh nylon, such as a stocking, over the lens to soften the image and smooth out fine details. This works best with high key lighting (*see p. 134*) and a wide aperture.

● To simulate moonlight, use a blue filter and deliberately underexpose the image.

● Improvise a neutral density filter with a piece of smoked glass.

● Rotate two polarizing filters against each other for a fade effect.

● For different effects, experiment by taking shots through coloured or frosted glass, plastic, prisms, distorting mirrors, kaleidoscopes, even the bottom of a whisky tumbler.

TELECINE TRANSFER

There are several advantages to teleciné transfer or the copying of your collection of 35mm transparencies (slides) and 8mm ciné or movie film on to video tape.

● The material is more accessible and easy to view, without the lengthy business of setting up a projector and screen.

● The material can be edited into your video tapes and will acquire a 'new look' by, for example, adding special effects (wipes or fades to link scenes, enhance the colour with lens filters as you shoot the transfer or change the shape with vignette effects, *see p. 116*). You can record a new commentary and/or music to an old travel film or compile a series of slides into sequences with introductory titles (of the date and occasion) produced with a caption generator.

● Slides and film will be permanently preserved and protected on video tape. They are easily damaged – the more you show them, the more vulnerable they become. Video tape, in contrast, can be run many times and, with proper care (*see p. 211*), will last indefinitely.

As with any copying process, the inevitable disadvantage is some loss of picture quality, but even this can be minimized with a little care.

There are several methods of teleciné transfer. Film-to-tape involves placing a unit between the film or slide projector and the camcorder (*see box*). Special carriers or adaptors can be attached to the camcorder lens for direct shooting (*see diagram*). The simplest method is to project the images on to a screen and reshoot them with the camcorder, as follows:

● Set up the projector in a darkened room to produce a small bright image on screen.

● Position the camcorder/tripod immediately alongside the projector. Both machines should be at 90° to the screen and closely aligned so that there will be no distortion ('keystoning') in the shape of the projected image. Using the telephoto position will help.

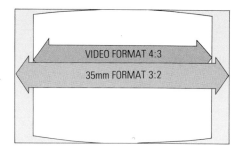

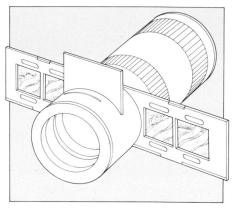

The format of a 35mm slide (3 parts wide to 2 high) differs to video. Reframe, and centre on image.

An adaptor fixed to the camcorder lens ensures proper alignment of slides and negatives for copying.

● Set the white balance to 'tungsten' and adjust focus precisely on the screen image.

● Connect the camcorder to the TV so you can monitor the process and check on picture quality as you shoot.

● View film material first to check for exposure. You may find that you can use a single manual setting for the whole reel; alternatively, you can rely on auto exposure, but there may be some lag or visible change in brightness with each new scene.

● If you want to retain the sound of the original film, connect the audio-out socket of the projector to the camcorder's audio-in (ie don't use a microphone).

Two common problems can be ex-

FILM-TO-TAPE TRANSFER

Copying ciné film or slides on to video tape is made easy with a teleciné attachment acting as an interface between the projector and camcorder. The image, bright and perfectly aligned for recording, is projected on to a translucent screen from one side. An internal mirror reverses the image so that the camcorder, placed at an aperture on the side of the unit, sees the image correctly. A close-up lens is used on the camcorder, which should be connected to the TV to monitor the transfer. A film's sound can also be copied, by linking the projector's audio-out to the camcorder's audio-in.

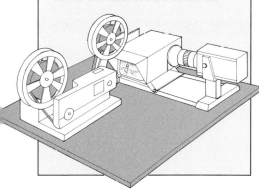

perienced. Some of the projected images may have too high a contrast range for successful video reproduction. The only solution is to set the iris to expose for either the bright area or the dark area of the image – detail will have to be sacrificed in one to register the other.

The second problem is caused by images flickering on screen due to the different frame rates of the film projector and the camcorder, and the intermittent action of the projector shutter. Flicker is particularly evident with pale images and 8mm film projected at 18 frames per second. The effect can be reduced by adjusting the speed of the projector, but this can result in some distortion of sound pitch. Check the effect of your adjustments on the TV screen and amend as necessary.

Since the format of a 35mm transparency is different to that of video (*see diagram*), you will have to shoot within the slide's frame. Even with horizontal compositions and by centring the video shot on the slide, you are bound to lose a fraction of the image on either side. With vertical compositions, even more will be lost off the top and bottom. You can reframe shots to improve their original compositions or pan, tilt and zoom within the frame. Be careful with tight zoom-ins – the grain of the film and texture of the screen will start to show up.

You can set slides up in a specific order and edit them in-camera, making a sequence as you shoot. Vary the length of each shot according to its content and importance, as you would with a live subject. Check the TV picture regularly during transfer, to monitor composition, contrast and exposure.

An alternative method is to use a special slide adaptor attached to the camcorder lens. Or you can simply fix the slide to the front of the lens with black tape (which will also prevent light leaking in) and set the lens to the macro position. Point the camcorder toward a light source (either daylight or tungsten, so long as it is even), so that the slide is backlit; using a white card to bounce light toward the lens is ideal. If the camcorder has a neg/pos facility, treat 35mm negatives and smaller formats in the same way.

This method gives better quality of reproduction than shooting the images off a screen, but you do not have the freedom to pan and zoom or reframe the subject that you have with the projector method.

Take advantage of film technology by shooting sequences specially to include on video tape. Film is ideal for recording slow motion and speeded-up effects, as well as animation of cartoons and puppets.

CREATIVE EDITING

> ❝ *Editing is crucial. Imagine James Stewart looking at a mother nursing a child. You see the child, then cut back to him. He smiles. Now Mr. Stewart is a benign old gentleman. Take away the middle shot and substitute a girl in a bikini. Now he's a dirty old man.* ❞

ALFRED HITCHCOCK, DIRECTOR
Rebecca (Oscar), *North by Northwest, Psycho, The Birds.*

Editing involves selecting particular shots and re-ordering their sequence to give visual sense and flow to the recorded material. But you can make editing a much more creative process by structuring and shaping the material to give it pace, mood and rhythm.

The creativity of your editing will depend partly on your imagination and partly on the facilities available.

Tape–to–tape assemble editing (*see p. 62*) is a good home method, but it has limitations since each edit you decide on becomes a fixed part of the final tape. If an edit has not worked, you must edit back into the previous shot to create a new edit point. Editing in at exactly the same point is not possible without severe picture disturbance.

However, with insert edit facilities on the edit-VCR, you can insert pictures and/or sound anywhere on an already edited tape. Because the control track remains continuous, both the in- and out-points of the edits will be 'clean' or free from electronic disturbance (*see p. 123*). You can edit in titles, illustrations and computer images at any stage. More important, you can insert cut-in and cut-away shots to link edited sequences, but their insertion needs careful placing and timing.

With an edit controller machine, you can override the tape-transport controls of both the camcorder and the edit-VCR. This enables you to fix more precise edit points (eg during the middle of an action shot). And the machine allows you to preview edits before recording them.

Apart from maintaining the elements of visual sense and flow in your editing, there are all sorts of creative techniques you can introduce at this stage to enliven or manipulate the images. These include:

● **Parallel action:** By intercutting shots from two different events, you suggest that they are related in some way. For example, if you cut back and forth between shots of a man hurrying along with a bunch of flowers, and a girl dressing herself for the evening, the viewer will assume that these two people have a date – until the end of the sequence, when the man gives the flowers to his mother and the girl goes out with her flatmate.

● **Split shots:** These can strengthen relationships. For example, if a shot of a cat drinking milk is followed by a longer shot of a child watching, the child's interest is established. But, you can convert the interest to 'fascination' by splitting the longer shot into 2 – cut from the child to the cat and back again to the child.

●**Juxtaposition:** Cutting between two contrasting subjects can suggest an association of ideas. For example, a shot of cattle being herded into a pen followed by a shot of milling crowds in the subway suggests the indignities of city life.

●**Pace:** Speeding up the rate of editing, by making shots progressively shorter, is a standard method to suggest an increase of pace, often used in chase sequences.

●**Montage:** A series of thematically linked shots can evoke mood or suggest the passage of time. For example, a slow-cut sequence of scenic views can evoke an air of tranquillity; rapid cutting from autumnal to wintery and then to spring scenes can suggest the passing of time as shown by the changing seasons.

●**Tension:** By repeatedly intercutting between the same 2 or 3 shots in a sequence, you can create expectation and increase tension.

●**Shock cuts:** By leading the viewer's expectations along a particular path and then confounding them, you create a shock effect. For example, a sequence of a person stealthily opening a door and peeping into a room might conclude with a shock cut of a hand reaching out to touch them from behind.

●**Jump cuts:** Distinct changes in people's positions or locations suggest the passage of time. For example, by cutting from a shot of a man ordering a meal to a shot of him draining his glass immediately suggests that time has passed.

●**Matched action:** Professional editing often creates smooth transitions between

By cutting together material from 3 separate tapes (shots of the children, statue and running horse), taken on different occasions, you can create a completely new story. Here, the sequence is edited to suggest that the statue has come to life for the children.

shots by cutting during an action. For example, a mid-shot of a person taking a drink could cut just as they lift the glass, then continue with a close-up of the glass at the mouth. For this to be effective, the movement in successive shots needs to be continuous (part of the same action) and precisely matched at the edit point.

Unfortunately, a home-editing set-up does not allow for this type of precision and unmatched action will produce distracting edits. The technique is possible with an edit controller and a shooting situation where you can record several shots of the same scene, as with a drama production.

Technical aspects: When a video tape is shot, a series of synchronizing pulses is recorded along one side of the tape. This 'control track' ensures that the tape will play back at the same speed.

With tape-to-tape assemble editing, the control track is copied along with the pictures and sound. For edits to be stable, pulses must be in step at edit points.

Insert editing makes use of an existing control track. This may be the track already present on the assembled material. Or you can lay down a new track, by 'blacking' a tape (ie a recording with no sound or pictures), then insert editing the material on to the 'blacked' tape.

Good sound, used appropriately, makes an important contribution to any video. Sound can also be used to manipulate the images, to suggest an atmosphere different to what the pictures imply. Think about the sound track when you are planning the images, particularly with drama and documentary subjects where live sound is often an essential aid to comprehension.

Sound will be recorded automatically as you shoot, unless you disconnect the camcorder's built-in microphone. At the editing stage of production, the sound track can be reassessed with the pictures for quality, relevance and creative value.

If it enhances the pictures, then all you need to do is smooth out any variations in sound level as you edit. This is done with a simple sound mixer inserted between the camcorder and the VCR being used as the edit recorder.

If, however, the sound track is not to your satisfaction, it can easily be expanded, enhanced or even replaced at the editing stage. Music, narration or commentary, and atmospheric sound effects can be introduced as new sound elements. They can be used individually or blended together, or even mixed with the original sounds recorded on location. The complexity of the finished track will depend on your video system and on additional facilities available. But even with the simplest of audio-dub systems, the results can be highly effective.

> ❝ *I'm really interested in mood and sound combinations ... You have to get the sound to fit a particular film. Certain lighting can create feeling — sound can alter mood even more.* ❞

DAVID LYNCH, DIRECTOR
Eraserhead, The Elephant Man, Blue Velvet.

MUSIC

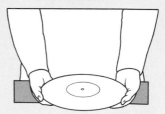

Music is the easiest, and often the most effective, element to add to a sound track. But never use it merely to fill a gap; don't be afraid of silent pictures.

Remember, there are copyright restrictions on the use of existing musical recordings which must be cleared with the proper authorities, even for private viewings. Specially composed and copyright-cleared themes are available for home use.

Both the choice of music, in terms of its tempo and style, and the way it is used are important. Avoid the well-known themes that will already have strong associations in people's minds, unless, of course, you want to exploit that association. Use music:
● To set the tone and style of a video. Run the opening titles to music and the closing credits to echoes of the same theme.
● To link sequences, eg by repeating a simple theme to bridge transitions.
● To establish atmosphere or reinforce a particular mood.
● To add pace to a sequence or provide a basis for editing, eg by cutting shots to an up-tempo beat.
● To add dramatic punctuation, eg discordant strings heighten tension.
● To reinforce the meaning of a scene, with the music acting as commentary, eg a protest song could enforce an environmental documentary.

COMMENTARY

For many home videos, you will want to write and record your own commentary over the pictures (*see p. 158*). Before recording, always rehearse first to check that the words fit with the images and to get the timing, pace and emphasis right. For the recording session:

● Record in a quiet room with balanced acoustics (*see p. 32*).

● Set up the TV so you can see the images; turn down its sound to prevent 'howl round' (*see p. 208*).

● The narrator should sit with the script (each page enclosed in a plastic sleeve to prevent paper rustle) propped up in clear view, to avoid lowering the head when reading.

● Place a unidirectional mic on a stand about 30cm (1ft) away and do a sound test to check voice level. Check the mic's position − too close to the narrator produces 'popping' sounds at the start of words or on certain letters; too close to the recorder picks up its sound.

● Beware of the voice dropping at the end of sentences and keep a glass of water nearby. Record only a few short paragraphs at a time.

● When recording, cue the narrator with a tap on the shoulder at the start of each commentary section.

● If a mistake is made, stop and re-record the whole section to ensure unbroken flow.

SOUND EFFECTS

Sound effects can be used in many ways to stimulate audience response. Commercial sound effects are available on disc or tape, but it is much more fun to record your own. You can improvise all sorts of sounds in your living room with simple equipment − coconut shells, sink plungers, combs, tin foil, a box filled with sand (*see also p. 127*). Or you can record specific sounds on location with a cassette recorder and directional mic.

Subtle or humorous sound effects will enhance a production, but don't overdo them. Use them to:

● Reinforce what is already seen on screen, such as the sound of waves for a beach scene or traffic sounds for a busy city scene.

● Suggest elements not seen, eg emphasize the tranquillity of a country scene with the chime of church bells or birdsong.

● Establish atmosphere and mood, with sounds such as thunder, wind, a dripping tap or distant laughter.

● Symbolize an emotional state, with sounds such as a heartbeat, ticking clock or approaching footsteps.

Because of the limitations of home editing, it is difficult to synchronize 'spot' effects, such as a crack of thunder, gun shot, ringing telephone or water splash. Work, instead, with atmospheric sounds that can be used over several shots or whole sequences.

Methods for adding a new sound track to a recorded tape vary according to tape format, the equipment available and the complexity of the track you want to create. With an edited in-camera tape, you can replace some or all of the original sound, or mix in any number of sound elements, as part of the dubbing process. If the format has the audio signal recorded in the picture track, sound can be replaced only during tape-to-tape editing.

The simplest way of adding sound is to dub on a new track, such as a commentary over a travel video, using the audio-dub facility on the camcorder or a VCR. If the VCR has twin tracks, you can record the commentary on one channel and retain the original sound on the other. However, with this form of parallel play, there is no way to control the balance of the two tracks, so do a test first to see if the results will be acceptable.

Use an auxiliary microphone for the recording, fed directly into the camcorder or VCR. Rehearse the words with the images on screen. Then, run the tape and press the audio-dub switch at the point where you want to lay down the commentary. Stop the recording at the end of each section. If unhappy with the result, you can re-record the section, but remember that with a single-track machine, the original sound track will have been erased.

The audio-dub method can also be used to lay down music or sound effects. Feed the relevant source (eg cassette recorder, compact disc or tape machine) into the audio-in socket of the camcorder or VCR, and proceed as before.

When dubbing on a new track on a camcorder, be aware that the machine's automatic gain control (AGC) will compensate for variations in sound level. During pauses in a commentary, for example, it has the effect of raising the background noise or with music, it will level out natural peaks and troughs. By contrast, many VCRs give manual control of sound levels.

LOCATION SOUND

Separate recording of additional atmospheric sounds on location (eg birdsong or running water) can be mixed in with other sound at the editing stage. In certain situations, however, it is important to make a separate continuous recording of the sound. For example, when shooting sequences with essential sound (eg a brass-band parade, speech-making scene or street market), you will want to cut between shots and move to various camera positions to get visual variety. This, of course, disrupts the sound track, which should therefore be recorded separately, using an audio recorder. Dub the sound track on later during editing.

Since both the action and the sound are happening simultaneously, you will need the help of a friend to act as sound recordist; they should get as close as possible to the source of the sound and direct the mic toward it, wearing headphones to monitor the level.

When recording outdoors in windy locations, stand with your back to the wind; avoid crackle and wind noise with a foam gag or sleeve around the mic's head, or improvise with a heavy sock or handkerchief.

At times, the camcorder itself can be used to record sound only; this can be useful for atmospheric effects, such as the sound of breaking waves to cover a seashore sequence.

MIXING

A simple sound mixer allows you to create an elaborate sound track with two or more sources mixed together. One method is to pre-mix the track on $\frac{1}{4}$in tape (using a stereo or 4-track machine) or on an audio cassette. Having recorded such a pre-mixed sound track, you can then dub it directly on to the video tape. With insert edit facilities, you can audio-dub sounds in at specific points.

The alternative method to pre-mixing is to link the sound mixer direct to the edit machine. For a combination of music and words, prerecord the commentary on tape, timed so that it matches neatly with the pictures. Then play this back and mix in the music at the same time, dubbing it directly on to the tape.

To be effective, this needs precision timing or an accurate tape counter. The skill is to dovetail both sound elements so that, for example, the music dips down to form a background just before new commentary comes in.

If you want to combine your original location sound with other elements (eg commentary, music and sound effects), it must be fed from the audio-out of the camcorder into the sound mixer, along with the other sound sources. The combined track can then be dubbed on to a new tape, with the pictures fed from the camcorder direct to the edit recorder.

BE CREATIVE

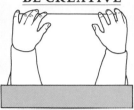

Whatever the sounds you add and whichever method you use to get new sounds on to your videos, there is great scope for experimentation. Some suggestions are:
● Make commentaries more lively and interesting by using a variety of voices. For family subjects, combine grandparents' reminiscences with children's voices, which often have great charm and value. Record them live, without rehearsal.
● Use music for humorous effects – dub a tango beat over a sports event or a romantic melody over monkeys engaged in communal grooming.
● Use amusing and unexpected juxtaposition of pictures and sound – dub chattering magpies over a conversational group at a party or traffic sounds over an underwater sequence of a shoal of fish.
● Improvise comic sound effects to add into simple story videos. Use your own voice to produce animal noises or atmospheric effects, such as whistling wind. Use household items for unusual sounds – shake a jar of beans, whisk an egg, grate a potato.
● An alternative to using prerecorded music is to compose your own. You can time it specially to the images; a synthesizer can provide some great effects. Or you could record your own version of a popular tune; remember, copyright has to be cleared for existing music.

GETTING SOPHISTICATED

Even with a minimum of equipment, the videos you produce can be imaginative and technically sound. But by using some extra facilities and techniques, you can expand your creative potential and achieve more sophisticated results. This section explains how you can give more impact to familiar subjects and experiment with new and exciting areas of video. 'Getting Sophisticated' need not be costly: consider joining forces with other enthusiasts for more ambitious productions.

The basic purpose of lighting is to get a proper exposure in order to improve picture quality, by ensuring sharp definition, saturated colours and control of the contrast range.

Lighting has many other, more creative uses. It can make subjects look more attractive by bringing out texture and detail; it can give a natural look to scenes, such as domestic interiors, by dispersing murky shadows and pools of brightness; and it can be used to suggest depth by, for example, making backgrounds darker than foregrounds, and vice versa. But most importantly, lighting can establish atmosphere and mood. Like music, it can appeal to the emotions of the viewer.

The complexity of your lighting needs will depend on the subject. For much home shooting, your aim will simply be to get well-lit shots. When making documentaries and promotional videos, you will have to take extra care to obtain attractive and effective images. For shooting drama, lighting is an essential element for creative manipulation.

In the simplest situations, a single video lamp can be a useful addition to daylight or ordinary room lighting, since it will raise the overall illumination. Even when lighting levels are good, an additional lamp can 'lift' the picture and improve close-ups of people by separating them from their backgrounds and adding sparkle to their eyes; it is also helpful for backlighting and contrast problems.

Remember, however, that a single lamp, used as the only source of light from on or near the camera, will create a flat effect on the subject, with harsh shadows cast on the background. By reflecting or diffusing the light off walls or ceilings, you can produce a more natural feeling.

An even spread of light can be produced by using 2 lamps, placed on either side of the subject and kept fairly high. With a set of 3 or 4 lamps, your creative control is even greater (*see illustrations*).

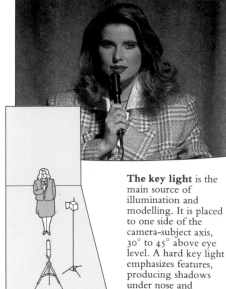

The key light is the main source of illumination and modelling. It is placed to one side of the camera-subject axis, 30° to 45° above eye level. A hard key light emphasizes features, producing shadows under nose and eyebrows.

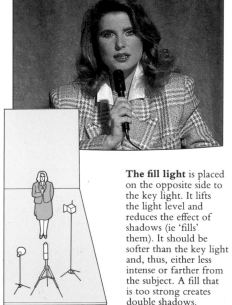

The fill light is placed on the opposite side to the key light. It lifts the light level and reduces the effect of shadows (ie 'fills' them). It should be softer than the key light and, thus, either less intense or farther from the subject. A fill that is too strong creates double shadows.

The backlight, placed slightly behind and above the subject, adds a rim of light to the hair and shoulders. It thus creates depth by separating, or isolating, the subject from the background. The light can be hard or soft, depending on the effect intended.

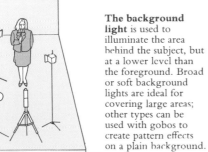

The background light is used to illuminate the area behind the subject, but at a lower level than the foreground. Broad or soft background lights are ideal for covering large areas; other types can be used with gobos to create pattern effects on a plain background.

With daylight alone, from a window off-screen right, the subject's face is shadowed on one side (*top*). For a more even lighting effect (*above and right*), use the daylight as the key light and add a single video lamp to provide the fill light and give a soft, even and natural look. With this mixed lighting set-up, use a blue gelatin filter over the fill lamp and set the camcorder's white balance to 'daylight'.

If the daylight source is weak, use it as the fill source and let the single video lamp act as the key light.

The 3- and 4-point lighting schemes are studio concepts that can easily be applied and adapted on location by using lamps of varying intensity. You can also make use of daylight as a general fill source.

CREATIVE LIGHTING • 2

Lighting your videos creatively means learning how to control, shape and modify light. Lighting can be direct, indirect or diffused. It is the way you use and combine these three approaches that will determine the 'feel' of your shots.

Direct lighting produces the most dramatic effects, including intense shadows, high contrasts and strong modelling of contours. The strength of these effects varies with the distance between the lamp and subject, and whether the lamps are adjusted to give sharp 'spots' or broad 'floods' of light.

Indirect lighting involves bouncing, or reflecting, light off white or pale surfaces to produce a more even spread of illumination (*see p. 38*). Reflecting light reduces the level of illumination produced by a lamp, so the closer the lamp is to the reflector, the greater the illumination.

A reflector should become an essential part of your lighting kit. It is particularly useful for close-ups, since reflected light is less dazzling for subjects and creates fewer shadow problems.

Diffusing light means scattering it to produce a gentle even effect, with lower contrasts and softer shadows. This is accomplished by placing a translucent material (the diffuser) between the light source and subject. Although this reduces the light intensity, the resulting low contrast is ideal for video.

A heatproof, wire gauze diffuser can be purchased which slips into a holder on the lamp. Or you can improvise your own diffuser, with thick tracing or greaseproof paper (two layers doubles the effect) clipped on to the front of the lamp or its barn doors. Professionals clip on spun-glass diffusers (and wear gloves to handle them). With a diffuser fixed to a large frame on a lighting stand and placed in front of the lamp, you can broaden the area of light to get 'shadowless' lighting.

For safety, be aware of heat hazards when using diffusers. Always keep the

Lighting conveys atmosphere. With only one lamp in use, heavy shadows are created by direct lighting (*top*). But with that light diffused (*above*), a soft, even and more natural effect is produced.

diffuser at least 7.5cm (3in) from the front of the lamp so that air can circulate.

A lamp's barn doors (the hinged metal flaps fitted to lamps) can be used to restrict the illuminated area and control shadows. You can adjust them to create narrow, horizontal or vertical slits of light.

Coloured gelatin filters placed over lamps can produce special visual effects, though remember that they will reduce the amount of light. Green and red can enliven a party scene. Orange or red simulate firelight; by shaking strips of paper in front of the lamp, you get the effect of flickering flames. Remember when lighting interiors that are partially lit by daylight to use a blue conversion filter on the lamp to raise its colour temperature to that of daylight (*see p. 39*).

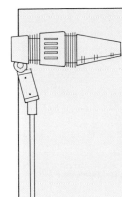

SNOOTS

A snoot is a cylindrical metal funnel fixed to a lamp housing to restrict and focus the beam. You can improvise a snoot with heavy card rolled into a cone shape and fixed on with tape. Use the round 'spot' that the snoot produces to highlight a subject (eg from behind to create a halo effect) or as an additional light source to improve a close-up. Or you can use it to simulate the effect of a spotlight falling on a painting or a torch beam in the dark.

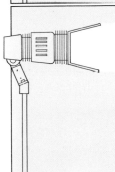

FLAGS

A flag is a sheet of opaque material, such as black card or thin plywood, placed between the lamp and subject to shape and control a light beam. When fixed to a stand, it can act as a mobile barn door and prevent light from a fill spilling on to the background or light from a backlight flaring into the lens. Flags can also be used to create shadows (eg over a subject's face to get a sombre effect). The farther away the flag from the lamp, the sharper the shadow.

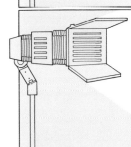

GOBOS

A gobo or cookie is a sheet of opaque material with cut-out sections. It is used to create shadow patterns on a background or subject. Fix it to a lamp or, like a flag, place it between the lamp and subject. With various cut-out shapes, you can create strong patterns on or behind a subject (eg the shape of a window or blind) or an overall mottled effect like the leaves in a forest Adjust the gobo in relation to the lamp to change the pattern's definition.

> ❝ One must try to discover a different and original atmosphere for each film and each sequence, to obtain variety, wealth and texture in one's use of lighting ... More and more, I tend to use only one light source, which is what usually happens in nature ... I have always tried to justify the direction of the light, whether it comes from the windows in daytime scenes or from lamps in night scenes. ❞

NESTOR ALMENDROS, CINEMATOGRAPHER
Sophie's Choice, Kramer vs. Kramer, Days of Heaven
(Oscar).

Different lighting styles will establish a variety of moods in your videos and help to provide characterization. High key lighting gives a fairly uniform level of illumination and suggests a general feeling of brightness. Low key lighting, with strong contrasts between light and dark areas, suggests an air of tension, drama and mystery.

Dramatic lighting can be made to present people in various guises. Lighting someone from below distorts their facial features, makes their eyes prominent and makes them look dominating. Lighting people from above diminishes them and creates a sombre claustrophobic air. You can subtly suggest both these effects by adding a single lamp to a conventional lighting set-up.

By using direct high key lighting with a diffusing filter on the lens, you can hint at romance. For close-ups, a backlight from directly behind a subject creates a halo around the hair; an extra front light puts sparkle into the eyes.

When shooting indoors, simulate daylight by using diffused and reflected light to cover the whole scene; add a key light to one side to suggest a window. When shooting a scene that includes a domestic

High key lighting produces an effect of uniform brightness. It is achieved with a key (*right*) and a fill (*left*) light of similar, but not identical intensities, and by lighting the background fully. The sources can be direct or diffused.

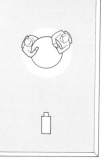

To top light a subject, rig up a lamp directly overhead, with the help of a crossbar or boom. Adjust the barn doors to confine the area you wish to light – in this instance, the couple and the table's surface. Top lighting adds a dramatic atmospheric feeling to the scene.

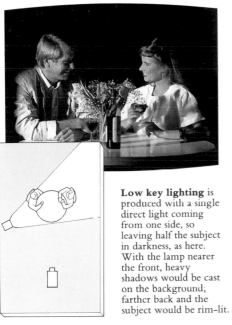

Low key lighting is produced with a single direct light coming from one side, so leaving half the subject in darkness, as here. With the lamp nearer the front, heavy shadows would be cast on the background; farther back and the subject would be rim-lit.

LIGHTING TIPS

● Always reset the white balance when the lighting set-up is changed.
● Reduce or cure unwanted bright spots on shiny surfaces by using diffusers, changing lamp height or adjusting barn doors. You can also spray on a proprietary 'duller'.
● For safety, splay lamp stands widely and use extension leads to avoid taut cables.
● Learn to look – it will improve your lighting judgments. Half-close your eyes to see effects more clearly. With the help of a portable monitor or TV, you can assess both lighting and colour.
● When shooting two people together, arrange the lamps so that the key light for one acts as the fill for the other.

Silhouette effects are created by using broad beams to light the area behind the subject, with both lamps set at the same distance from the background. Use flags or barn doors to make sure that no light spills directly on to the subject.

light, such as a table lamp, boost its effect with a hidden light pointing in the same direction. Treat this as a key light and add fill and backlights.

When subjects change position within a scene, you may need to set key and fill lights for two positions and use extra lamps to cover the area in between. For a pan shot, put a lamp near the camcorder and swivel the lamp's head to follow the person's movement.

Where there is a lot of activity in the scene, provide overall illumination by bouncing lights off the ceiling; use one or two keys to suggest the main source of light. With nighttime interiors, it is acceptable, and more realistic, to have people moving through areas of shadow.

To light a large area, you will need more, and stronger, light. Broad-beamed lamps (see p. 37) are ideal; set them as high as possible and use the beams either direct or bounced off the ceiling. For safety, weight their bases.

MULTI-CAMERA TECHNIQUES

Certain events, such as weddings, stage dramas and sports, benefit from coverage by more than one camcorder. This 'multi-camera' approach, using two or more machines, gives a sophisticated and polished production.

Form a team with other video makers and arrange your coverage strategy in advance. There are two approaches you can take. In the first, material is recorded separately by individual camcorders and the tapes edited together later. In this case, it does not matter if the camcorders used have different tape formats since the collective sequences will be edited on to a single format, but there may be some variation in picture quality between them.

The second multi-camera approach involves the use of a vision mixer. This machine enables coverage to be switched between cameras (use similar models ideally, since shots will be intercut) and recorded on to a single VCR.

Multi-camera coverage obviously involves more planning than if you were shooting on your own. You have to work the system to advantage and avoid simply duplicating each other's shots.

Weddings: At a wedding, for example, one camcorder could be positioned outside the church and a second inside. The arrival of the bride at the altar can then be covered in full, so that there is continuity between shots of her walking from the car to the church door and up the aisle.

Alternatively, you could have both camcorders in the church, one concentrating on the main participants of the ceremony and the other picking up important incidental cut-aways of the onlookers.

Although there may be a temptation to cover other events with both camcorders at the same time (eg groups outside the church), it is a better policy for one person to 'leapfrog' ahead of the action and set up the next sequence, leaving the other to continue coverage. This way, you are sure to be in the right place at the right time.

With speechmaking, however, coverage by 2 cameras can produce ideal results. One covers the speechmakers, while the other records cut-away shots of the guests' reactions and close-ups. These shots can be inserted later into the 'speechmakers' tape, thereby retaining sound continuity and breaking up what will otherwise be a lengthy static shot of the speeches.

Sports: Multi-camera coverage of sports events is ideal since, with most games, there are several potentially good camera positions (*see pp. 92–7*). Each camcorder should shoot from one of the key positions and concentrate on a particular aspect of the game, such as the activity around the goal or touchline.

With lengthy events, editing is made easier if all the operators use the stopwatch function of their caption generators to coordinate the recordings.

Track events, too, can benefit from multi-camera coverage from key positions. Remember, however, to retain continuity of direction (*see p. 48*) when shooting any sort of track event. The final tape will have a professional look when edited together with shots taken from various angles. You can even use one of the tapes as the edit master and insert edit shots on to it from the other tapes, thus retaining the original's quality for a great part of the programme.

With 3 camcorders shooting as a team, you can get comprehensive coverage of a sporting event such as an ice hockey match (*left*). Use one camcorder from an elevated position on the stands to get an overview of the game. Place the other 2 at a lower level to follow the players and cover the action around the goals.

With a vision mixer, you can cover a stage event (*right*), such as a school play, with 2 cameras shooting from either side of the stage. A third independent camera in the aisle records cut-aways. The pictures and sound are fed separately to the vision mixer, where the fourth team member coordinates coverage by switching between the pictures displayed on the monitors and recording directly on to the VCR.

Stage events: Using a vision mixer is the alternative approach to multi-camera shooting and is particularly good for covering stage events, such as school plays, concerts or presentation ceremonies.

This production accessory (which can also function as a special effects generator, *see p. 138*) enables you to feed the pictures and sound from 2 camcorders or video cameras into a single VCR. You can not only cut between cameras, but you can also mix or electronically wipe between the two machines and edit your programme as you shoot.

For the system to work, the synchronizing pulses of the 2 camcorders must be 'genlocked' together for disturbance-free transitions. Therefore, at least one of the machines needs a genlock facility.

When covering a school play, try and get to rehearsals and prepare a shooting plan. Ideally, use 3 cameras to get perfect continuity: one on either side of the stage to offer alternative shots, with both connected to the vision mixer, and the third not connected and roving over the performers to get cut-aways, which can be insert edited into the vision-mixed tape.

ELECTRONIC EFFECTS

A range of special effects can be created by simply manipulating the electronics of your video equipment or by shooting images direct from the TV screen. With the help of a special effects generator (SEG, *see box*), you can produce many more visual effects, some of which are illustrated opposite.

● A black and white, or monochromatic, image can be produced with most VCRs. During editing, you can use this control to convert some of your shots into monochrome to give them a 'dated' or documentary look.

● Picture reversal is possible with those camcorder models that have a negative/ positive switch. Its intended purpose is to convert colour negatives into positive video images (*see p. 121*). But you can exploit this facility to include striking negative images in pop videos, nightmare and fantasy sequences. Even more abstract effects are possible by deliberately over- or underexposing the shot and by setting the white balance incorrectly.

● A form of solarization, eerie and ideal for certain dream scenes, can be created by significantly overexposing a shot. The most effective results are got from bright, high-contrast subjects. By shooting such images from a TV screen in a darkened room, you can control the effect by adjusting the TV's contrast, altering the camcorder's white balance or shooting with filters on the lens.

● Video feedback can be used to great effect with graphics. Try it with titles laid on a sheet of acetate and taped to the TV screen. By feeding the picture from the camcorder into the TV at the same time as recording it, the result is a series of repeating images, as in a hall of mirrors.

● To create unusual transitions between scenes, produce a special wipe effect with a simple vision mixer (incorporating a fader and wipe generator) inserted in the editing chain between the camcorder and VCR/edit recorder.

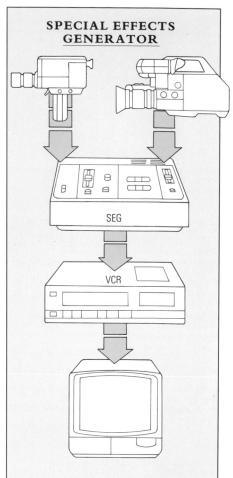

SPECIAL EFFECTS GENERATOR

SEG

VCR

The special effects generator (SEG) can combine images from at least 2 camcorders (or one camera and a video input) to produce wipes, visual mixes, split screen, fades, 'key' effects and superimpositions; it can also mix sound and electronically colour titles and backgrounds.

The SEG either generates its own sync pulses or may need a camcorder with a 'genlock' facility. Effects can be previewed before recording.

A colour negative effect is possible using the neg/pos control of the camcorder to reverse the colour and brightness.

Solarization can be produced in-camera by overexposure of a high-contrast subject. Use filters to colour highlights.

A superimposed title can be produced in various colours by the SEG and placed anywhere on a background scene.

Hold a wipe in the centre of the frame to create a split screen effect. Or wipe one scene off by wiping another in.

Use a key effect to inset one picture into another. The keyed-in shot can be placed anywhere on screen in any shape.

A key title, made of large letters, can be cut into a background scene and filled in with contrasting images from another shot.

POP VIDEOS · 1

Pop videos are exciting to watch and even more exciting to make. Combining pictures and music creatively is the basis for such productions. You can add in striking electronic effects by imaginative manipulation of your video and TV equipment. And with the help of a special effects generator (SEG), there are even more creative possibilities – wipes, key effects, mixes, superimpositions and split screens (see p. 138).

Remember, if you are using professional artists' recordings, you will need to get copyright clearance before copying music on to video, even if you are only showing the tape privately.

The simplest approach to making a music video is to visualize images that will fit with the words or beat of the instrumental or song chosen. Some suggestions about how to adapt your images to the music are:
● Ask friends to act out the lyrics of a song and record them in locations that seem to express the mood of the music.
● Create your own storyline to interpret the music, so that the images and lyrics are juxtaposed to evoke an emotional response, whether tragic or comic. Make use of dramatic devices such as irony; create a powerful and poignant effect by cutting lyrics extolling the joys of life with scenes of poverty or conflict. Or you could intercut pompous martial music with scenes of children playing with toy soldiers.
● Use a visual theme to link the music, for example a heavy rock number could be accompanied by quick-cut scenes of bustling city life, or the spirit of a romantic ballad could be reflected in slow pans and leisurely editing of a scenic landscape.
● With a playback system (see p. 142), you can have fun with a friend miming the lyrics of a song – get a female friend to mime a male voice, and vice versa.
● Shoot a montage of various stills material with a rostrum camera (see p. 114).

You might include album covers, publicity photos in magazines or posters of the artists themselves (once again, you will have to consider copyright restrictions), together with some personal photos, slides or 8mm film as additional sources.
● For a more abstract approach, record images produced from a computer or TV screen, using video feedback images (see p. 138). Shoot moving subjects deliberately out of focus or use special effects filters (eg multi-image or prism).

To make a pop video, work out a shooting plan first. When editing in-camera, start by drawing up a storyboard

The storyboard for a pop video provides a matrix for the production, around which you can extemporize and make improvements when recording the visuals. Besides the type of shot planned, the relevant lyrics or their timing (or counter readings) should also be noted under each shot, so that the images can be recorded to length at the time of shooting. This is important when you are editing in-camera.

1. Long s
to group
playing i
bars (use sta

5. Mid-shot

with the relevant lyrics or their timing noted beneath each shot. It is vital to know the precise time taken for each line or verse (choose the unit that is appropriate), so that the recorded images can be synchronized with the lyrics.

To ensure synchronization, record the music first on to the camcorder's tape (allow a 30-second lead-in of blank tape). Then play back the music and decide on the exact in- and out-points for each image you have planned, noting the numbers on the tape counter. The music will be erased automatically when you shoot, but you can dub it on again later.

Editing a pop video tape-to-tape allows much more freedom at the shooting stage and can give greater precision at the editing stage. A storyboard is still a useful starting point, to provide a structure for shooting and a basis for pacing the edits.

Good edit points will depend on the music itself. With strong percussion sounds, you can cut on the beat to produce a satisfying effect. Or you can cut to a new image at the start of a verse or musical phrase, or where a new solo instrument takes over. Fast cutting works well with fast music to get impressionistic effects.

Try to match the camerawork with the mood of the music. A strong visual effect can be created by, for example, matching a slow zoom with the sonorous notes of a clarinet or horn, or combining a sweeping pan shot with flute phrases.

1. Track in stage introductory (filter).12 secs.

2. Close-up of lead singer in wide hat, turns to camera (use multi-image filter). 3 secs.

3. Long shot, street corner, with 2 band members. Singer enters screen left. 5 secs.

POP VIDEOS · 2

> **" I think the video revolution, where equipment used for filming is light and portable, and where you don't need huge crews, has made it possible to break into the film business. "**

LOL CREME of GODLEY AND CREME
POP VIDEO DIRECTORS
for The Police, Duran Duran and Elton John.

Slick pop videos of well-known groups and bands are regularly seen on TV. These usually involve a playback system with the artists miming to a studio-produced tape. You can have fun making your own pop videos with a group and help promote them at the same time. If the material is their own, you will have no problems with copyright.

A simple playback system can be set up, by copying the sound directly on to the camcorder (better still, a VCR with the camcorder pictures feeding into it) at the same time as playing it back to the group through an amplifier and loudspeakers. This ensures synchronization.

Take a master shot of the entire performance, zooming in at appropriate moments to feature individuals. Then shoot additional material, such as close-ups of faces and instruments, and any other action going on which does not have an obvious sync element. All these shots, together with any location material, can then be insert edited into the master shot later.

Use a creative approach that not only reflects the content of the music but also the image the group is trying to portray. This is a great opportunity to let rip and experiment with effects that would be inappropriate in most other video subjects. Break the rules – try jump cuts, deliberate breaks in continuity and repetition of actions. Add greater impact with the use of a special effects generator (SEG, *see p. 138*) and an electronic 'paintbox' to produce fantastic coloured images.

Give full rein to your creativity when making a pop video. Exploit the whole range of visual techniques. Take advantage of distinctive locations, costume and make-up. Experiment with dramatic lighting, trick effects and special filters. Make use of supplementary lenses, striking angles and moving camera shots.

THE MOVING CAMERA

Shooting with a 'mobile tripod' gives noticeably slick sophisticated results. Mounting the camcorder/tripod unit on a set of wheels, called a dolly, allows you to follow the action with smooth camera movements.

This extra piece of equipment gets you into the professional world of 'tracking', 'trucking' or 'crabbing'. Tracking means moving along parallel to the action or to move toward or away from a stationary subject. (In a professional set-up, the camera actually moves along a track or rail, hence the name.) Trucking or crabbing is a sideways movement across the action or past a stationary subject.

Both movements give striking 'zoom-like' effects. But shots taken from a dolly should not be confused with zooming shots, where the camera is stationary and only the lens focal length is changed. The effect with a zoom-in is to tighten up the frame and make the subject progressively larger. The process is one of magnification, in which all the objects in the scene retain their relative positions and there is no change in perspective.

In contrast, the effect of a tracking shot is much more realistic, like the experience of walking toward something. Objects in the scene approach, change position in relation to each other and finally pass by on either side. (The speed of movement is accentuated by moving past out-of-focus objects or people in the foreground.) It is this qualitative difference that makes dolly shots so distinctive. Use them to:

● Follow action, such as a person crossing a room or walking down a corridor. Adjust framing by combining with other camera movements, eg panning and tilting.

● Highlight a static subject; a favourite shot in detective mysteries is to track in to an overlooked piece of evidence. For a really eerie effect, track out from a subject and zoom in at the same time, giving a striking distortion of perspective.

● Dramatize an emotional moment, such as tracking in on two lovers engaged in their first embrace to emphasize the intimacy of the scene.

● Reveal or present a subject, such as tracking out from an unfinished painting to reveal the artist at work or crabbing around a room to show off its decorative features.

To be effective, a dolly shot must be executed smoothly (and noiselessly, when recording sound) over a flat even surface, so that there are no distracting bumps. Keep the lens set to wide angle to minimize vibrations; avoid tracking in telephoto.

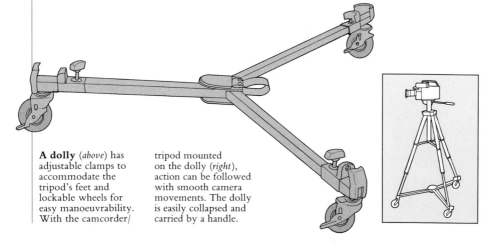

A dolly (*above*) has adjustable clamps to accommodate the tripod's feet and lockable wheels for easy manoeuvrability. With the camcorder/ tripod mounted on the dolly (*right*), action can be followed with smooth camera movements. The dolly is easily collapsed and carried by a handle.

A wheelchair makes an ideal improvised dolly. It is easy to push and steer, and works well in confined spaces. Steady your elbows on a board if necessary.

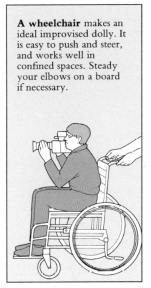

A supermarket trolley gives a steady shooting position. Your weight will help to stabilize the steering. Oil the wheels to avoid recording irritating squeaks.

A home-made platform on wheels can serve well as a dolly. Design it with room for the camera operator and tripod, and maybe even a light stand and assistant.

The dolly 'pusher' should move at a steady pace, starting and stopping without a jolt. Furniture, rugs and lighting cables should be cleared out of the path. Mark the front and end positions of the dolly movement on the floor or ground with tape. An assistant may need to move alongside the dolly to 'follow focus' during the shot.

Follow focus: With the help of a friend, this useful technique allows you to alter focus during a shot when the distance between the subject and camera is constantly changing, as with a track-out from a subject. You could rely on the auto focus, but operating manually gives much greater control over the situation.

'Follow focus' needs practice to perfect and rehearsal before each take. Note the focus distance on the lens barrel for the front and end images of the shot; mark both positions with a piece of tape. As the camera tracks out from the subject, your assistant should turn the focus ring smoothly between the two settings. You can then concentrate on the composition of the shot in the viewfinder.

Improvised dollies: Anything that can be moved along smoothly, preferably on wheels, can serve as a dolly. For example, you can be pushed around in a supermarket trolley, wheelchair, baby carriage or chair with casters (*above*). You could sit on a rug and be pulled over a polished floor. Or you can shoot from the open window of a car that is being pushed, to get smooth silent shots.

In all cases, steady the camcorder by bracing it against your body, tuck elbows in or prop them on raised knees, and shoot in the wide angle to avoid vibrations.

Make your own 'dolly', with a base board wide enough to accommodate a tripod (with legs fully splayed) and the camera operator. Wheels should be at least 7.5 to 10cm (3 to 4in) in diameter. Build the rear wheels to swivel so that you gain full steering. Fix an upright handle to the back board for pushing; with a hinged bracket, you can fold it down for easy transport. To ensure the tripod does not slip forward, drill 3 holes for its legs to fit into or add a board along the front edge.

COMPUTER GRAPHICS

Anything that can be generated by a computer and displayed on its monitor screen can be recorded on to video tape by linking the two systems. You can use computer graphics to build up simple figures, using a combination of colours. By storing the shape in the data memory, you can repeat it on screen to create graphic designs or produce simple animated effects.

You can start a Christmas video with a representation of the tree surrounded with festive gift boxes. Or you can enliven a travel video with an arrow moving across a map to show the route taken. When covering track events, you could introduce the subject with an animated figure of, say, a sprinter. And you can enhance any business presentation with colourful pie and bar charts or moving graphs to show the progress of the company.

The hardware may consist of any home or business computer, though models specially designed with video in mind are more versatile. Get professional advice from a dealer on hardware potential.

The real artistry comes with the software. You can get ready-made graphics programs on computer tape or disc. Or you can create your own graphics on screen (see box).

To get computer images on to video tape, you can simply point the camcorder at the computer's display screen, and shoot. This should be done in a darkened room to avoid reflections on screen. The recording may, however, be degraded by loss of picture sharpness and vertically drifting 'frame-beat' bars.

A better way to record computer images is to insert them at the editing stage, thus obviating any shooting problems. Connect the computer directly to the VCR to be used as the edit recorder. Wire the two machines according to the instruction manual or get advice from your dealer.

For a first exercise, try recording from

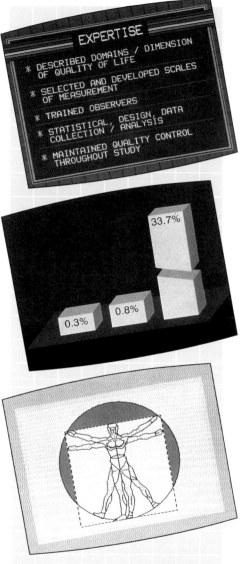

Modern computer graphics come in many varied forms. A text layout (*top*) can be used for titles, captions and credits. A 3D bar graph (*centre*) can be used for business information. A high-resolution image (*above*) might form the basis for an animated cartoon.

an ordinary personal computer an eye-catching title sequence at the beginning of your tape. Wipe up the screen a block of colour containing titles made of large graphic blocks. Hold the titles on screen long enough for them to be read and then wipe them down. Then, bring up another block of colour with the next series of titles. Follow these basic steps:

1 Set up the titles in the computer, either from an existing program or by keying them in.

2 Connect the computer to the VCR that is acting as the edit recorder and set it to record-pause.

3 Run the titles program on the computer and simultaneously release the pause on the VCR.

4 At the end of the titles sequence, pause the VCR. You have now recorded the titles and are ready to insert them on your video tape by the assemble editing process (*see p. 62*).

If you want to end the tape with a series of credits, pause the VCR after the editing process and revert to the computer as input. Set up the credits on screen (these can be a scrolled-up list or individual lines) and run the program, simultaneously releasing the VCR pause button.

More sophisticated computers (with genlock facilities) combined with vision mixers allow you to get superimposition effects, cross wipes and cross fades. A dedicated-video computer, with suitable software, offers such effects as dot matrix, chroma key and explosion. Explore such techniques with other computer enthusiasts, or you can hire the equipment or attend video workshops.

Computer-generated sound has creative possibilities, too. You can record the sounds the computer makes (whether these are just 'bleeps' or electronically produced music) by directing a microphone at the machine or, better still, by plugging your camcorder directly into the computer.

CREATIVE GRAPHICS

The home computer or 'micro' has become so versatile that it can be used to produce a wide range of graphic effects, all of which can be transferred to video tape. Use these effects, say, at the beginning and end of a tape, to break up lengthy sequences or to introduce hard information in a palatable and attractive form.

● The most basic graphics program allows you to key in simple shapes, such as circles, squares or rectangles. These shapes can be used singly or in combination to produce figures or abstract designs. This program is ideal for displaying statistics of any kind, eg bar or pie charts.

● Simple graphic shapes or 'modules' (such as coloured squares) can be made to repeat themselves all over the screen in a pattern. Certain areas can then be wiped out and titles inserted in the space. The colour of the background can be changed regularly, eg to introduce a new sequence.

● A more sophisticated program allows you to change the size and position of the modules on screen, to create an animated cartoon, with shapes that expand and contract.

● With a graphics tablet (a drawing board which plugs into the computer), you can draw images freehand using a special stylus. The results are only limited by your own artistic ability and the resolution of the computer screen. The image is created from a series of minute dots or 'pixels' (picture elements); the more pixels that the computer can generate, the higher the resolution and, therefore, the better the image, with fine details and smooth outlines. A 256×192 dot matrix is adequate for use with home video formats.

SCRATCH VIDEOS

Making scratch videos is a fun way of producing entertaining tapes without straying from the comfort of your home or having to go out on location – it is a sort of 'armchair' video making. Once you have built up a library of tapes, collages of images can be compiled by editing together material from all the recordings you have made.

Because the copyright laws are so complex, the creation of scratch videos should be confined to your own domestic tapes. It is possible to reproduce commercial material, but only when all the necessary permissions have been granted by the lawful copyright owners. If in doubt, don't use commercial sources, otherwise you may find yourself at the end of a civil, or possibly even a criminal, complaint.

A simple exercise is to exploit the conventions of interviews and eyelines to create humorous and often bizarre juxtapositions. Since many of the interviews you have shot will have used a similar format – with the interviewer looking off-screen in one direction and the subject looking in the other – you have only to intercut two such interviews to create a whole new conversation.

For example, create an amusing interchange by cutting between questions addressed to a local police officer (asked as part of a documentary you have made) and answers supplied by young children (taped during a session about their views on school regulations).

The important thing to remember when creating a scratch interview of this kind is that the edited shots must have matching eyelines, be of similar shot size and have complementary screen directions. If they do not, the 'joins' will be too obvious and the scratch tape will lose its credibility.

You could also take an exciting selection of vox pops interviews, such as local reaction to the building of a new highway, and preface it with the recording of a totally different introduction, shot for example as a preface to a tape of people's thoughts on hearing that the town was to be visited by a famous movie star.

The fact that viewers have preconceived notions of what they expect to see in a sequence of shots is another starting point for making scratch videos. Shots of people looking or pointing off-screen can be used to create curious new relationships. Close-up shots taken on vacation of your children watching a street entertainer could be intercut with shots of speeches taped at your company's sales conference, a PTA meeting or a political rally.

A shot of a child taken at the zoo, pointing and laughing at the antics of the chimps, could cut to show her parents dressing in their best for a wedding. Or a high-angle shot of someone looking up can cut to a matching low-angle shot of a disdainful dog.

If you have been using your video equipment long enough to have plenty of material of one person (your partner, say, or one of your children), you can even edit together material of them reacting to themselves or acting in a seemingly nonsensical fashion. For example, you could cut together pieces of dialogue, so that a person is seen to ask a question and then respond to it themselves, with a completely irrelevant answer.

By experimenting with parallel action, some of your most precious tapes could be re-edited for comic effect. Shots of a wedding video could be rearranged so that the bride's arrival seems interminably delayed – by repeatedly intercutting between the preparations, the same shot of the groom waiting outside the church and the church clock.

Make a scratch video by intercutting shots from tapes taken at different times and places. Be convincing by matching the eyelines, screen directions and sizes. Juxtapositions (*opposite*) are just some of the amusing effects you can create.

MAKING DOCUMENTARIES

A video documentary communicates ideas and information, and can be both entertaining and educational. 'Making Documentaries' introduces techniques specific to the art, including interviewing and commentary writing, showing at the same time how to extend your creative abilities and reach a wider audience. The best documentaries are often collaborative efforts, produced by a team of people sharing ideas, skills and resources. There are any number of subjects you can cover, from demonstrating how to do things to promoting a community cause.

THE VIDEO CREW

Travel, weddings, nature, family occasions, sports – all these subjects can be adequately covered on your own. Of course, it always helps to have someone around who can hold a microphone or light, or conduct an interview.

More elaborate productions, however, need a team of people working together. This is particularly true with documentary projects, which can involve research, writing, directing, interviewing, lighting, camerawork, sound, production of captions and editing. One person cannot cope effectively with all these areas. But, by forming a small production group, you can share these tasks, as well as get new ideas, pool resources and collaborate creatively to make more imaginative tapes.

Each member of the video crew should feel that they are getting experience and satisfaction from their efforts. But, to be effective, a crew needs to be organized. One way to tackle this is to follow the professional model: assign specific production roles to each member of the team and allow them to concentrate their skills in that area. One person acts as the 'director', leads the group and coordinates the creative aspects of the production.

Another way is to combine some of the tasks so that, for example, the director also does the interviewing or the lighting person handles the camerawork as well. A third approach might be to do the tasks in rotation, so that each member of the group has a chance to learn a new skill.

With drama productions, you may need to bring in additional people to your crew, to help with design and continuity.

Whatever scheme the group adopts, it is important that each member is clear about their job so that they can operate at maximum efficiency.

A model group might contain 6 people. Their roles are defined here, but flexibility is the key to group work and no one should become so specialized that they cannot take on other tasks.

The interviewer liaises with the director to work out a strategy and list of questions for each interview. While the director works with the crew, the interviewer runs through the main areas with the interviewee and gets them to relax. The interviewer can be on- or off-screen during the shoot and can also speak direct to camera as a presenter.

The production manager organizes the group, produces a budget, coordinates the shoot, makes the schedules, arranges for the availability of equipment and locations (including transport, access and catering) and keeps the financial records.

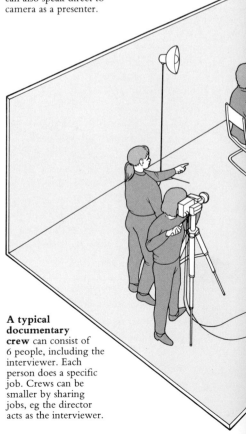

A typical documentary crew can consist of 6 people, including the interviewer. Each person does a specific job. Crews can be smaller by sharing jobs, eg the director acts as the interviewer.

The camera operator liaises with the director and lighting person, looks after composition, focus, exposure and camera movements, and ensures equipment works.

The sound recordist handles the acoustics, chooses and places the mics, including the manipulation of a boom mounted mic. Separate recordings may also be made for dubbing later.

The lighting person creates the lighting style the director wants, arranges the lamps for each shot, attends to electricity and safety, and watches for shadows cast by the mic boom.

The director leads the group and makes creative decisions from the research stage to the final shoot, directing the cast, leading the crew and supervising editing.

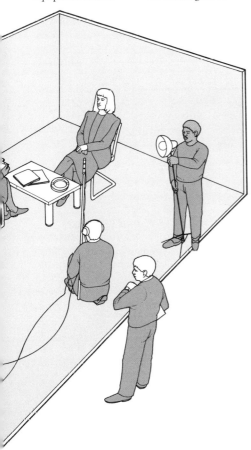

TIPS FOR CREW MEMBERS

● The director and production manager should go on location recces to check out lighting and acoustics.

● The production manager should check on the facilities for parking and access for equipment and arrange for catering during breaks.

● The director should run through the planned shoot with the crew, shot by shot, and decide on the lighting style for each scene.

● The sound recordist could consider mounting a directional microphone on a boom or 'fishpole', which can be held at arms length above or below the subject, just out of shot; check this during camera rehearsals. A mic boom is easily improvised with a broom handle; secure the mic and cable with tape or rubber bands to prevent any audible rattle.

● During the shoot, the start of each shot should be identified, either with a caption generator or a marker board, giving the shot and take numbers. Any member of the crew who is free can do this.

● Whoever is doing the editing could be present to take notes on continuity, ensure that each shot is identified and make suggestions for additional coverage to help during editing.

Interviewing is an integral part of documentary video making and a skill that is well worth developing. A good interview starts long before you face the subject to pose your questions. Research, planning and preparation are the keys to good interviewing; later come the skills of relaxing a subject, asking the right questions in the right form and, above all, listening to the responses.

The first priority is to get to know as much about the topic as possible and then to decide who you want to interview, what they have to contribute and how to get the best from them.

There are several types of interview subjects, each with a distinct contribution to make and each demanding a different approach on the part of the interviewer. There are the experts or specialists who provide explanations, opinions or authoritative statements in answer to specific questions; there are witnesses who simply recount their experiences or describe an event as they saw or participated in it; and there are personal opinions gathered from the public at random, including vox pops.

All three types of interview subject may be relevant to your topic. In the case of experts and witnesses, it is important to meet the subject first and establish a rapport, with both parties clear on the reason and content of the interview.

From this information-gathering, you can compile a list of key questions on which to base the interview and develop it in a logical order. You don't have to stick rigidly to this order – if interesting points emerge during the interview, you should, of course, respond and ask supplementary questions, but beware of straying too far from the main topic. Tell the subject the areas you will be covering but not the actual questions, so that you can retain spontaneity during the interview itself. Avoid at all costs a rehearsed, artificial feeling – an interview should be stimulating and informative.

There are two ways of covering an interview with one camera:
● The 'off-screen' interview, frequently used in TV news and location reports, where the question is not heard but the subject is seen making a statement obviously looking at and responding to someone out of shot who has posed a question. A series of statements can be edited together, from the same person or several people, to form a continuous 'interview' sequence. In such situations, the questions must elicit statements in the form of self-contained answers. To achieve this, the interviewer should begin questions with the words who, what, where, when, why or how, so that a 'yes' or 'no' answer is made impossible. They should also avoid making verbal responses during the interview, since these will be extremely difficult to edit out later.
● The 'on-screen' interview is the conventional 'conversation', often used for in-depth interviews, with the interviewer and subject facing each other. You can cover this type of interview with one camera by shooting the subject and interviewer separately and then cutting between them in succession (see p. 156).

For an in-depth interview to be successful, it is vital that the subject is relaxed and confident. This is not only the job of the interviewer; all members of the video crew should cooperate. Ideally, a familiar environment is the best setting, where the subject will be at ease. If this is not possible, your set should be comfortable and organized, with lighting and sound preparations completed before the subject is brought into the room.

Before the start of the interview, a sound test for voice level should be done and the camera position checked. The interviewer could relax a nervous subject by asking a neutral question, such as 'Where did you go on vacation last year?' If the subject is very nervous, you could start into the interview gently, leading into the areas you want to cover, while recording this informal 'chat' unknown to the subject. You may well get the best out of them in this atmosphere.

Shoot plenty of tape during the interview and, at the end, offer to redo sections if the subject is unhappy or wants to raise further points.

Vox pops: Short interviews with people in the street are often used to demonstrate public opinion on issues. They can be shot as a series of close-ups, but try to vary the backgrounds, screen directions and eyelines to reinforce the 'roving interviewer' out of shot. Edit the shots together later to form a continuous sequence.

> 66 *Interviewing seems to me reasonably simple — it consists only of finding an interesting person, and then finding questions to ask him ... do enough research in advance ... I rather prefer doing an interview with the camera working over my shoulder, so that the subject is in fact rather talking to the audience* 99 *instead of me.*

ED MURROW, CBS NEWSCASTER/INTERVIEWER
See it now, Small World, Person to Person. Vice-President CBS

Use a transcript to edit an interview into a continuous statement, with the questions deleted. Mark up the passages to keep and where to insert new shots.

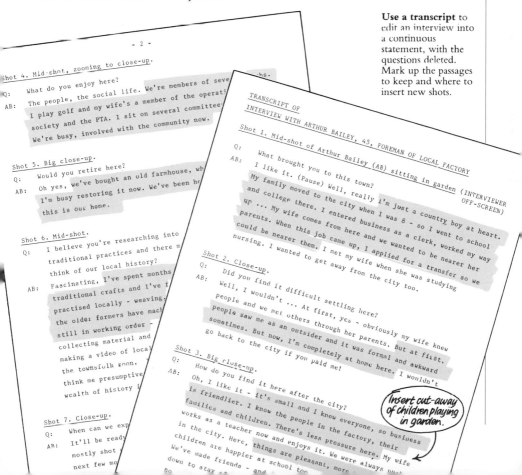

- 2 -

Shot 4. Mid-shot, zooming to close-up.
Q: What do you enjoy here?
AB: The people, the social life. We're members of seve...
      I play golf and my wife's a member of the operati...
      society and the PTA. I sit on several committee...
      We're busy, involved with the community now.

Shot 5. Big close-up.
Q: Would you retire here?
AB: Oh yes, we've bought an old farmhouse, wh...
      I'm busy restoring it now. We've been he...
      this is our home.

Shot 6. Mid-shot.
Q: I believe you're researching into
      traditional practices and there m...
      think of our local history?
AB: Fascinating, I've spent months
      traditional crafts and I've f...
      practised locally - weaving...
      the older farmers have mach...
      still in working order -
      collecting material and
      making a video of local...
      the townsfolk soon,...
      think me presumptive...
      wealth of history i...

Shot 7. Close-up.
Q: When can we exp...
AB: It'll be ready...
      mostly shot...
      next few mo...

TRANSCRIPT OF
INTERVIEW WITH ARTHUR BAILEY, 45, FOREMAN OF LOCAL FACTORY

Shot 1. Mid-shot of Arthur Bailey (AB) sitting in garden (INTERVIEWER OFF-SCREEN)
Q: What brought you to this town?
AB: I like it. (Pause) Well, really I'm just a country boy at heart.
      My family moved to the city when I was 8 - so I went to school
      and college there. I entered business as a clerk, worked my way
      up ... My wife comes from here and we wanted to be nearer her
      parents. When this job came up, I applied for a transfer so we
      could be nearer them. I met my wife when she was studying
      nursing. I wanted to get away from the city too.

Shot 2. Close-up.
Q: Did you find it difficult settling here?
AB: Well, I wouldn't ... At first, yes - obviously my wife knew
      people and we met others through her parents. But at first,
      people saw me as an outsider and it was formal and awkward
      sometimes. But now, I'm completely at home here. I wouldn't
      go back to the city if you paid me!

Shot 3. Big close-up.
Q: How do you find it here after the city?
AB: Oh, I like it - it's small and I know everyone, so business
      is friendlier. I know the people in the factory, their
      families and children. There's less pressure here. My wife
      works as a teacher now and enjoys it. We were always...
      in the city. Here, things are pleasant. We've made friends...
      children are happier at school too...
      down to stay...

Insert cut-away of children playing in garden.

The first thing to decide when shooting an interview with one camera is whether you want the interviewer and the microphones in or out of shot.

For a 'statement' interview (with interviewer off-screen), the shot size of the subject should be varied to avoid jump cuts when the answers are edited together into a series of statements (without the intervention of questions). By shooting with the camera alongside the interviewer, the subject will be seen almost full-face and looking slightly off-screen; a change in shot size (eg from a mid-shot to a close-up) should be done as a new question is being posed. You can tighten in when the subject is talking, but never pull out as they talk — it gives the impression you are losing interest in them.

A conventional 'conversation' interview (with the interviewer on-screen), shot with one camera, involves covering one person at a time (*opposite*). Start with a long shot of the subject facing the interviewer, who is positioned nearest the camera and whose back can be in shot to add depth and orientate the viewer.

Record the whole interview, concentrating your camerawork on the subject and changing the shot size as new questions are put. Don't frame so tight that you cannot accommodate the subject's movements (eg leaning forward or hand gestures). When the interview is over, record the reverse angle sequence of the interviewer, running through their list of questions. Retain the eyeline established during the interview and close in for cutaways of the interviewer's reactions.

If you want your sound set-up to be out of shot, fix an omnidirectional or cardioid microphone to an improvised boom and move it between the people as they talk but keep it above or below frame. You can also use mics on stands. If you are using clip-on lapel mics, fade down the one not in use by connecting both to the camcorder via a sound mixer.

Establish the interview setting in a long shot of the subject with the interviewer in the foreground, to add depth to the scene. Hold this shot for the first question and answer. Then, tighten in to an over-the-shoulder medium close-up of the subject as the interview proceeds. Only pull out between answers, never during.

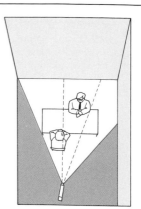

Move in closer, to the second camera position beside the interviewer, to shoot the bulk of the interview. Start with a mid-shot, as the subject warms to the topic (don't lose gestures by framing too tight) and zoom in during a question to a close-up shot. Framing even tighter, to a big close-up, intensifies the mood of the interview.

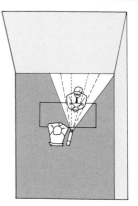

When the interview is over, shoot a separate reverse angle sequence of the interviewer from the third camera position. Retain the eyeline established during the interview. Get various sized cut-away shots of the interviewer listening or reacting, to be used in editing later to bridge jump cuts or to allow long answers to be cut and tightened up.

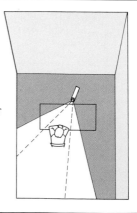

The old adage 'a picture is worth a thousand words' is as valid for video making as for any other visual medium. But sometimes you will want to broaden the picture by adding extra information not evident in the images. You may want to draw the viewer's attention to a detail that might otherwise be missed. You may wish to convey a very different concept to what the images seem to say. Or you may simply want to link events in a way that cannot be done visually.

Commentary can meet all these objectives, but it must sound natural and be well presented and to the point. It can entertain and inform at the same time, but it must never make the pictures redundant, by stating the obvious.

A frequent use of commentary in documentaries is to interpret images for an audience, to offer a particular viewpoint or define the picture. For example, take a beautiful scene of a river, held for several seconds; the image is idyllic, but the commentary states that beneath the surface lurks death, for river life is dying because of the pollution upstream from a factory discharging its poisonous waste. The viewer's emotions change from peaceful enjoyment of the scene to regret and concern at man's profligacy.

Commentary can be used to introduce interviews ('We talked to a local skipper about the fishing around the islands', then cut to the skipper talking). It can also be used to link disparate sequences or to provide a continuity that does not exist in the images. For example, take 2 shots seen in succession – a tropical rain forest and a hamburger. Most viewers will not understand the connection, unless a commentary explains that vast areas of forest are being cleared to make way for grazing land for beef cattle so that the world's need for hamburgers can be satisfied.

A commentary should be written after the images are edited, when you can run through the tape and decide where words are needed. Most of the time, you will have to write to fit specific timings and shot lengths. This will influence what you say – if you have only 10 or 12 seconds in which to make your point, you will have to be brief and simple. Calculate a reading speed – 3 words a second is regarded as a 'fast' commentary by professionals. You will want a more relaxed pace.

The words of a commentary will colour the viewer's opinion, so choose them carefully – they are easily misinterpreted or their significance lost. Your own thoughts on a subject must be clear before you can write them clearly. A good test is to record the words on audio tape, instead of writing or typing them. Then you will know if they sound right and flow well, or if you are indulging in clichés or hiding behind meaningless pedantry (eg 'It is also of great importance to fully understand the profound meaning of . . .').

Every word in a commentary must be made to count. Compose short simple sentences and use them dramatically, telling the viewers what they need to know only when they need to know it. 'Wall-to-wall' commentary is to be avoided at all costs – leave good breathing spaces when the viewers can relax, take in the pictures and enjoy atmospheric sounds or music.

Once you are satisfied, type out the commentary, double-spaced on one side of the page, leaving wide margins for amendments and cueing notes (below). Now you are ready to test it for fit against the edited images. Rehearse before recording; read aloud while viewing the pictures on the TV. Decide on the in- and out-points for each section of commentary by using visual cues from a particular shot or by watching the tape counter. Mark these cues at the beginning of each section of your working commentary document. If you want a word to fall on a precise shot, use the tape counter to time your approach and remember to breathe in before the cue comes up.

THE FOLLOWING COMMENTARY COULD ACCOMPANY THIS VIDEO SEQUENCE.

On the road to Skye, Eilean Donan castle was reduced to a ruin in 1719 by three English men-of-war. Jacobite sympathies and the Spanish garrison provoked this bombardment. The castle was restored in 1932 and is now a museum.

We sailed for Lewis – the largest and most northerly island of the Outer Hebrides – from the Kyle of Lochalsh.

NO COMMENTARY; NATURAL SOUNDS OF WATER LAPPING, DISTANT GAELIC MUSIC, SHIP'S ENGINES.

Stornoway – once the rallying point for the Norse invaders – is now the capital of Lewis and the unique and vital heart of Gaelic life.

Many of the islanders earn a living from fishing, crofting and cloth-weaving. They are a proud and independent people . . .

CUT TO INTERVIEW WITH FISHERMAN.

USING ARCHIVE MATERIAL

Include archive material in your documentary programmes to broaden their content. Or you can construct completely new programmes – historical documentaries – based on old material, such as photographs, movie film, paintings, manuscripts, in fact any source you can trace and shoot. Or intercut old stills with new live material to create an effective contrast between past and present.

With an imaginative sound track, there are any number of ways you can enliven stills and evoke the period. You can dub on the sound of horses' hooves over hunting prints, factory sirens over industrial landscapes or contemporary popular music over street scenes. And you can read short dramatized passages from literature of the day to portray the style of life.

Archive sources to explore include local historical societies, museums, art galleries, libraries and private collections of memorabilia. Old machinery, such as steam engines and threshing machines, is sometimes put on display in full working order during public open days. Research the subject, interview operators and enthusiasts, and arrange a live action shoot. Precision camerawork is a pleasure with this type of subject – enjoy your compositions and the rhythm and sound of the machinery.

To shoot archive material, take the rostrum technique (*see p. 114*) out of the 'studio' and on to location. Consider the following guidelines:

Shooting through glass: With permission from a museum or art gallery, you can shoot paintings, prints and etchings. These will usually be protected behind glass and so you will need to light the subject evenly.

Set up the camcorder on a tripod and, to avoid distortion, position it parallel to the centre of the subject. Ensure it is level. Position 2 video lamps at 45° to the subject on either side and use diffusers to soften the beams. Make sure the light is not reflected in the glass by checking in the viewfinder.

If you have to move the camera to avoid reflections, stay as close to the centreline as possible and use the telephoto position to flatten perspective. Any visual distortion caused by an off-centre camera position will also be minimized by cropping out the frame of the subject, thereby removing the strong vertical and horizontal elements that would otherwise draw attention.

Wear dark clothing when shooting and drape a black cloth over the camera/ tripod, so that you avoid reflections in the glass. If this does not work, try changing the angle of the subject by tilting it slightly – wedge a matchbox under the frame and compose the shot more tightly.

Another way to reduce reflections is to rotate a polarizing filter on the lens until the reflections are less visible. But, remember, any filter will cut down on the amount of light passing through the lens, so lighting levels may have to be increased to compensate.

A polarizing filter is also very useful to reduce glare on the highlights of oil paintings that have been specially lit to show off modelling of the brushwork or canvas. Cross-polarization is a professional technique, in which large, heat-resistant polarizing filters are used over the lights as well as on the camera lens. The effect is to eliminate nearly all of the glare and reflections.

The **statuette** from a collection of memorabilia (*below*) can be shot on a rotating turntable, and lit by diffused lighting from the side, which is bounced off a reflector board.

To shoot items in a display case, such as scientific instruments or jewelry, shoot at an angle to the surface, mask the camera with a black cloth and use soft fill lighting bounced from a reflector board.

Camera narrative: Dramatize paintings and photographs by treating them as live action, with the camera tracking, tilting and panning over their surface (*see p. 115*). Rehearse these camera movements – they will have to be very smooth and steady, since the subject is static and there is no action to disguise any camera shake.

The gliding movement of a tracking shot avoids the change in perspective that is inherent in a zooming or panning movement. You could continue your coverage of the painting by tracking out to reveal a guide or lecturer commenting on its merits or history. A whole programme on paintings of a particular subject or period could be compiled in this way.

A demonstration video is the simplest kind of documentary you can produce and is a good exercise to undertake as an introduction to this form of video making. Its aim is to demonstrate, clearly and succinctly, the stages of a process and it combines the need for logical exposition with the skills of commentary writing.

The tape can be made for educational or training purposes and the subject of the demonstration can be anything from baking a cake or mending a puncture to wallpapering a room or making a model airplane.

The easiest method is to record someone doing something in sequence and edit the shots in-camera, as you shoot. A commentary can be dubbed on later, to give additional information that the pictures have not shown. You can also superimpose titles over the images with a caption generator to reinforce the commentary or to sum up technical data (eg tyre pressures or amounts of ingredients).

To make an edited in-camera demonstration tape, research the process and rehearse the actions involved. A storyboard is the best way to summarize your shooting plan (*opposite*) and break it down into self-contained shots, the timing of each carefully planned in anticipation of the words you may wish to add later to accompany the images.

Brief the demonstrator so they know exactly what is to be done and when. Start with a wide shot to establish the subject and use mid-shots to focus attention. Plan cut-aways to condense time and cut-ins and close-ups to show detail. Use fades to indicate the passing of time, as during the cooking of a dish.

Observe the 180° rule of continuity (*see p. 48*) – don't cross the line of action and confuse the viewer by reversing the screen direction. Keep camerawork simple, but do change shot sizes and angles to create visual interest and avoid jump cuts. Light the whole area with soft bounced light, to

9. Long shot. Table in foreground; decorator hanging plumb line to right of window.

10. Cut plumb marked exit

13. Cut-away close-up of decorator concentrating, looking down at table.

14. CL past fold off

avoid throwing distracting shadows on the background and so that you can change camera positions quickly. Record live atmospheric sound only where it is helpful to the understanding of the process (eg air escaping from a tyre).

An alternative approach is to record the whole demonstration from one angle, with the demonstrator giving a running commentary. Then, ask them to repeat the

in close-up.
line being
'n wall. Hands
'ottom left.

11. Long shot. Decorator moves left to table, starts pasting cut length of paper.

12. Close-up of paper being pasted on table.

'se-up of
'd paper being
'd, then carried
'ight.

15. Long shot (as 9). Decorator moves right, climbs steps, hangs paper.

16. Cut-in close-up. Detail of paper in position, being smoothed with brush.

process while you concentrate on shooting cut-aways and close-ups to insert edit later. Crafts (eg pottery or glass-blowing) are ideal subjects. The script must be carefully written and the demonstrator rehearsed, so that timing and pace are right. If the demonstrator is not moving around, use a single microphone position to maintain sound continuity or clip a mic on the lapel (but beware of clothes rustle).

It is best to plan a demonstration video with a storyboard, especially when editing in-camera. Most of the images will speak for themselves; you can dub on commentary later to give technical information (here, you might speak over shots 9 and 10 to elaborate on the use of the plumb line). With tape-to-tape editing, you can shoot out of sequence and cover all the long shots together (ie 9 and 15), then concentrate on the closer shots.

THE VIDEO PORTRAIT

People are natural subjects for documentaries. Choose the right person and you will have a memorable video portrait, which can be not only artistic but maybe functional as well, for promotional purposes.

The subject should be visually interesting and provide lively comment. Ideal people might include artists, crafts people, musicians, farmers or elderly people with fascinating memories. If you can focus your portrait around a public concert or art exhibition that the subject is involved in, so much the better.

A video portrait is a delicate collaboration, built on your interest in the subject and their trust in you. Approach them gently, but openly, to get the facts. Talking, listening and observing will give you an insight into their character. This is the hallmark of a good portrait, but it takes time and effort on your part to research the real person. All the time you are researching, think visually about what will appear on screen and how you can show the subject's life in pictures.

Get to know biographical details of their background and working history. Spend as much time as possible with them; conduct in-depth informal interviews and make notes of the conversations to help you build up a script. Observe them carefully and look for telltale gestures and mannerisms that reveal character. Watch them at home, with their family and friends; study them at work and learn as much as possible about their particular skill and technique. Let them tell you about their beliefs, attitudes and influences, so that you can construct a complete and honest portrait.

Each sequence in the programme should build on the last, so that the portrait is multifaceted and the viewer will be lead on to learn new things about the subject with each new scene.

The opening sequence of your video portrait should aim to intrigue the viewer by providing an initial glimpse into the subject's life. For example, you could show a potter mixing clay or an artist sketching out rough lines; whatever the theme, shoot this sequence with care for maximum impact. Add a simple commentary to serve as an introduction.

Shoot an extended interview with the subject. This can be edited for use at various points throughout the programme or used as a voice-over commentary, accompanied by relevant supporting visuals. The interview should be as relaxed as possible, since it will provide a vital element in the finished documentary. Remember to phrase your questions so that you get self-contained answers and to vary the shot sizes in case any of the material will be edited together later.

Flesh out the portrait by including interviews with other people who know the subject – agents, family, partners, other artists and critics. Their insights can provide a wealth of informative and entertaining material. If there is a special dinner party or awards ceremony in your subject's honour, make sure to shoot interviews and speeches for later use as short statements to broaden the portrait.

Produce a storyboard of a sequence that explains the technique or process of the subject's work. Sketch a rough commentary at the script stage, so that you have an idea of the timings for each shot.

Plan to use natural sounds to enhance the atmosphere of the portrait. These can be related to the subject's work – a paintbrush drawn over canvas, a potter's wheel turning, the sound of pruning shears. Music can be used effectively to portray the subject – their favourite piece can be used as a theme throughout the video. Perhaps you can construct a montage sequence of their work and cut it to music, with no commentary.

Look for a clear crisp ending – perhaps a comment from a peer that sums up the subject and their work.

A potter is an ideal subject for a video portrait. Show the subject at work and edit an interview with them, so that their voice-over takes the viewer through the process. If the visuals are self-explanatory, use music or the natural sounds of the work to accompany the images.

The quickest and least obtrusive way to shoot a subject at work is to use available light. Most artists' studios will be flooded with daylight. Fill in the shadows by bouncing light off walls and ceilings to create an intimacy that allows the subject maximum freedom.

Complete the work sequence by showing the final product of the subject's efforts. Include as much of their working environment as possible and little touches of their personal lives – a pet, a close-up of an empty coffee mug, an overall hung up at the end of the day.

STORY OF A TOWN

Shoot an historical documentary portrait of the town you live in. This project can be compiled over several months and will involve you and your team in all the skills of documentary work – research, scripting, planning sequences, conducting interviews, shooting on location and editing the material.

Working with a group means sharing and developing ideas together. Everyone should contribute their thoughts and opinions on what makes your town an interesting place; cover a range of ideas, all of which may be valid, and reach a consensus on the areas to be covered.

Your research should include people (past and present) and places (historical and contemporary) to show the history of the town and why it has grown to what it is today. Sources will include local historical societies and museums, which will have collections of memorabilia to show the history of the town (paintings, photographs, old movie films, machinery, documents, newspapers). The local chamber of commerce can help with the town's business development over the years. And the private collections of local residents will provide a more personal view of the town's life.

Most people in your group will have their own areas of interest, so take advantage of this and form similar-interest working units that will research a particular aspect in depth.

Interviews will form an important part of your documentary portrait. Research likely subjects and aim to cover a wide range of people – from local dignitaries to ordinary townsfolk and sports teams. Having talked with potential subjects, the researcher should draw up a list of key questions, to show the main areas to be covered.

Commentary. can be used to link sequences or to introduce subjects; interviews can be used as voice-overs. For example, elderly residents might recall their early days in the local factory; use their voice-overs to accompany rostrum-shot photographs of the factory as it was, all those years ago.

A script coordinator should then produce a written treatment that outlines the subjects to be dealt with and the general approach to take. Discuss this document and then draw up a documentary script (*opposite*), which should detail the contents of each sequence and the areas to be covered by interviews and commentary. Keep in mind the overall length of your programme – a maximum running time of 30 minutes is best.

The production manager's job is vital to the success of the programme; it is their job to schedule the shoots, check equipment, seek permission to use certain locations and coordinate the availability of subjects and crew.

To get an overall picture of the town, you will need general and detailed shots. Do recces over several days and choose camera positions in advance. Check out the lighting and sound aspects of each location and anticipate the technical requirements for each shoot. Consider the best time of day to shoot in natural light, especially important for buildings (*see p. 171*). Schedule certain sequences for times when locations are not too busy.

Aim to capture the life of the town – busy shopping scenes, quiet Sundays, night life, details of architecture (street signs, shop fronts). Record atmospheric sounds – the early morning factory whistle, church bells and school playgrounds. Taking shots from a slow-moving car on a quiet Sunday morning is a good way to give an introductory impression of the whole place.

A neat way of ending the programme could be to focus on a big event in town (harvest festival, Labor Day Parade) and cover it with several video teams. But remember, multi-camera coverage by different camcorder formats and models will produce varying picture quality, which may be a problem at the editing stage.

Edit all your recorded material tape-to-tape. Gaining access to an edit controller machine in a community arts centre will make the job much easier and the result more professional. Appoint one person to coordinate the editing. Be prepared to do a rough edit first to see if the structure is right and the portrait complete. Then re-edit, to include any suggestions the group has to make.

A working documentary script is laid out to show the plans for each sequence. The details of the images occupy one side of the page, with the sound elements opposite.

PICTURES
Sunrise. Shots of a rural landscape seen from a car; a signpost flashes by and we see buildings ahead. SUPERIMPOSE MAIN TITLE Our Town.

High-angle shots of main street and town centre; busy shopping arcades with people loading trolleys.

INTERVIEW with MAYOR, with the town hall in background. Shots of central business area, offices and modern factory units. Archive stills (from museum) of busy street market and early industries.

A sequence showing tree-lined avenues of the new suburbs with parents collecting children from school.

INTERVIEW with DON LANGFORD, manager of the Railway Hotel, seen in background. Private archive stills of the original hotel. Archive film of passengers disembarking at station; stills of customers in town stores.

Deserted canning factory. LOU HAMMETT, retired foreman, is seen wandering around the empty yard and derelict factory floors.

8mm home-movie footage of the ROBINSONs at home with their young family.

INTERVIEW with TILDA ROBINSON in her living room, surrounded by ... photographs.

SOUND
MUSIC: a mellow tune on harmonica and bass guitar.

MUSIC fades down.

COMMENTARY: Our's is a small town, but busy - the main centre for the region in fact. You can buy anything here, from caviar to combine harvesters.

MAYOR talks about town as an expanding business centre, the arrival of firms from outside the region and the changes in local economy from agriculture to industrial technology.

COMMENTARY: People are moving into town to take advantage of new housing and good schools. But this town is proud of its history.

DON LANGFORD explains that this was the first hotel in town, established when the rail connection was made. Early customers were mainly wealthy farmers in town on spending sprees.

MUSIC: a melancholy refrain on harmonica gives way to VOICE of LOU HAMMETT talking about life in the old factory and its significance to the town.

COMMENTARY: But as old industries faded, others started, offering new lives to some.

TILDA ROBINSON talks about the children growing up in the town and how much they have enjoyed life here.

PROMOTING A CAUSE

A video programme that is well made and to the point can communicate a message in a punchy direct way. The message may be your own feelings or views on a subject or it can be those of an interest group, such as a youth organization, community pressure group or charitable trust.

Because of the nature of video, an audience will unconsciously compare your programme with broadcast TV. So your production must be as professional as possible, with carefully constructed sequences and a logical well-argued case presented in an authoritative manner. It must also be relatively short – 15 to 20 minutes is a good length. If there are vox pop interviews, keep them short and to the point. Work with a small team and exploit collective skills and ideas.

The key to making a persuasive documentary is to aim it at a specific audience. This will define your approach; for example, if you are trying to drum up support for a worthy cause with the general public, you may have to introduce the subject and expand it step by step; with a more specialized audience, you can dispense with the more general approach and get right down to the facts.

Whatever the subject, start by thinking the argument through on paper; then produce a written outline, which should make clear the documentary's objective, structure and content. When the outline is agreed by all parties concerned, proceed to detailed research so that you become an expert on the subject. Think visually all the time when writing the script. Finally, produce a full script and visualize it in a storyboard. Sequences can be connected by linking commentary or you can move from scene to scene by editing together statements made by interviewees.

All persuasive documentaries, whether on environmental issues, social injustices or tidy-town campaigns, tend to follow the general pattern described here.

THE PROBLEM

The opening sequence of a persuasive documentary should 'hook' the viewers' interest and draw them into concern for the subject. Opening images should, therefore, be visually strong with carefully composed shots that introduce the subject in precise terms. Appropriate music can set the scene or reinforce the impact. Use a narrator to outline the 'problem' succinctly and strong interviews with witnesses recounting experiences related to the subject.

PUBLIC CONCERN

Move on to establish the need for action. Reveal the public sentiment through vox pop interviews with the local residents; include headlines from the local newspaper and an interview with an independent expert who expresses concern about the situation. Shots of demonstrations and residents' meetings are valuable, as are punchy interviews with sympathetic community leaders.

THE CAUSE

The middle section of the documentary should develop the individual arguments in detail. Statements made by the narrator and interviewees should be illustrated with sequences covering the subjects being referred to. Pace the flow of information so that it is not too dense; remember, 'wall-to-wall' commentary is tiresome. Use diagrams to illustrate technical points or simple animation to clarify processes.

THE ARGUMENT

As in any form of persuasion, deal with the counter arguments. Your research should have uncovered the motives of those supporting or causing the present situation. Tackle any financial or political arguments head-on. Allocate part of this section to interviews with the opposition and let them have their say; then follow with your own arguments. Use the caption generator to superimpose titles to identify the name and status of each of the speakers.

By intercutting the pros and cons, you can produce a dramatic and effective sequence. For example, if the opposition state that there is no problem, cut to images of the polluted river or eroded hillside; they will speak for themselves.

THE SOLUTION

Now is the place to offer solutions to the problem. Offer a positive image for possible change and outline how immediate improvements can be made. Show examples where a similar problem existed and has been set right. Build up the edited pace of shots and the musical tempo to create a sense of urgency.

ACTION

Conclude the documentary by re-capping the argument. Hold a shot of a caption listing the main points. Repeat some of your stronger images and use music to lift the viewers' spirits. End with a clear explanation of what you would like them to do. Don't blunt the message by rolling up endless credits.

A persuasive documentary about an environmental problem needs to present the case in a logical manner. The argument must be developed in order to evoke audience concern. Highlight the problem in the opening sequence (*top*) and move on to show public concern (*centre*). Then explain the causes (*above*), through commentary or interviews. Conclude with possible solutions to the problem and the role that the audience can play.

CREATING AN ARCHIVE

A series of video tapes that documents the local life of a community over the years can be progressively built up to create a permanent audio-visual record of local history. In time, your video archive will become a unique collection, a veritable databank of value to both present and future generations.

Creating such a local archive can be made easier and more fun with the help of friends, who can contribute ideas to the project, help you with the research and assist in the shooting, by either handling the camcorder or sound, or by acting as an interviewer.

One of your chief sources of information will be elderly local residents. Collect oral history by shooting informal interviews with them in comfortable surroundings, with soft diffused lighting to relax and flatter them. Operate the camcorder from the mains, so that you don't have to stop and disrupt the flow of talk.

With a little gentle prompting, you can lead the conversation around to their memories and experiences of the locality. Discussing such matters in a small group often works best, since one person's memories will stimulate the others to talk.

Research and record local customs and traditional practices, many of which are disappearing fast; you may well be recording history. Traditional crafts are still to be found in small pockets of many countries, mainly in rural communities. Dry-stone walling, thatching, basket-weaving, timber-frame building, dying cloth, milling flour – all these crafts and the people who work them make good subjects; by recording an interview separately and then editing it to expand on the story of the pictures, with only the voice-over of the craft worker heard (not the interviewer's questions), you can produce a polished piece on traditional lifestyles.

Industries, too, are disappearing; once, a whole area may have depended on them. Record old methods that are being phased

Record local traditions before they vanish forever. Your tape may be of historical value some day. Preserve the uniqueness of an ancient folk custom (*above*); shoot fast-disappearing skills, such as dry-stone walling (*centre*) – you may not get the chance again – and cover community events (*right*).

out in our modern world – manufacturing and agricultural examples abound.

Annual events, such as a Labor Day parade, Christmas pantomime, big football matches and church festivals, are worth shooting. So are special events – local elections, the circus coming to town, a visiting dignitary opening a school. You will be amazed at the wealth of material around once you get going. Try to show the history and celebration of these events in the locality by interviewing the organizers and participants.

The architecture and streets of your area will also provide a major source of visual material for your video archive. Research old photographs and prints to see how the area used to look and record these with a rostrum camera. Then go out on location and try to match the same views and perspectives to get the contemporary reality of the area. Intercut the old with the new and add the voice-over of an elderly resident's memories of the area to flesh out the pictures and evoke life as it was.

If old factories or houses are being demolished in an area to make way for the new, try to get inside the buildings (ask permission first and only go in if they are safe) and record interior features before they are destroyed forever. With an appropriate musical sound track, you can produce an effective sequence and capture some of the style and quality of former years.

Natural perspective is an important part of architectural video making. Shooting from a tripod will give the best results, especially if it has a spirit level to check that horizontals are straight. Find a position where you can shoot head-on, on a level with the subject, to reduce visual distortion. You may be able to find an elevated position in an adjacent building; ask permission to shoot from various floors (once people know what you are doing, you should have no problem in gaining access).

Another important factor to consider when shooting buildings is the time of day. Choose a time when the sun falls across them dramatically, but avoid shooting into the light. By studying a local map, you can orientate yourself and decide when the building will be best lit for your purposes. If you plan to be on location all day, schedule your shooting for the direction of the light and arrive early enough to watch the scene develop.

Collections of memorabilia dating back over the years – old photographs, prints, dolls, newspapers and documents – are an invaluable source of material. They can be sought out from local residents and from the local museum or public library. Stills material can be shot with a rostrum camera (*see p. 114*) and 8mm movies and slides transferred by the teleciné method (*see p. 120*). All this material can be edited into 'live' tapes later. Cataloguing on video will not only serve to preserve it (since excessive handling causes damage), but will also make it more accessible to researchers.

Long-term storage of tapes: Tapes will last indefinitely when kept in a controlled environment. Remember to remove the safety tab from the cassette to avoid accidental erasure of the tape.

Store tapes upright in individual plastic containers, ideally in a constant humidity (35% to 40%) and at about 60°F. They should be rewound every two years to maintain tension and to make sure they do not stick. Colour and sound quality are not affected by light, but may suffer deterioration if stored close to a large magnetic field (such as a motor or loudspeaker).

A local museum or public library may provide the most controlled conditions and safest place in which to store your archive material.

PRESENTING YOUR BUSINESS

*The simplest of video presentations can act as a powerful
sales aid to promote your business. By extending the use
of your equipment in this way, you may even recoup
some of its cost. Once you are competent and confident in
production techniques, including lighting, camerawork and
editing, you can put these skills toward presenting and
promoting your business both internally and externally.
An attractive video production might even be a means of
selling your home. This section shows you how.*

SELLING YOUR HOME

You can use video to help sell your home, to rent it or to exchange it for vacation periods. To work well, your programme should be a personal tour of your home, rather than a 'hard sell' promotion tape. Aim for a maximum viewing time of 15 minutes.

Planning is your first priority. Work out a script and shooting plan that will take viewers through the house in logical order. The script should emphasize the advantages of your home – size and number of the rooms, fittings (especially in the kitchen and bathroom), garage capacity, garden and so on. When developing the shooting plan, take account of the best daylight to show off each room to advantage. This may mean shooting out of sequence with the script, but you can edit the tape later. Plan your coverage over several days and include pets and family members in the shots to give rooms a homely, lived-in feeling.

Plan to bring in additional lighting to make the house look brighter, especially in the naturally dimmer areas such as the basement or hallway. Work out possible compositions for each room in advance, including people and objects you will want in each shot.

Smooth tracking shots around a room or along a corridor will greatly enhance the presentation. A dolly may be too large to manoeuvre in most rooms, but being pushed around in a baby carriage will give the same effect (see p. 144).

Set up your shooting arrangements before the light falls across the room, so that you can compose shots carefully and make any last-minute adjustments (eg move lighting stands and cables out of shot). Start with a wide shot to establish each room, then show the details. Pan across a fireplace or frame a doorway or window; then cut to the reverse angle and show the rest of the room. As you shoot, use the caption generator to add information on the dimensions of each room.

Prepare for shooting a video of your home by working out the best angles for showing rooms and special features. Natural daylight is important, so check when the sun will show up each room to best effect. Take advantage of balconies or galleries for high-angle shots of rooms. Shots taken from upstairs windows will give attractive views of the garden and immediate surroundings.

Brighten your home with fresh flowers and use them in attractive compositions, as in the foreground. Include children playing a game in one part of the room to give a 'homely' feeling.

Make the patio look inviting with garden furniture and plants, but tidy and sweep it first.

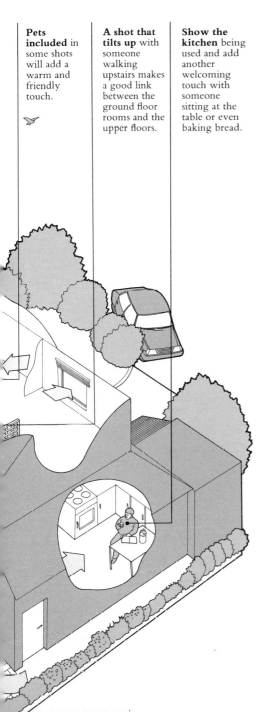

Pets included in some shots will add a warm and friendly touch.

A shot that tilts up with someone walking upstairs makes a good link between the ground floor rooms and the upper floors.

Show the kitchen being used and add another welcoming touch with someone sitting at the table or even baking bread.

A storyboard for a video of a typical home might be constructed as follows:

● Wide shot of street, showing the general surroundings and family car approaching the house from the most favourable direction. Pan with the car to bring the house into view.

● Long shots of exterior features, such as the garden, garage, patio and pool.

● Wide shot of the building itself; zoom in to show any special architectural features.

● Track-in shot (taken from an improvised dolly) of front door opening in welcome.

● Shots of individual rooms, including slow pans and reverse angles. Add a homely feeling with children playing on the floor or pets dozing peacefully.

● Close-ups of decorations, special features and fittings.

● Tilt with someone as they walk upstairs. This is an effective way to link the downstairs rooms with the upper floors.

● Treat the upstairs rooms as you did the downstairs.

● Long shots from the upstairs windows to show the best views of the garden and surroundings.

● Sequence showing the best of the neighbourhood – nearby amenities such as the shops, transport, swimming pool, public library and cinema. Edit in material from other tapes to show any colourful local events, such as markets and fairs.

● Track away from the front door as it closes, then superimpose a caption showing the address of the house, its price and availability.

A commentary, recorded independently of the visuals, should emphasize the practical advantages of your home, especially things that cannot be seen, such as the central heating and burglar alarm system. Use music (eg a cheerful classical piece) for the opening and closing sequences.

Finally, prepare a plan of the house, with room dimensions and all the relevant data to support the video tape.

SELLING YOUR PRODUCT

Video can act as a powerful sales and promotions aid for your business. It is a versatile medium and, depending on your audience, can be used for direct sales, desk-top promotions, in-store presentations or display purposes at exhibitions, trade fairs and conferences.

A sales video that is thoroughly planned, well made and creatively used will help promote you and your product or service. The promotion must be aimed at a specific audience. Are you trying to sell to sales representatives, wholesalers, retailers or the public? Once you have identified the target group, you can plan accordingly.

Work out a shooting strategy in advance by compiling a storyboard from photographs of the product or service. You could even make a video 'rough' from such stills material to see if your idea is effective and test it out on colleagues.

The sound track will be an important element. Music can set the tone of the

DIRECT SALES

When you are selling a product or service direct to the public, you should make a 10- to 15-minute video that can be shown in a waiting room, shop or office. Copies of the tape can also be sent to customers, but check the viewing format first (*see p. 212*).

In planning the production, choose music that will convey the mood and use it creatively to pace the presentation and get the audience involved. Show off your product or service to best advantage. If appropriate, add short interviews with satisfied customers. If you are a landscape architect, for example, choose a sunny day for shooting, use elevated positions to show overall layout and close in on details of special features. Or a clothes designer would need to pay special attention to lighting in order to show off the colours and textures of the garments.

To help clarify technical information (eg the acoustic or thermal insulation qualities of double glazing), edit in simple colourful graphics, produced either from artwork or generated by a computer (*see p. 146*).

DESK-TOP SCREENING

Portable, all-in-one, desk-top video units can be bought or hired, and enable you to present your case to fellow professionals conveniently and quickly.

A 10-minute tape is long enough to introduce your product or service; remember you are dealing with busy people. You may not need any music, but you may need to use a professional voice-over artist to lend an air of authority.

Choose graphics (professionally drawn or computer-generated) that explain product advantages clearly and link the images closely to the commentary. You may also need graphs and projections that compare your performance and cost-effectiveness with that of your competitors.

Aim to be concise and clear. Be prepared to supply back-up literature that makes the same points and includes the same graphics as your presentation. To show technical details, you may need to use additional lighting to get a good depth of field and show subjects in sharp focus.

presentation and get attention. Scripting also needs consideration; decide where you need commentary to sell the product and where it can sell itself on a purely visual basis. Use words that your audience will understand; don't get too technical or too bland. Use a master script and adapt it for the various audiences, so that work is not duplicated unnecessarily.

If your budget will allow, you might invest in a professional to read the commentary. But, with certain audiences, it may be better to retain the personal touch by doing the voice-over yourself. Because you want to convince people that yours is the best product or service of its kind, add testimonials to support the claim.

Although you may be competing with rival big-budget advertising, remember that you need not spend vast sums to help your business do better. With careful thought, and by hiring certain equipment (such as lights, vision mixers and desk-top players), you can make a low-cost video.

IN-STORE PRESENTATION

This type of video presentation is usually shown independently of your sales team and will be played by the store's staff at specified times. Alternatively, provide a video recorder that members of the public can operate themselves, or use a VCR with an auto-repeat facility.

Your video display must draw the attention of busy shoppers, so position it to attract the most people. A 5-minute tape is long enough to inform and entertain viewers, and short enough to hold them. Supply supporting back-up literature. Music, relayed on good speakers, can be a crowd-puller, but make sure that there is no conflict between the commentary and music. The sound track must also be audible in a noisy store environment.

Visual effects will also catch the eye, so it may be worth paying extra to have your production polished up in a commercial editing suite. Here, you can incorporate some sophisticated editing techniques and appropriate effects, such as wipes, mixes (where one shot dissolves into the next), key effects and superimposed titles (*see p. 139*).

EXHIBITION DISPLAY

When you promote your company at exhibitions, trade fairs or conferences, your audience could be fellow professionals and/or members of the public. If necessary, make separate tapes to address each audience, using similar approaches to those described for desk-top and direct sales presentations.

Your video might be used on an exhibition stand rather like an in-store presentation. Or you may have access to a darkened room or area with a video projection system. (Such systems can be hired.) Make sure that the area is as quiet as possible; select a video projector bright enough to deal with the prevailing light conditions and with a good sound system.

You may find that the expense of hiring an exhibition stand also justifies the cost of an in-vision presenter – a TV actor or radio personality who will endorse your product on tape and provide professional polish. You might also hire them to make publicity appearances on your stand during the exhibition to help attract customers.

A camcorder can be a valuable tool for anyone in business, whether they are engaged in large or small enterprises. It can be used to:

● Improve communications between people who are too busy, or located too far apart, to meet face to face.

● Disseminate business information, ranging from videos of interviews, seminars or conferences, to audio-visual summaries of business trips. Data can be recorded, copied and relayed to everyone who needs to be 'in the know'.

● Create reports and training courses.

● Outline products and services on offer.

The use of video to disseminate information, both within and outside a company, can be done at many different levels and for a variety of purposes (*see diagram*). A manager could put video to good use in the creation of reports. These could be updates for staff members on company progress, briefings for new personnel or outlines of new projects.

By making an informal presentation direct to camera, you can often be more informative, lively and realistic than you would be in writing. A video briefing such as this can effectively be done as an interview, with the questions coming from off-screen. Follow these general guidelines:

● Work out a soft lighting arrangement to create a relaxed informal atmosphere.

● Use a microphone on a stand or desk.

● Make sure the presentation is scripted and well rehearsed beforehand.

● Be relaxed and confident; make sure you are comfortably seated and have a glass of water to hand.

● Direct the production as much as you need, but allow the person operating the camcorder to be creative too.

● If necessary, do several takes until you get it right.

● Incorporate graphic aids, such as pie charts and graphs, and stills of documents, if appropriate, and insert edit these into the master tape.

The video interview has other interesting uses in business communications. By making a video of candidates for a position within the company, you can be sure that the person is 'seen' by everyone involved in the decision-making process, even if they cannot meet the candidate in person. It could also be used to introduce newly appointed members of staff to other employees in the organization and to detail their functions. Or a series of video interviews, involving everyone from the managing director to the office junior, might form the basis of a company video 'magazine' for, say, quarterly distribution. A recording such as this could be a useful tool to improve company communications and strengthen team spirit.

Reports on work-in-progress at building or engineering sites are another ideal subject for video. The tapes will provide a constant update and can easily be integrated into the company's communications network. They will also save time and money spent on travelling and meetings. To tape the work done during a single day, you can use a camcorder linked to an intermittent controller. Set up the camcorder in one place and program the intermittent controller to take one shot every few minutes. The resulting tape will be like a time-lapse film. A wall that took a day to build would appear to rise from the ground, as if by magic.

For long-term projects, you can produce a similar result by taking a series of shots separated in time by days, weeks or months. If you do this, it is vital to have the camcorder in the same position each time, so that the audience always has the same viewpoint. Mark the camera position permanently on the ground so that it is always easy to find. Alternatively, replay a little of your previous take and match the opening shot of the new sequence closely in the viewfinder. With an adjustable eyepiece, you can trace the framing of the shot with a wax pencil (which rubs off easily) and use

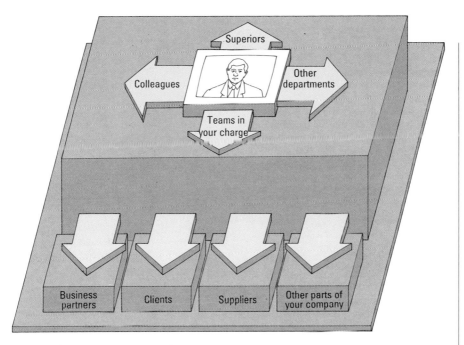

Superiors

Colleagues

Other departments

Teams in your charge

Business partners

Clients

Suppliers

Other parts of your company

Video makes communications easy with people at all levels within a company's hierarchy. It can also widen the scope of your communications network if you make it available for viewing by employees in other locations and by your clients and suppliers.

the outline to match the composition.

Keep camerawork simple and consistent for this kind of works report; avoid elaborate camera movements, such as zooming. A caption generator is very useful to insert dates, statistics and other technical information over the relevant pictures. Record a simple commentary by speaking into the built-in microphone as you shoot. This can always be modified in the final editing if necessary.

Sales personnel, who spend most of their time away from the office base, can make similar 'on site' recordings of their work and use them for reporting. A video could provide valuable feedback, including the reactions of buyers, customer complaints and competition in the market.

CONFERENCE CHECKLIST

When using video to record a conference, don't forget to:
● Obtain a conference timetable well in advance and plan accordingly.
● Visit the conference venue beforehand to check out shooting plans, including lighting, acoustics and microphone positions. Work out all potential camera positions to cover both the speaker and the audience.
● To get the best possible sound, find out if you can take a direct feed from the public address (PA) system to plug into the camcorder's audio socket. Test this out in advance to check for hum (caused by electrical mismatch of equipment).
● If possible, read speeches ahead of time so you can shoot selectively.
● Make sure you take enough blank tapes for your needs and use mains power to save on batteries.

TRAINING AND SAFETY

Training or safety videos can entertain as well as inform. Good videos set high standards and stress the importance of carefulness and common sense.

Video has important applications for improving business performances in, for example, the areas of training, safety and skills analysis. Before you produce such a tape, make sure you carry out logical, clear and accurate research. Nearly all countries and industries have institutes of safety standards, industrial advisory bodies and regulations which are legally enforced. These must be followed and clearly explained in step-by-step scripting.

> 66 *We all know the power of good comedy to capture and hold the attention of an audience, and we also know how long it stays in the memory ... What is less well understood is how this great power of comedy works as a teaching instrument ... Once you have seen a character on film behave like an idiot, an alarm bell rings in your head next time you are on the verge of making the same mistake yourself.* 99

ANTONY JAY, FOUNDER, DIRECTOR AND SCRIPTWRITER VIDEO ARTS LTD and co-author of *Yes Minister* (3 British Academy Awards) and *Yes Prime Minister*.

TRAINING

Training videos can be used in business to illustrate the correct procedures for using equipment and machinery, or for carrying out specific and specialized tasks. They improve performance and help foster good team spirit.

A simple and direct approach is to make a video that introduces the background principles underlying a specific task before it is performed. It might explain to a receptionist, for example, the principles of good customer relations before they start operating the switchboard.

Another direct approach is one that shows trainees how to do something step-by-step, or demonstrates in stages how a piece of machinery should be used. Such a tape should include details of proper procedures, such as the correct order in which switches should be turned on, and cautions concerning abuse of machinery.

A more sophisticated version of the stepwise approach is to make a tape in segments. Trainees play one section, then go away to perform a certain specified task (and maybe also read a training manual). They then return to the tape and play the next, more difficult section, and so on. A tape such as this can be made so that trainees are set written as well as practical tests at the end of each section.

A less direct, but equally valuable type of training video is one that provides valuable insights or background knowledge. A tape that explains how roads, buildings or bridges are built would be useful for construction workers, while a tape explaining how a product is made would provide excellent background information for sales personnel.

SKILLS ANALYSIS

A skills-analysis video provides managers and their workforce with a way of examining individual performances in detail. The idea is that seeing themselves at work will alert people to their mistakes. This kind of training tape must, however, be made with tact and care. You should never make staff think that you are 'spying' on them or be destructively critical of their efforts. The video should always be discussed with the personnel involved in a sympathetic way.

The efficiency with which staff perform specific tasks can be greatly improved with the help of video. A tape on packaging procedures, for example, showing how much time and energy people waste in walking around the packing room floor, would highlight the problem and could provoke a discussion on how this aspect of the job might be improved.

Videos of people communicating with each other are also revealing. These can be used with success to help people see themselves as others see them. Videos of meetings, whether these involve colleagues or customers, are especially useful in improving performance. Just showing someone how defensive or offhand they appear to be provides a lesson that only needs to be taught once. Negotiating, interviewing, selling and dealing with customer complaints are aspects of business life that might benefit from this approach.

Psychiatrists, psychologists, social workers and teachers find skills analysis particularly helpful during their training. By seeing the way in which they behave, and the responses they illicit, skills can be improved.

SAFETY

Video can play an important role in stressing safe working practices and the risks incurred if they are ignored.

The sort of safety videos that work best are those that portray actual accidents or 'near misses' because this is what people can identify with most easily. The events you portray should be carefully staged as dramatic reconstructions – never endanger life by re-enacting the event.

The detail in a safety video can be deliberately understated, often to better effect than showing the obvious. For example, you could stress the importance of wearing proper clothing near running machinery with a sequence of fast intercut shots between the undone cuff of an overall and the whirling cogs of a wheel. The pace of editing builds up tension and the viewer's anticipation of what might happen can act as a more effective lesson than showing the actual accident itself.

You can add more impact to the video with chilling music and interviews with workers who have witnessed accidents or been victims.

Video can be used to demonstrate to workers what to do when accidents actually do happen and to underline the everyday safety procedures that should be followed. These could include the correct way to wear any protective clothing, how safety guards on machinery are set to the 'on' and 'off' positions and the proper start-up and close-down procedures.

Underline your message by using a bold repeated caption, such as 'carelessness costs lives' and insert this between sequences. You could also add impact with graphics of accident statistics in related industries.

DRAMA ON TAPE

Video opens up the creative world of visual narrative, of story-telling and drama, and offers you the chance to combine acquired technical skills with imagination and flair. 'Drama on Tape' explains how to get your ideas from script to screen — by writing a narrative that really works, by casting and directing the players, and by working as a team to produce entertaining and dramatic programmes.

WRITING A SCRIPT

Narrative drama is among the most creative and rewarding forms of video making. But first, get your script. Polished technical skills, good performers, interesting locations – these will count for nothing if you don't have a strong workable script to begin with.

There are endless subjects to be explored and sources to exploit. Coming up with the right idea is the hardest part. Once you have this, the subject, or content of the plot, is simply a matter of expounding that idea. Your own experience and imagination are the most valuable sources. But you can gain your confidence by picking up on human-interest stories in newspapers and magazines, or turning to literary sources (though remember, you may need copyright clearance to use these).

Begin by writing down the idea, the basic premise of the drama. It need only be one sentence. Then write an 'outline' of the story (a few paragraphs will do) and discuss it with the group who will be helping you produce the drama.

The next step is to follow the professional model and produce a written 'treatment'. This should give the structure and development of the plot in a summary, scene-by-scene, and written in the present tense. It should convey the mood and style of the story and can include snippets of significant dialogue (but no technical details at this stage).

Having discussed the written treatment with members of the group, now you can get down to the actual script. Work out details of the plot, descriptions of settings and actions, and the dialogue for each of the characters (see script, opposite). Remember that dialogue is written to be spoken – make sure it works and sounds natural by reading it aloud. Avoid declamatory speeches (they rarely work on screen) and keep lines succinct.

Writing a character sketch for each of the main protagonists can be helpful. To be authentic, a character's personality and behaviour must be credible and consistent. They should also be seen to develop and change during the course of the plot. In the script, a character's traits will be built up through details of action and dialogue, by showing how the person reacts to situations and other people.

Think of a drama video as a story told with pictures. Don't rely on dialogue alone to develop characters; action is vital. A good first exercise is to shoot a drama with no dialogue and make the actions and gestures convey the story.

Drama, including comedy, emerges from conflict. Successful narratives are based on this principle and follow certain patterns of development, whatever the content of the story. Conflict can be within a character (psychological), between characters (emotional) or with society (social). Once you have established the basic storyline, the various conflicts will provide the dramatic action.

In structuring your story, try adopting the following model – which can daily be observed in any TV series or film.
● Start by providing your character with a motivation or goal, such as trying to solve a crime, find happiness with a partner or achieve great success in business.
● Create conflict and confrontation by placing obstacles in their way – clever

> 66 *In a book you might start with some dialogue, and then describe the room ... some more dialogue, and then describe your clothing, and more dialogue. The camera gets that in an instant. Boom, and you're on ... The camera is relentless ... The single most important thing contributed by the screenwriter is the structure.* 99

WILLIAM GOLDMAN, SCREENWRITER
Butch Cassidy and the Sundance Kid (Oscar), *All the President's Men* (Oscar).

criminals, a rival lover or a business competitor.

- Show complications and progressions within the pattern of struggle – positive leads in the crime-solving and false trails, emotional ups and downs between lovers or financial loss and gain.
- End with a resolution to the conflict (it does not have to be happy or predictable) – the crime solved, triumph of the rival lover or a successful business coup.

The opening scenes of any video drama are particularly important. It may be your only opportunity to 'hook' the viewers and get their attention. Aim to set up the scene, introduce the main character's objective and reveal the obstacles in the first sixth of the script. You must get the viewers involved and evoke emotion, so that they will have empathy with the main character, want to see how the plot develops and how it is resolved.

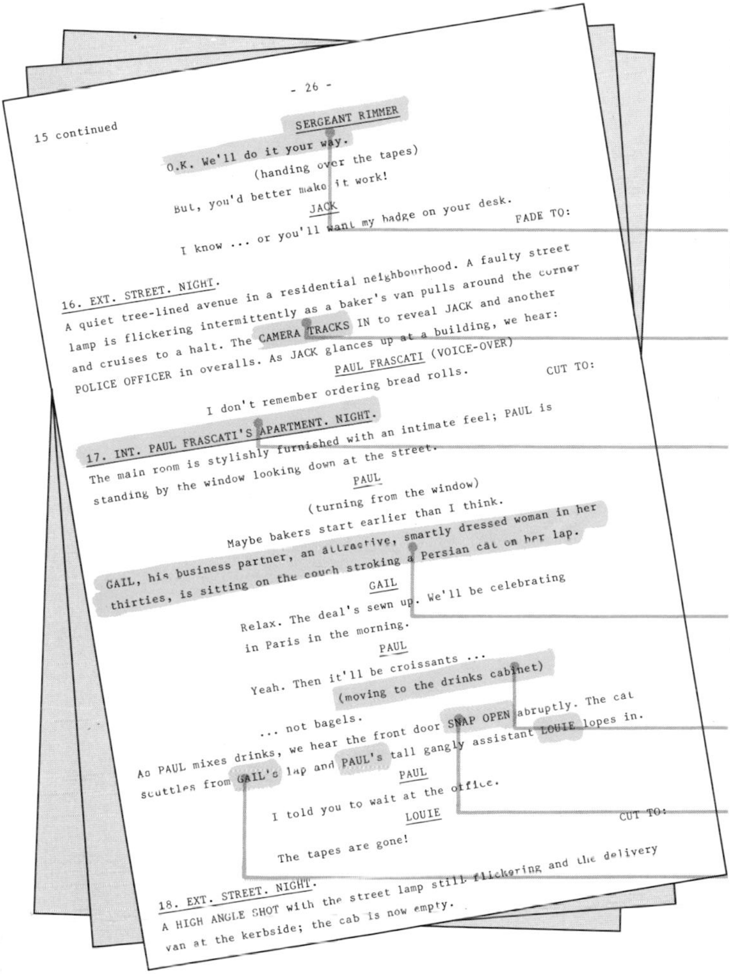

\- 26 -

15 continued

SERGEANT RIMMER

O.K. We'll do it your way.

(handing over the tapes)

But, you'd better make it work!

JACK

I know ... or you'll want my badge on your desk.

FADE TO:

16. EXT. STREET. NIGHT.

A quiet tree-lined avenue in a residential neighbourhood. A faulty street lamp is flickering intermittently as a baker's van pulls around the corner and cruises to a halt. The CAMERA TRACKS IN to reveal JACK and another POLICE OFFICER in overalls. As JACK glances up at a building, we hear:

PAUL FRASCATI (VOICE-OVER)

I don't remember ordering bread rolls.

CUT TO:

17. INT. PAUL FRASCATI'S APARTMENT. NIGHT.

The main room is stylishly furnished with an intimate feel; PAUL is standing by the window looking down at the street.

PAUL

(turning from the window)

Maybe bakers start earlier than I think.

GAIL, his business partner, an attractive, smartly dressed woman in her thirties, is sitting on the couch stroking a Persian cat on her lap.

GAIL

Relax. The deal's sewn up. We'll be celebrating in Paris in the morning.

PAUL

Yeah. Then it'll be croissants ...

(moving to the drinks cabinet)

... not bagels.

As PAUL mixes drinks, we hear the front door SNAP OPEN abruptly. The cat scuttles from GAIL's lap and PAUL's tall gangly assistant LOUIE lopes in.

PAUL

I told you to wait at the office.

LOUIE

The tapes are gone!

CUT TO:

18. EXT. STREET. NIGHT.

A HIGH ANGLE SHOT with the street lamp still flickering and the delivery van at the kerbside; the cab is now empty.

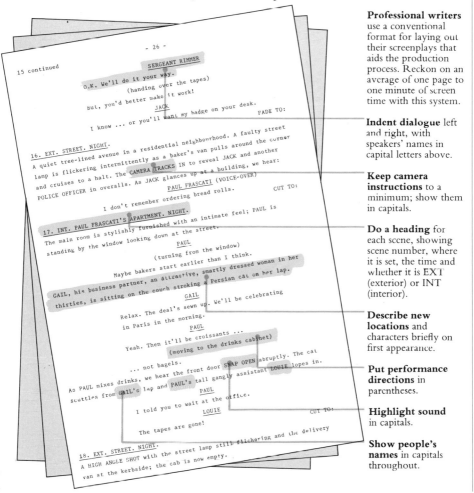

Professional writers use a conventional format for laying out their screenplays that aids the production process. Reckon on an average of one page to one minute of screen time with this system.

Indent dialogue left and right, with speakers' names in capital letters above.

Keep camera instructions to a minimum; show them in capitals.

Do a heading for each scene, showing scene number, where it is set, the time and whether it is EXT (exterior) or INT (interior).

Describe new locations and characters briefly on first appearance.

Put performance directions in parentheses.

Highlight sound in capitals.

Show people's names in capitals throughout.

PLANNING A PRODUCTION

The key to get you successfully from script to screen is in the planning sessions held prior to shooting. Their object is to ensure that the actual shooting goes smoothly and that the script is fully realized. All members of the video-making team should be involved at this stage; although there is collective responsibility for the production, each individual should undertake to do a specific task.

SCHEDULING

A video drama is not necessarily shot in script order. Often, it is simply not practical: if the same location crops up several times, shoot all those scenes together.

● The first task of the scheduler is to break down the script into a logical shooting order. This may require juggling with times, so that availability of locations and cast coincide, with travelling times built in.

● Overall shooting time will vary according to the complexity of the production and the demands of the script. A 10-minute narrative, with no dialogue, set in one exterior location, could be shot in a day. With more elaborate dramas, involving lighting interiors and breaking scenes down into several shots, a day's shooting may only give you 3 to 5 minutes of edited screentime.

● Take account of tasks that you know will be time-consuming, such as elaborate lighting set-ups and clearing the area for dolly shots.

● Professionals always allow for 'weather cover' in their exterior shooting schedules. At any location, take exterior establishing shots first while the weather is fine before doing interiors. Also, allow for shooting at particular times of day, eg romantic scenes at sunset.

LOCATIONS

When scouting out locations, there are certain practical considerations.

● Permission may be needed, even when shooting in public places. Seeking permission is not only a courtesy, but may be a necessity if you want to get people's cooperation. Make sure to tell the relevant authorities in advance about your group and plans, so that there will be no objections on the day. Inquire about parking facilities, convenient to your shooting set.

● Direction of sunlight on the subject is important for both exterior and interior shots. A street scene may look better with one side completely in shadow, so consider the time of day for shooting. Note the position of windows indoors and the amount of sunlight the room receives at different times of day.

● Lighting requirements need to be assessed for each location. Bring a camcorder on 'recce' sessions to calculate lighting needs.

● Power points, their number, type and position, need to be checked carefully. Ideally, run only one lamp from each socket. Assess the need for extension cables and adaptors.

● Unwanted sound can be a problem in exterior locations – traffic, aircraft, road works, distant sirens and noisy crowds. Choose another location or ask local residents about the quieter times of day.

Even 'quiet' interiors can have problems: airconditioning, fridges, fans, all can produce an annoying hum on the sound track. Perhaps you can turn them off temporarily. Check the acoustics of the location (see p. 32). If there is reverberation, you may need to bring in sound baffles.

BUDGET

With a crew and cast giving their time willingly, a small-scale drama production can be made for little more than the cost of a couple of tapes. But, as your creativity expands, your budget will need to keep pace. It is only prudent to make some basic cost calculations before committing the group to a production.
● **Transport:** Moving the equipment, crew and cast between locations may require 2 or more cars or a van. Even if the vehicles are free, the petrol is not.
● **Facility fees:** You must expect to pay a fee in certain locations. Many public organizations charge video or film makers as a standard practice, especially frequently used places such as airports, national monuments or art galleries. With private homes, it is good policy to offer a nominal sum to cover electricity used.
● **Props and costumes:** Most can be borrowed, but allow for scenes involving food and drink, breakages and for decorating sets.
● **Equipment:** Allow for hiring costs (eg lamps) and purchase of little extras (eg bulbs, gels, diffusers).
● **Tapes:** Drama inevitably involves shooting more material than will be used, so have enough tape to cover at least 5 times the planned programme length (professionals operate at a ratio of about 10 to 1). Also, allow for audio tape if you plan separate recording of additional sounds.
● **Insurance:** If your production becomes at all elaborate, you must cover the group for third party and property damage.
● **Contingency:** Always allow for a margin of error and unexpected costs; 10% is a fair rate.

PROPS AND COSTUMES

The content and style of your video drama will be greatly influenced by its props and costumes.
● Make a list of all the necessary items. Most can be either donated by members of the group or borrowed, but some may have to be bought.
● Decide on each performer's costume, which will be an important expression of the character they portray. You can hire costumes from costumiers or theatre companies.
● Having ascertained where all the items will come from, make a final checklist for each scene. If deliberate breakages are involved (eg glasses), have several items on stand-by.
● One crew member should organize for the props and costumes to be in the right place at the right time.

PRODUCTION

Once locations, transport, props and costumes are organized, the production manager can make up the 'call sheet'. This is a detailed schedule of arrangements for each day of the shoot and should set out:
● Date of shooting.
● Scene numbers to be shot.
● Address and telephone of location.
● Rendezvous point for the crew.
● Cast required.
● 'Call' times for the cast.
● List of props and costumes needed.
● Additional equipment to be used.
● Any special location problems, eg parking, dirty environment.
● Time planned for end of shooting.
The production manager should keep the names, addresses and telephone numbers of all involved.

Once a script is complete, the process of directing a video drama can begin. First, a series of creative decisions has to be made, about locations, casting and visualization.

The choice of location is governed by artistic as well as pragmatic considerations. For example, if the script calls for a scene in which two lovers have a clandestine meeting in a bar, the choice of setting must be both apposite and credible to reflect the nature of their relationship.

Casting an amateur drama production often involves using friends and family. But it may be worth looking around to fill the lead parts, by advertising in your local newspaper or contacting drama groups. You can hold auditions, reading from a strong scene in your script, and record them for later review. Do a second take with promising applicants to see how they respond to your direction. Remember that video dramas are not like stage productions: acting is on a smaller scale, voices must be natural and gestures toned down.

The director needs to be closely involved with the design of the production, from the adapting of interiors, with furnishings and fittings, to the selection of appropriate props and costumes. Discussions should be held with the technical crew on the visual style of the video drama – the kind of lighting for each scene (eg high or low key), the use of dolly shots or the inclusion of special filter effects.

Pre-rehearsal sessions are important for the cast. Time should be devoted to outlining the details and motivations of each character and reading through the script together so that the plot and theme is fully understood. Once these familiarization sessions are complete, rehearsals can begin and character movements worked out, with the cast contributing ideas about how best to play each scene and the director deciding on how best to shoot it.

The director marks up the final shooting decisions on a copy of the script (*opposite*) or summarizes them in a storyboard. The shooting order is worked out, with a shot plan for each scene (*below*).

The order of shooting will not necessarily follow the order of the script (*see p. 186*). Start with your widest, master shots and then move in for close-ups. (Remember, video likes close-ups, so don't shoot too much in long shot.) This will help you sustain continuity of lighting throughout the scene. Take all shots looking in one direction at the same time; then, reset the lighting and do the reverse angle shots.

As a video director, you need, above all, to have good working relationships with the crew and cast. You must have clear ideas and intentions on the production and an ability to communicate these to both parties. You must be sensitive enough to

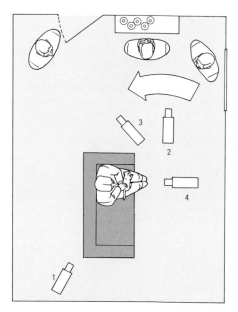

The shot plan for Scene 17 (*opposite*) shows the camera positions to cover the action and the order of shooting.

To keep lighting continuity, start in the wide angle (**1**), then move in to mid-shot (**2**) and close-up (**3, 4**).

listen to the suggestions of others and flexible enough to adapt your own ideas. Once on set, trust the crew's skills and don't interfere on technical details. Concentrate instead on giving support and encouragement to the cast.

For each scene, rehearse the action and camera movements fully. When everyone involved is satisfied, ask for quiet. Tell the camera operator to start recording and, after a short pause, call 'action' (and 'cut' at the end of the take). Check immediately with the crew about technical problems and ask if the cast want another take. Review the tape if there is uncertainty. To help with the editing later, use a caption generator or marker board to show the scene and take number. Try to keep the shooting momentum going, so that everyone stays involved with their roles.

> *A good director is like a good psychiatrist. He knows what conclusions he wants you to reach, but he lets you discover them for yourself. He acts as a guide rather than a commander.*
> **ROD STEIGER, ACTOR**
> *On the Waterfront, In the Heat of the Night (Oscar).*

> *Of course, you're mad if you don't take up ideas as they come along, especially when you're working with children ... On the other hand you hear an awful lot of good lines ruined by improvisation.*
> **ALAN PARKER, DIRECTOR**
> *Bugsy Malone, Midnight Express, Fame, Birdy.*

A drama script can be marked up to show the shooting treatment intended for a particular scene. Number each shot and indicate its size and content. Coverage can involve overlaps, where part of the action will be shot from different angles to allow greater choice at the editing stage.

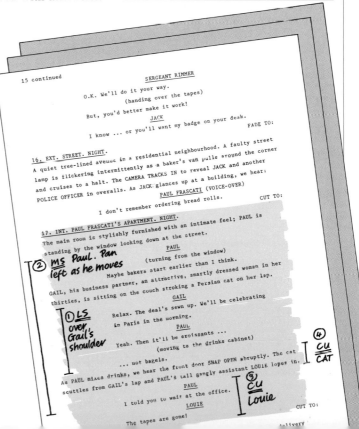

15 continued

SERGEANT RIMMER

O.K. We'll do it your way.
(handing over the tapes)
But, you'd better make it work!

JACK

I know ... or you'll want my badge on your desk.   FADE TO:

16. EXT. STREET. NIGHT.
A quiet tree-lined avenue in a residential neighbourhood. A faulty street lamp is flickering intermittently as a baker's van pulls around the corner and cruises to a halt. The CAMERA TRACKS IN to reveal JACK and another POLICE OFFICER in overalls. As JACK glances up at a building, we hear:

PAUL FRASCATI (VOICE-OVER)

I don't remember ordering bread rolls.   CUT TO:

17. INT. PAUL FRASCATI'S APARTMENT. NIGHT.
The main room is stylishly furnished with an intimate feel; PAUL is standing by the window looking down at the street.

② MS Paul. Pan left as he moves

PAUL
(turning from the window)
Maybe bakers start earlier than I think.

GAIL, his business partner, an attractive, smartly dressed woman in her thirties, is sitting on the couch stroking a Persian cat on her lap.

GAIL

Relax. The deal's sewn up. We'll be celebrating in Paris in the morning.

① LS over Gail's shoulder

PAUL

Yeah. Then it'll be croissants ...
(moving to the drinks cabinet)
... not bagels.

As PAUL mixes drinks, we hear the front door SNAP OPEN abruptly. The cat scuttles from GAIL's lap and PAUL's tall gangly assistant LOUIE lopes in.

④ CU CAT

PAUL

I told you to wait at the office.

③ CU Louie

LOUIE

The tapes are gone!   CUT TO:

PERSONAL VIEWS

By turning the camera on yourself, you will see yourself as others see you. 'Personal Views' explores ways to analyze your own performance in any area, such as speechmaking, interviewing or entertaining, and so prepare you for public appearance. By contrast, you can also record the more intimate moments of your life – as a friend, lover or parent. Finally, your personal experience and enthusiasm can be used to encourage and train the next generation of video makers.

THE VIDEO LETTER

As an alternative to a conventional letter, try compiling a video letter to send to distant friends and relatives, or to give as an unusual Christmas or birthday gift. Keep your audience in mind while putting the tape together. Vary its contents to include a mixture of existing material and specially shot material.

A round-up of the year's events is a good subject for a video letter. Edit in recorded highlights of family news from previously shot tapes, such as the main events of holidays, travel, weddings and other family and local occasions. Preserve any humorous or dramatic moments and, above all, avoid being repetitive or boring.

The material you shoot specially for the 'letter' can include family and friends, house and garden. Informal sequences work best. Show how the children have grown and what their current interests are by shooting a series of simple scenes from their daily lives. Tape toddlers having fun at bathtime and children playing in the garden or by the pool. Show any new pets introduced into the household and how the children interact with them.

Another topic that will be of interest to relatives and friends will be major new items in your life, such as a new home. Tape a guided tour of the house as you might do for a prospective buyer (*see p. 174*). To show off the way your garden grows, do some slow gentle pans and long-held shots, cut together with music and commentary. Shoot flowers and shrubs from a low level and with the light behind them or to the side, so that they are backlit for a translucent effect. For close-ups of your prize specimens, use the macro setting or a supplementary close-up lens.

If you have acquired a new car, make a fun tape akin to a commercial, with a series of shots from striking angles cut together in rapid succession and with special effects and up-tempo music. Shoot action sequences of your car by taking shots of it on the move from another vehicle and low-angle shots from the roadside of it passing. Cut to close-ups of interior details and any special features. Use a star filter to add sparkle to shots of gleaming chrome and a graduated filter to create dramatic backgrounds.

Find a way to link disparate sequences in the tape. You could, for example, use a

Compile a video letter from existing tapes and from specially shot material, eg of new arrivals like pets.

series of children's drawings to act as appropriate backgrounds for titles or captions, with lettering hand-written or produced by a caption generator.

Create an informal talking commentary throughout the tape. Get the whole family to contribute by sitting them comfortably in a semicircle with an omnidirectional mic placed equidistant between them. Run the video tape on the TV (with its sound turned down) and record their comments and responses to the material as

it is played. You can either record the sound directly on to the tape or make a separate sound tape for dubbing on later (*see p. 126*). Let the talk run freely; direct them only enough to prevent them talking over each other.

Another informal approach is to tape an actual family conversation, recording the images and sound live. Record in daylight, either indoors (no lights) or in the garden to get a relaxed feeling. Shoot from a low level (about at people's eyeline) and start in the wide angle to include the whole group, then close in on individuals.

Arrange for one person to lead the conversation and to get the others talking. The 'leader' can then cue you for close-ups of individuals, by saying something like: 'Ann, do you remember that day at the zoo?' You can then move to cover 'Ann' before she starts speaking. When the conversation gets animated, with everyone contributing, shoot in the wide angle. Make sure to get shots of people listening as well, to edit in as cut-aways.

SENDING VIDEOS ABROAD

● Always check that the recipient of your tape will be able to play it on their video equipment. Compatibility depends on the broadcasting system of a country (PAL, NTSC, SECAM) and on tape formats. (For full details on international video standards, *see p. 212*.) Tapes can be converted to conform with different systems, but this is expensive and impairs quality.

● Enclose the tape in a plastic casing, rather than the manufacturer's standard cardboard box. Then package it in an envelope padded with 'bubble' plastic.

● Don't worry about tapes going through modern X-ray machines at customs – they will not be harmed.

SELF-ANALYSIS

Turn the camera on yourself and you have an instant way of analyzing yourself, your personality and public performance – as an entertainer of any kind, whether you be a musician, comedian, dancer, juggler, magician, ventriloquist or puppeteer, or as a lecturer, teacher or public speaker.

An analysis video can also be useful to help someone else (say, your children or partner) to prepare and practice for such a performance.

Video has the great advantage of easy playback, so you can record rehearsals and analyze them immediately, polishing your performance at each stage.

Although you will be recording in private, it helps to arrange the 'set' so that it is as close as possible to the public venue. Create the effect of stage lighting with strong directional lights set high on their stands to shine down on you and give a spotlight effect. A strong backlight will also help to isolate you 'on stage', creating a limbo effect.

Set the camcorder on a tripod so that it is directly in front of you and address your performance to the lens; it is your audience in this case. Use an angle that is wide enough to show the whole performance; this is vital when you are recording yourself and cannot operate the controls. If your act needs close-up analysis (as with the lips of a ventriloquist or the hand movements of a magician), break the performance down into sections so that you can stop and change the shot size between sequences. Set up the TV so you can check the shot on screen. You can edit the tape later to create a coherent flow.

Good quality sound is important to your analysis. For rehearsals, put the mic where it works best and don't worry if it appears in shot. If you are working on a dance routine, record sound directly on to your video tape from an audio cassette or record player by connecting it via the line socket of the camcorder. You can then play it simultaneously through the loudspeakers.

At the end of the recording, play back the tape on the TV and review your performance. Once you are confident enough, show it to a partner or friend for comment and analysis. Don't overreact to criticism; use it constructively to improve your act. Keep rehearsing and playing the tape back until you get it right.

The same self-record/analysis technique can prepare you for public speech-making, whether in business (as at a sales conference) or at social events (a wedding reception or community meeting). Again, try to simulate the conditions in which you will be performing; stand on a podium or behind a desk, or sit at a table.

Set the camcorder for a head-on medium shot, taken from the waist up. Use lighting that produces a soft overall effect and is evenly balanced. For sound, use a unidirectional mic set up not more than 60cm (2ft) away. Then, let the tape roll, step into shot and speak your lines.

When you have finished, play the tape back and analyze it closely. As well as noting how you sound, look particularly for any nervous actions, such as excessive blinking, unnecessary hand movements or facial grimaces.

Although you might use a self-analysis video such as this for a special occasion, it could also prove of value in more everyday situations. People often get a shock when they see themselves on screen. Everybody 'edits' their own view of themselves. But, with video, self-editing is not so easy, and you will find it much more revealing than, say, looking at yourself in a mirror.

The self-revelation that video allows could be important in preparing yourself for a job interview. You could tape a mock interview in which you answer questions, put by a friend, direct to camera. On replay, you can assess your responses and reactions, and improve on them.

Improve your personal performance, and make a better impression on your audience, by using video as a form of self-analysis. All kinds of performers will benefit from seeing themselves as others see them. You can shoot the video on your own by simply letting the tape run and stepping into shot. For dance routines or comedy acts, keep to the wide angle setting to take in the whole scene. Other acts, such as those of a ventriloquist or magician, will need close-up shots, so shoot the performance in stages. Start with the lens wide, then stop to change its focal length and get closer views of details.

You can also involve friends to operate the camcorder and handle the sound or lights. If the tape you make is good enough, you could use it to promote yourself and get bookings.

To create the right atmosphere, rehearse in the costume and make-up you will be wearing 'on stage'.

PROMOTING YOURSELF

Once you have perfected the performance to the best of your ability (see p. 194), you can use your final video tape to promote yourself – by booking your act directly or sending the tape to an agent or casting director. A tape of yourself could also help promote your career or even find you a partner for life.

The final tape of an entertainment or stage performance should be recorded in front of a live audience: real reactions will increase its credibility value. This might involve setting up a special performance with invited guests or you can shoot on location for such acts as a fairground juggler, cabaret artist or children's entertainer.

To make an effective tape, you will need the help of at least one person, to operate the camcorder; lighting and sound assistants would also be useful. You can direct the show yourself, based on your experiences during practice sessions. You could use multi-camera coverage to vary the shot sizes and angles (see p. 136). An alternative approach is to use one camcorder and cover the same act in the same location but on different nights. Shoot from different angles on each occasion and edit the tapes together later. Cut-aways will be an important element in the final tape, so spend time getting good audience reaction shots – clapping hands, smiling faces, uproarious laughter.

It can help to make a separate sound recording, especially of verbal acts (such as comedy), for use at the editing stage. Lines of dialogue or jokes can be dubbed in over shots of the audience, and applause and laughter used with shots of the performer.

If you are an actor, singer or musician, you might find it more advantageous to put together a tape that shows your range and versatility, rather than showing a single performance. The skill in this is in the editing – you want to show enough, but not too much, of each section and the whole tape needs to have a running theme of some kind for coherence.

Another way of promoting yourself or a friend is to make a video-dating tape. It can be sent to prospective partners in response to an advertisement placed in a newspaper or magazine. A tape such as this should be a rounded portrait of the subject, made to appear as attractive as possible.

Taking the storyboard illustrated here as a model, start with a montage sequence of stills from the family photograph album, shot with a rostrum camera (see p. 114). A voice-over introduces the subject and describes the personal history as the pages of the album are turned. Cut in for close-ups of details in the photographs.

One of the main sequences in the tape should be an informal interview with the subject about interests and attitudes. The questions are posed by an off-screen interviewer and, at the editing stage, the answers are run together to form a continuous 'statement' from the subject.

Set up the interview in comfortable home surroundings, using soft sympathetic lighting. It may be useful to 'dress' the setting with items important to the subject and which reflect their interests and character, such as including a pet being stroked, books on shelves or pictures on the walls. Take care with this sequence and be sure to get some good mid-shots and close-ups so the subject's personality will emerge naturally.

The interview should give the subject the chance to talk about hobbies and special interests. Use the responses as cues to cut to sequences of the subject 'at play', pursuing their favourite leisure activities. Include shots of the subject at a social occasion, relating to other people.

The workplace can offer good opportunities to reveal more about character. Most people appear comfortable and confident when talking about their work, so tape a short interview with the subject covering their job and career ambitions. You could also include taped interview statements from friends, family and colleagues to serve as personal testimonials.

Tape a final interview with the subject, shot exclusively in close-up. This is the time for the subject to talk frankly about the sort of partner they are seeking. Conclude the tape with a well-composed close-up of a smiling face. Use the caption generator to give the subject's name, age and telephone number. Add something extra to the tape's atmosphere by editing in the sort of music the subject likes to listen to, or even a recording of their own musical talents, if appropriate.

A similar approach to this video-dating tape could be used to produce a testimonial video. This might be built around interviews with users of the product or service you are promoting.

A video-dating tape could find you a partner. A storyboard, detailing each shot and the voice-over, is the basis for organizing the shots into a logical sequence, designed to show the subject off to best advantage.

1. Close-up. Family album with hand turning pages. Voice-over (V/O) introduces subject.

2. Long shot. Subject relaxed at home, being interviewed. Zoom in for mid-shots.

3. Medium shot. Subject at ease. V/O talks about painting hobby.

4. Long shot. Subject playing tennis. V/O talks about varied sporting interests.

5. Long shot. Subject relaxing with friends. Live sound.

6. Close-up of subject. A friend's voice describes subject.

HOME EROTICA

Because a video tape can be made in the privacy of your own home, and played back immediately without having to be processed or developed by outsiders, it is ideal for recording your private world of personal experiences and intimate moments. Above all, your aim in making an erotic video should be to experiment and have fun. Stop at once if you feel it is threatening your relationship in any way.

For a video to be erotic, it does not have to be explicit. Subtle suggestion – the things the camera does not quite manage to show you – and loving sensual gestures and sounds are often much more stimulating and appealing than graphic sex scenes. The impression you give depends as much on the context of the tape, and the atmosphere you create, as on the actual content of the shots.

A simple 'live' approach might be for partners to take turns at being the video maker and for each to make a record of the other's sensuousness. Treat the human form like a contour map and have the camera track, pan, tilt and zoom over it in exploratory fashion.

With the help of a storyboard and script, you can produce a narrative in which each partner is seen on the screen in turn, even though they were recorded alone. By anticipating the needs of continuity editing (such as screen direction and eyelines), you can construct and edit a continuous story or fantasy sequence. For example, intercut a shot of one partner looking off-screen with a point-of-view shot of the other.

For both partners to appear together, set the camcorder on a tripod, with its legs fully extended to give elevated shots from above the 'set'. With the lens at wide angle, check the area that will be in shot before you join your partner. Run the camcorder from the mains and use a tape of maximum playing time, so that you can let the situation develop on camera and forget about technicalities.

Relaxation is vital, so get into the right mood well before you start recording. Forget your inhibitions, perhaps by giving each other a massage or bathing together. Have some romantic music playing (this can be erased later) and warm up the room beforehand. Remove tight items of clothing well in advance (such as belts, underclothes and socks), so that any marks have time to fade.

Lighting is critical to atmosphere. If you are shooting during the day, or with strong domestic lighting, you may not need additional lamps as long as you use the low-light control on the camcorder. Exploit the camcorder's ability to shoot at candlelight levels by using groups or banks of candles, placed out of shot, to give a romantic glow to the scene. When lighting in this way, beware of the fire hazards.

Filters can be used to create other effects, for example, a diffusion filter softens the appearance of the scene. For a more abstract treatment of the subject, use a multi-image filter to break the shot up into several images. The fracturing effect is enhanced by using the neg/pos facility on the camcorder to create a negative image.

A single lamp placed to one side creates an attractive low-key effect, with part of the figures always in shadow; this adds intrigue and accentuates the contours of the bodies. With 2 lamps illuminating a white or pale backdrop, the figures will appear in silhouette. A rim effect, outlining the shapes, can be created by placing a single lamp almost behind the subjects.

Live sound, recorded with a microphone suspended over the set, will add a realistic dimension to an erotic video. Music can be particularly evocative and provides both mood and momentum. Add polish to the production by editing in a sequence of favourite love songs or extracts from the classics, to synchronize with the pace of the sequence. Romantic or erotic verse, read by you or your partner, could also be dubbed on later.

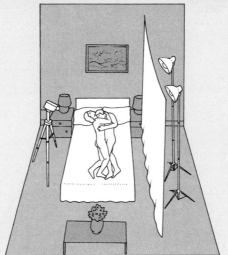

Soft romantic lighting enhances any erotic scene. Experiment with diffused lighting by hanging white or pale-coloured sheets around the bed and position lamps behind them. For a really smooth effect, add orange gels to the lamps or a pink filter to the lens. A simpler way is to set the camcorder's white balance to 'daylight', even though you are shooting in tungsten light. This gives a tanning effect to pale skins.

IN AT THE BIRTH

The news that a baby is on the way presents the opportunity to make a video record of pregnancy, birth and the early days of a baby's life that will deserve a special place in your family archive.

As soon as the mother-to-be has had her pregnancy confirmed, you can begin to chart her progress. The sorts of shots to include might be typical episodes of the pregnancy, such as checking her weight on the scales or decorating the nursery.

Video can be particularly useful to the expectant mother in helping her with the exercise routines recommended to keep her fit and prepare her for labour. Get permission to record the instructor doing the exercises, then play them back at home. Taping the mother-to-be as she exercises will also provide a self-analysis tape for her to assess progress (see p. 194).

Throughout pregnancy, record informal discussions with the expectant mother and the rest of the family, including grandparents-in-waiting; encourage them to talk about their reactions to the forthcoming event.

In planning to make a video record of the birth itself, it is vital to be well prepared. Attend some antenatal classes with your partner, so that you know exactly what to expect. This may also provide the opportunity for some interesting pre-birth shots, such as a group of women doing their exercises, the doctor listening to the heartbeat of the unborn child or other fathers-to-be rehearsing baby-bathing or nappy-changing.

As part of your preparations for the birth day, tape a sequence of shots to show the hospital or clinic where the event will take place, since you are unlikely to have the time or the inclination to shoot these on the day itself. Include a variety of views of the approach road, the hospital name plate and grounds.

Accompany your partner when she visits the labour and maternity wards, so you can check out acoustics and lighting,

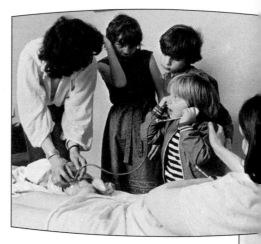

Capture spontaneous reactions as part of your video recording the events of pregnancy, the birth itself and the days following. Be ready, when the family come to visit their mother after the birth, to get happy shots of, say, a child's wonderment on hearing the heartbeat of his newly born brother or sister, and recording the sound.

and familiarize yourself with the layout. Talk to the hospital staff, discuss your plans with them and seek their permission and cooperation. Establish where and when you will be free to shoot your record of the birth itself and work out some precise camera positions in advance.

The labour room may well have many reflective surfaces that will produce reverberation. Check the acoustics by clapping your hands once; ideally the sound should die away naturally. If you anticipate acoustic problems, plan to use a directional mic attached to the camcorder. If you are allowed, shoot a short test sequence to check the lighting.

At the birth, there are some important things you must remember:

● The main priority is the health and safety of mother and baby. Nothing must be allowed to interfere with either.

● Do everything the hospital staff tell you and do it immediately. They are in charge, you are only a spectator.

● Be as unobtrusive as you can.

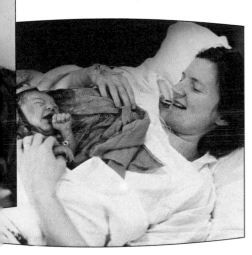

Record the intimacy of the moment by taking close-ups of the mother and her newborn baby. These shots can be edited to form an attractive montage sequence reflecting the happiness of the occasion.

- Be ready to put down the camcorder to hold your partner's hand or support and comfort her whenever she needs you.
- Be patient: labour can take many hours, particularly for a first baby, so don't expect to be recording continuously.
- Operate the camcorder from batteries. Power leads might get in the staff's way.
- Lighting your video will almost certainly involve making do with whatever exists in the labour room; if, however, your baby is being born at home, you can organize your own lighting set-up.

Lighting in the labour room may be bright and fluorescent, although many modern obstetricians recommend that babies be born into a dimly lit world, to reduce the trauma of the birth experience. Fluorescent lighting can create an unpleasant blue or greenish cast, so use a colour-correction filter on the lens. It can also appear as a slight flicker (caused by the differing pulse rate of the light and recording rate of the video tape). The only solution to this is to use additional lights on

stands, if this is allowed; if not, try using a video lamp mounted on the camcorder, but make sure that you do not shine it directly on to the newborn baby.

As the birth proceeds, try to vary your shots, between the mother and the attendant staff. If you are in a fixed position, with the camcorder on a tripod, use the zoom to get separate close-ups of the participants, so that the material will edit together naturally. If you are hand-holding the camcorder, move around the mother to get reverse angles from her perspective. If labour takes a long time, get some cutaways of the clock to accentuate the passing hours.

Add an authentic touch to the proceedings by using the date and stopwatch functions of a caption generator to show the date and timing of the labour, as well as the precise time of birth. Superimpose the information at intervals during shooting.

When the baby is born, zoom in and record his or her first cries. Follow this by showing the mother's first contact with the baby (babies are often delivered straight to the mother's breast); then record the cutting of the cord, the cleaning, weighing and wrapping. Try to get close enough to the scales to show the weight and superimpose the figures on screen using the caption generator.

Follow the birth sequence with shots of family and friends visiting the new mother. Set yourself up in advance near the mother's bed, or the baby's cot, so you are in position and pre-focused, ready to record the visitors' first reactions as they enter. Intercut these shots with close-ups of the mother and baby. Apart from smiling faces, many of the reactions will be verbal, so use a directional mic mounted on the camcorder to catch them.

A final sequence at the hospital or clinic could show the mother thanking the staff. This would be a good moment to superimpose a caption giving the date, the child's full name and current weight.

VIDEO FOR KIDS

Once you are adept at video making, you can pass on your knowledge to the younger generation. Children aged from about 8 upward are old enough for their first video-making experience; older children will be particularly intrigued by the technical aspects such as lighting and sound. The best sort of equipment for younger children to experiment with are the small, easy-to-handle, lightweight camcorders, which have simplified controls and functions or else are fully automated.

Simple 'point and shoot' camcorders have a fixed lens and pre-set focusing distances, so there are only 2 or 3 functions that have to be set. A costlier alternative is a camcorder with many functions, all of which are automatically controlled, including focus, exposure and white balance. The great advantage of such a camcorder is that it has an electronic viewfinder and allows instant playback, which the 'point and shoot' model does not.

Explain how the camcorder works by going through the functions systematically and demonstrating each of the controls. Allow children to manipulate the focus and zoom controls, iris and white balance, and have the camcorder linked to the TV so that they can see the effects on screen. Start with some basic shooting exercises around the living room, so that they can test their skills and experiment with composition and camera movements.

Once they are confident in their handling of the machine and understand any potential hazards, encourage children to make programmes of their own. Their first efforts will be full of technical errors and visual mistakes, but view the results with them, explain the problems and offer solutions.

Children learn quickly and you will see an improvement in their production capabilities with each new exercise. Some suggestions for children's projects, varying in complexity, are included here.

1 **Hobbies:** Get children to make a short video demonstrating their skills in cooking or crafts, and explaining the activity's intricacies. There should be a detailed sequence of the finished work.

2 **Pets:** As well as recording children playing with cats and dogs, there is scope for making tapes of other pets. With small animals in cages, extra lighting may be needed. This should be bounced or reflected so that creatures are not dazzled or frightened.

3 **Interviews:** These involve children in simple research and preparing questions, as well as camerawork. They should concentrate on composition and shot sizes, and on using the zoom lens. Good sound can be recorded using an auxiliary hand-held mic.

4 **Sports and games:** Select outdoor activities that can be shot in one location and concentrate on dramatic and novel camera angles. Roller-skating or riding bicycles are good subjects for practising pans, tilts and zooms with the action. Add a running commentary as sound track.

5   **Putting on a show:** This can consist of individual acts performed on a simple stage with lights on either side (*left*). Follow full-length shots with zoom-ins to close-ups of the high points of each act. An omnidirectional mic at the front of the stage will give good general sound; 'comedians' could hand-hold a mic as well. Introduce acts by using the caption generator.

6   **The story video:** Children have wonderful imaginations and could easily compile an adventure plot. Get them to draw a simple storyboard and work out the script. Stress teamwork.

7   **Dance demonstrations:** This gives children the chance to see and analyze their own performances. Playback music can be recorded by the camcorder's own mic or fed into the audio-in socket from a cassette machine.

8   **Pop group or band:** To get good shots of live music, it helps if the camcorder operator is familiar with the performance, so that it can be broken down into separate shots of the musicians that will edit together into a continuous programme. Try special visual effects.

9   **Location dramas:** Take a stage production outdoors on location and shoot it as a video programme. This gives you more freedom to cover the action from a variety of angles. Take care with sound recording outdoors. Edit shots to emphasize the drama.

10   **Group discussions:** A recording of children talking about life as they see it is demanding of camera and sound-recording skills. The event must be sufficiently controlled so that the shots can be edited into a coherent whole.

Children making their first videos should use a camcorder that is light and easy to handle. They can become familiar with the camcorder's functions while shooting a variety of subjects.

TECHNICAL REFERENCES

Although the operation of most camcorders is straightforward, it is helpful to understand some of the technicalities of video. This section explains the significance of a specification, how to read it and make comparisons with other models. It also shows how to care for your equipment to ensure trouble-free shooting. And it maps out the international standards that affect the playing of video tapes around the world. Finally, the glossary explains a wide range of technical terms and professional jargon that you will come across in video making.

When selecting and using equipment, it is important to understand the meanings of the terms used so you can get the best out of your equipment and compare it to other models. Standard features are mixed with specific details in the 'hybrid' specifications described here, in order to illustrate their meaning in terms of how they affect the video maker in practice.

LENSES SPECIFICATIONS

A typical specification for a lens might read $f1.4$; f = 9–54mm; 6:1 power zoom; diameter 52mm.

● THE f NUMBER describes the maximum aperture of a lens. The lower this number, the more light that is admitted to the image sensor. In practice, this partly determines the lighting conditions under which you can shoot.

● THE f NUMBERS refer to the focal lengths of the zoom lens at each end of its range.

● THE GREATER THE ZOOM RATIO, the more 'magnification' available from the (typically) 47° arc of the wide angle setting.

● LENS THREAD DIAMETER is important mainly when selecting filters to screw on to the lens; 46, 49 and 52mm are the most common.

CAMCORDER SPECIFICATIONS

● ILLUMINATION RANGE 10–100,000 LUX: This describes the range of light intensities over which the camera can work. The lower limit gives the intensity of light needed for 'acceptable' (rather than 'good') pictures, and the 10 lux here corresponds to a face illuminated at close range by a candle. The picture from a 10-lux camera becomes 'good' at about 900 lux; 100,000 corresponds to strong sunlight outdoors at noon.

● IMAGE SENSOR CCD 17mm/$\frac{2}{3}$in: The pickup device may be a tube (*Newvicon, Saticon*, etc) or a solid-state device (ie CCD or MOS). The latter is more rugged

electrically and mechanically, and in the latest models is as sensitive as the *Newvicon* tubes. The larger the sensor size (ie $\frac{2}{3}$in or 1in), the better the performance.

● SIGNAL/NOISE (S/N) RATIO 40dB: 'Noise' in a picture appears as a grain, snow or confetti effect, and is worst at low-light levels. The higher the decibel (dB) figure, the better; in normal viewing conditions, noise becomes perceptible at about 38dB S/N ratio.

● RESOLUTION 270 LINES: This indicates the maximum number of vertical black and white lines that the camera can distinguish. The greater the number quoted, the more detail in the picture. A resolution capability greater than about 300 lines is wasted in home-format recorders, which have limited bandwidth.

● VIEWFINDER ELECTRONIC 1in B/W (BLACK AND WHITE): Most camcorders have a mini-monitor built in or included as a clip-on/plug-in accessory. This shows exactly what the camera is recording and allows immediate replay of the pictures on location. It also indicates other functions, such as stop/run, low light or low battery. However, it cannot show the colour fidelity of the picture being recorded.

● WHITE BALANCE 3,200K/5,600K: Light can vary widely in colour, from the warm red of tungsten lighting to the cold blue of an overcast day. Typically, a 2-position switch sets the colour temperature to 3,200°K for artificial light and 5,600°K for outdoor conditions, while an auto-white button sets the electrical circuits of the camcorder for true white reproduction from a wide range of light sources. Check, with a colour monitor on location.

● SYNCHRONIZATION INTERNAL ONLY: The scan timing of most camcorders is governed by an internal 'clock'. This raises no problems when the camcorder is used in isolation. But where the outputs of more than one machine are to be mixed, the second and subsequent camcorders need a 'genlock' facility, indicated by an 'external sync-in' socket (*see p. 137*).

● POWER REQUIREMENT 9.6V DC. 8W: The voltage (V) quoted will match that of the supplied battery or mains power unit. It becomes significant when you want to run the camcorder from an external source, such as a car or boat battery. Equipment rated for 12–14V can be operated direct from a 12V car battery or battery belt. For camcorders with a lower rating (eg 6V, 8.5V or 9.6V), you must use a suitable adaptor to reduce the voltage.

The wattage (W) figure shows how energy-hungry the camcorder is – the lower the figure, the longer a given battery will last, Excessive use of the auto focus, auto zoom, pause button and tape rewind will run down the battery.

● AUTO FOCUS: Two types are in general use. Infra-red auto focus uses a triangulation system, 'bouncing' an invisible light beam from the object in view. The alternative system is the TTL (through the lens) image-sensing by a CCD array. This system is less liable to be confused by such surfaces as windows and mirrors.

● NEG-POS: This facility allows all brightness and colour characteristics to be reversed, so you can make positive pictures from colour negatives, and create special effects.

● REMOTE CONTROL: In some cases, remote control facilities are provided to and from a camcorder. These systems will only work between matching equipment from the same manufacturer.

● WEIGHT/SIZE: For transportation, the lighter and smaller the camera, the better. For use, balance and convenience are more important factors, particularly relevant when hand-holding the camcorder.

● STANDARD: This matches the broadcast system in the country in which the camcorder is sold. International standards become relevant here (*see p. 212*).

● FORMAT: This describes the type of cassette and its maximum playing time.

● LP: Many camcorders offer a choice

between SP (standard play) and LP (long play). Where possible, stock enough tapes to shoot SP mode – it gives better quality reproduction.

● FLYING ERASE HEAD: This describes an erase head that is mounted alongside the read/write heads on the spinning head drum. It gives clean edits, with no electronic disturbance.

AUDIO SPECIFICATIONS

● SIGNAL/NOISE RATIO 47dB: Noise on a video sound track appears as hiss and hum in the background. Depending on the circumstances of recording *and* listening, video noise becomes noticeable at 40–45dB ratio. The best audio performance (typical S/N 80dB) comes from Video 8 and VHS Hi-Fi equipment.

● INPUT/OUTPUT LEVELS: Zero decibels (dB) represents about 0.75V. Each 6dB below this point represents a *halving* of the signal voltage. A microphone delivers typically 500 microvolts (−62dB). To exchange audio signals between two pieces of equipment, an approximate match between their dB levels is required. An attenuator is used to reduce a level.

● FREQUENCY RESPONSE 200Hz–15KHz: The wider the range, the better. The low-frequency response of a Video 8 camcorder has been deliberately curtailed to suppress lens-motor and handling noises.

TAPE SPECIFICATIONS

● RUNNING TIME: In VHS, the 'type' figure gives the SP (standard play) running time in minutes, preceded by 'E' for Europe (ie a 3-hour tape is E180) or 'T' for the USA/Canada.

For Video 8 tapes, the first letter indicates the material (P for metal powder, E for metal-evaporated type). The next figure indicates the system (5 for Europe, 6 for USA). And the final two figures give the SP running time in minutes. Thus, P590 is a metal-powder, European-system tape with a running time of 90 minutes.

TROUBLE-SHOOTING

Many problems that arise in video equipment are due to human error or simple forgetfulness, rather than to failure of the equipment itself. This checklist gives several commonly encountered problems and their possible causes and solutions.

PICTURE TROUBLES

● NO PICTURES: Lens cap on; camcorder not switched on; battery flat or power not connected. Check all these.

● GRAINY PICTURE, WASHED-OUT COLOUR: Insufficient light, so increase if possible – about 900 lux is the minimum desirable.

● BURNT-OUT HIGHLIGHTS: Pale areas overexposed in strong sunlight, so adjust the iris manually and fit a neutral density filter, if necessary.

● DIM 'FLAT' PICTURES: Condensation in lens, so leave camcorder in a warm (not hot) place until dew has cleared. This problem can also be due to iris, fader or sensitivity controls being wrongly set.

● SPOTTY FLICKERING PICTURE OR 'SNOW' EFFECT: Dirty video heads, so use a cleaning tape or, better still, have them hand-cleaned by an engineer. In Video 8 and VHS Hi-Fi machines, dirty heads also affect sound.

● EXCESSIVE 'DROP-OUT' AND 'SPARKLE': Tape is worn or the recorder needs servicing.

● COMET-TAILING FROM HIGHLIGHTS WHEN PANNING OR TILTING: Normally this is only present with tube-type image sensors and is solved by increasing the light level.

● PICTURE WOBBLE: If not due to unsteady camerawork, a servo fault could be present, in which case call an engineer.

● GEOMETRIC DISTORTION: Camcorder is too near a magnetic field, such as a transformer or loudspeaker, so reposition.

● COLOUR CAST: Use the correct white-balance setting, or auto balance. Sometimes, the hue cannot be corrected within the camera, typically on teleciné-transfer or in difficult light conditions; a colour correction filter may help.

● GREENISH TINT TO INDOOR PICTURES: May be due to the effect of fluorescent lighting, in which case use an appropriate filter (eg violet).

● AUTO WHITE BALANCE NOT WORKING: Insufficient ambient light, so increase the lighting level. Another cause could be that the white balance is beyond its correction range (eg shooting the intense red light from a bonfire), but a colour correction filter will improve the situation.

● NO COLOUR ON REPLAY: TV incorrectly tuned, so retune.

● STATIONARY SPOTS OR LINES ON PICTURE: Foreign bodies on the lens are defocused and rotate or move with lens action, so clean the surface with photographic tissue. A sharply defined blemish is usually due to damage at the sensor faceplate. Prolonged exposure to strong white light, with the camcorder operating, can sometimes 'heal' a damaged faceplate in the case of tube sensors.

● DEGRADED PICTURES AND/OR SOUND ON COPIES: Some deterioration is unavoidable, but it can be minimized by (1) using high-grade tapes; (2) getting the best possible standard in the first generation or original recording; (3) connecting the camcorder to the VCR by audio and video leads, rather than by radio frequency (RF) leads; (4) ensuring that both machines are in top condition.

● INSTABILITY OF PICTURE AT EDIT POINTS: Ensure that the VCR being used as the edit recorder has a backspace or an insert edit facility for smooth transitions.

● HORIZONTAL BARS OF 'SNOW' ON PICTURE: Adjust tracking control. If there is no improvement, have the machine serviced. These 'noise' bars are normal during the 'search' (cue and review) operation.

● PICTURE ROLLS VERTICALLY: Check if the TV has an adjustable vertical-hold control. See if cleaning the heads improves matters. If not, get a professional service.

● AUTO FOCUS NOT WORKING: Auto-focus window may be dirty or obscured by your hand. With a 'difficult' subject (*see p. 20*), rely on manual focusing.

● FOCUS CHANGES WITH ZOOMING OPERATION: Set up focus at the full zoomed-in position.

SOUND TROUBLES

● EXCESSIVE HANDLING/LENS MOTOR NOISE: With a built-in or a camcorder-mounted microphone, handling and operation sounds are transferred directly via the camcorder body. The problem is aggravated in quiet surroundings by the action of the automatic gain control (AGC) circuit, which turns up the level of the sound channel. Minimize handling noise or, better still, use an auxiliary microphone.

● WIND NOISE OUTDOORS: Fit a foam-rubber sleeve or shield around the microphone and hold it in a sheltered position to the leeside of the camcorder.

● HOWLING NOISE OR OSCILLATION: 'Howl round' is picked up when the recording mic is too close to the TV loudspeaker. Turn the TV sound down completely.

● 'WOW' OR PITCH CHANGE AT EDIT POINTS: This is sometimes inevitable in the copying/editing (tape-to-tape) process. Professional servicing of both camcorder and VCR will minimize it.

● LOW MUFFLED SOUND, HIGH BACKGROUND NOISE: Clean the audio heads.

● SOUND IS EITHER WEAK AND NOISY, OR LOUD AND DISTORTED AFTER COPYING/EDITING: Interchange levels are wrong. Use an attenuator to reduce excessive signal voltage level.

OPERATIONAL TROUBLES

● CAMCORDER NOT FUNCTIONING: Dew condensation; battery flat, power unit not plugged in or switched on; no tape in machine. Check all these items.

● NO TAPE MOTION OR JUMPS TO REWIND OR FAST FORWARD: In excessive light, the camcorder's tape-end sensors are triggered into stopping the tape. Decrease the amount of light.

● SHORT BATTERY OPERATION: Excessive use of auto zoom, auto focus, pause and stop/start controls; battery not fully charged or worn out; low ambient temperature; internal presets may require adjustment by an engineer. Check all these items. For prolonged operation on location, it is best to use a battery belt or a car-cord, if practical.

● NO RECORD FUNCTION: Check that the safety tab on cassette has not been removed.

● STOPS DURING FAST FORWARD/REWIND: Check that the counter memory or tape index switch is off.

● ALWAYS STOPS AT WELL-DEFINED POINT IN TAPE: Damaged tape is triggering the tape-end sensors to stop. Discard tape.

● NO REWIND OR FAST FORWARD: Tape is already at the beginning or end.

● CASSETTE CANNOT BE REMOVED FROM THE COMPARTMENT: On some models, this will be the case if the battery is exhausted.

● THE PLAYBACK PICTURE IS UNCLEAR: The recording was underexposed or out of focus.

● LONG DELAY BEFORE USE IN 'DEW' CONDITION: Use mains power unit where applicable; many camcorders are fitted with head-heaters that operate only from the mains power unit.

● EQUIPMENT MALFUNCTION OR FAILURE TO RESPOND TO CONTROLS: All modern equipment is internally controlled by microprocessor chips. Sometimes, their internal programs can become disordered by interference on power lines, local static changes, etc. This can normally be overcome by resetting the program – disconnect all power sources for a few seconds, then reconnect and switch on in the normal way.

● CAMCORDER SWITCHES ITSELF OFF AFTER A FEW MINUTES IN PAUSE OR STOP: This is normal, a design feature for power-saving.

CARING FOR YOUR EQUIPMENT

Video equipment is expensive, so it is clearly worth taking certain precautions to protect it from damage and possible breakdown. Some useful hints and ground rules are summarized below.

GENERAL CARE
● Shield the equipment against dust, sand, foreign bodies, rain and salt spray. If shooting in wet conditions, a camera raincoat will protect both you and the camera. For frequent and prolonged shooting in such situations, it is worth investing in a splashproof housing for the camcorder.
● When storing or transporting equipment in damp or humid conditions, place bags of silica gel inside the equipment case to absorb atmospheric humidity. The bags can be reactivated by heating them in an oven.
● Always protect the equipment from bumps and shocks while in transit. Keep it in a sturdy hard case, each item fitted into a shaped nest cut out of the foam lining.
● Do not leave video gear exposed in a vehicle. Not only does this invite theft but, on a hot day, it can lead to electrical failure, tube deterioration or distortion of the plastic casing.
● Never attempt to dismantle, lubricate, repair or internally clean your video equipment; you risk damaging or contaminating it. Always have your equipment serviced by professionals.
● Clean the outside of equipment with a damp cloth; if you must use a cleansing agent, use the mildest of detergents. Abrasives and solvents will damage surfaces and printed legends.
● To protect yourself and the camcorder, don't operate it from mains (line) power during severe electrical storms. Stop shooting outdoors when there is lightning.
● For long-term equipment storage, the optimum temperature is 20°C to 30°C. Store the battery separately.
● Always switch off before changing batteries and when connecting accessories.

● Ensure proper cooling, and avoid overheating, by keeping ventilation slots clear.
● Never pick up or carry the camcorder by its viewfinder.
● Replace any blown fuses with the exact type specified.
● Always ensure that you are using the correct voltage and polarity with external power sources. Excessive voltage or reversed connections can 'blow' the electrics.

CARING FOR LENSES
● Never point the camera directly into the sun or a bright light at close quarters. It can permanently damage a tube-type sensor or the lens components of a CCD/MOS device. Tube sensors are also vulnerable to 'burn-in' if you are shooting a fixed bright scene for many hours; an image can be permanently burnt into the tube.
● Keep the lens cap on when not shooting. Image sensors can be damaged by excessive light even when the camera is off.
● Use a UV filter to protect the lens and clean with a blower brush and lens tissue.
● Avoid turning the focus ring during auto-focus shooting. It strains the motor and wastes battery power. Similarly, do not impede the action of the motor zoom or keep its button depressed at the zoom end.

CARING FOR CAMCORDERS
● Make sure that the camcorder casing is not getting too hot when shooting close to an operational video lamp.
● Keep the viewfinder lens out of direct sun, which will damage the rubber and plastic surfaces inside.
● Clean the viewfinder screen with cotton buds on sticks.
● With tube-type image sensors, it is important to avoid any physical shocks when the lens is pointing downward; particles can get deposited on the internal target areas.
● Do not store the camcorder unused for

more than about 6 months, otherwise the tube sensors will deteriorate. Run it for 1 to 2 hours every 6 months to prevent this.
● The most vulnerable part of a camcorder is its cassette housing. When inserting a cassette, make sure it is face-up, flap forward and of the correct type. If the machine will not accept it, check for obstructions, then consult an engineer Never force a cassette in − you will not solve the problem, only cause expensive damage.
● Never re-insert cassettes containing polluted, chewed or creased tape. You can damage the heads or block them.
● It is rarely necessary to clean the heads if the tapes you use are in good condition. Only use a head-cleaning tape when there is evident deterioration of the picture and sound, and then follow implicitly the cleaner-manufacturer's instructions. An annual clean-and-service by a dealer or engineer is recommended.

CARING FOR TAPES
● Metal-detectors and modern X-ray surveillance equipment, as used at air and sea ports, will *not* harm magnetic tapes or their recorded material.
● Keep tapes away from strong sunlight, magnetic influences (eg transformers), direct heat and dusty or humid environments. When a cassette is not in the machine, it should be protected in its box.
● Before storing a partially used cassette, it is wise to fast-wind it fully forward, then back. This equalizes the tape's tension.
● Tapes should be stored upright in their containers, at room temperature in a dry dust-free environment.
● If tapes have been damaged by mishandling, they can be spliced, provided the correct equipment is used. Do not use makeshift tools − the join you make can damage the recorder heads. Good commercial splicers for home use are now available, but there will inevitably be some visual disturbance at the join.

CARING FOR BATTERIES
● Portable video batteries will last their full lifespan (2 to 4 years) only if they are carefully looked after. Follow the manufacturer's instructions on charging and storage. In particular, avoid overcharging, for example by too much 'topping up' of a partly exhausted battery.
● Never use a video battery for running other equipment. However, a battery-belt pack can power a portable video lamp.
● Do not short-circuit the battery terminals.
● Store lead-acid batteries charged, and nickel-cadmium batteries discharged, in a cool place. Charge batteries fully one day before use.
● Dispose of 'dead' batteries, but *never* burn them.

CARING FOR LAMPS
● Avoid using video lamps in wet conditions. One drop of water on the bulb is sufficient to make it explode.
● During replacement or use, do not touch the bulb with bare fingers (always wear cotton gloves) to ensure the bulb's maximum life.
● After bulb failure, replace the fuse; even if it is not blown, it will have been stressed.
● Continually turning the lamp on and off will shorten the bulb's life considerably. Only turn off the lamp if breaks in shooting are likely to exceed 10 minutes.

SECURITY OF EQUIPMENT
● Insure your video equipment against theft and damage. Check the exact terms of the policy, which will not usually cover wear and tear.
● To aid detection of theft, use an ultra-violet marker pen to inscribe all equipment with your address, including post or zip codes.
● When travelling, always carry equipment as hand luggage and take a copy of the original purchase receipts with you for customs purposes.

INTERNATIONAL STANDARDS

There are several types of video standards in use throughout the world. These standards affect the playback of video tapes that have been recorded or purchased in another country. The map shows the global distribution of each standard and the chart summarizes their compatibility. For more detail on specific countries and offshore islands, you should refer to their local embassy, consulate or tourist office.

In general, the compatibility of video hardware is the same as for video tapes, so long as the mains voltage requirement is satisfied (*see below*). In some cases, however, the link to local equipment may have to be made via 'baseband' audio and video leads, rather than by aerial sockets, to avoid difficulty with transmission bands and sound-carrier spacing. These standards are defined by a letter (G, I or M) in the equipment specification.

Most camcorders sold in Europe have a concealed G/I sound switch in the RF converter/modulator, which permits their use with TV sets in the UK, Ireland, Hong Kong and South Africa (system I), as well as in western Europe and some Middle Eastern countries. Video 8 hardware, thus equipped, will work with TV sets in all the 625/50 areas shown on the map opposite, except in Argentina and Uruguay.

For those who travel widely, several multi-standard (ie PAL, SECAM and NTSC) homebase VCRs are made, primarily intended for markets in the Middle East. These machines are not usually designed for System I operation, however, which restricts their use in the UK, Ireland, Hong Kong and South Africa. Conversion of these machines (and single-standard machines) can be undertaken by specialist workshops where it is economically viable. Equipment manufacturers can usually put you in contact with such specialists.

A multi-standard or imported, purpose-designed video recorder will re-play tapes recorded in an 'incompatible' country, but it is important to understand that the standards for colour and scanning rate are not changed during replay or record. A suitably equipped TV set (multi-standard or purpose-designed) is also required.

A cheaper and simpler way of viewing tapes in the 'X' (or 'no results') and B/W (black and white) categories of the chart is to have them transcribed and standards-converted by a facilities house, many of which advertise regularly in video magazines. In general, 'home movies' can be converted, but not commercially produced or broadcast programmes, which carry a copyright.

Video on holiday: A battery-operated camcorder will, of course, work anywhere in the world. And you can replay material via its earpiece and built-in viewfinder/monitor.

Difficulties can arise, however, when you want to replay the tape on a local TV set. There may also be problems with local power sources and battery-charging. Where applicable, avoid such problems by using a 'car-cord' adaptor to run the camcorder whenever you are within range of your car or boat, thus avoiding the need to run down the portable battery.

Some video manufacturers offer a battery-charger accessory to work from the car/boat cigar-lighter socket. In other cases, it is necessary to recharge batteries or operate equipment from local mains supplies.

Mains (line) voltage supplies: Before going abroad, always check with the relevant embassies about the mains voltage supply in operation, since there may be local variations. Generally, the countries of the world divide into two groups as far as domestic AC mains voltage supplies are concerned.

● Low-voltage countries (110–127V) tend to follow the NTSC 525/60 areas of the map.

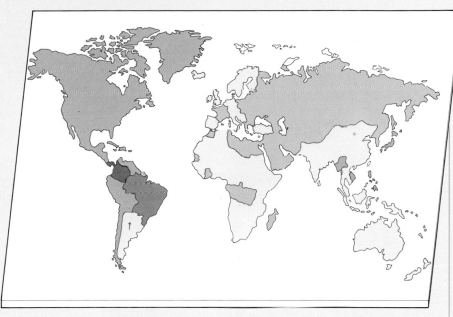

OK				
B/W	OK			
X	X	OK		
X	X	B/W	OK	
X	X	B/W	B/W	OK

▢ 625/50 PAL

▨ 625/50 SECAM

▨ 525/60 NTSC

▨ 525/60 PAL

▨ 525/60 SECAM

The several types of video standards in use around the world are summarized in the map (*above*). Their compatibility for global tape swapping are explained in the chart (*right*), to be read across and down the squares.

COMPATIBILITY KEY
B/W = replay in black and white only.
OK = tapes are compatible.
X = no results.
● = compatible with Video 8 tapes.
† = B/W OK; colour depends on design of the VCR.

● High-voltage countries (220–240V) largely correspond with PAL and SECAM 625/50 areas on the map.

AC frequency may be 50Hz or 60Hz, but this is unimportant for chargers and power units, all of which can cope with either rate. What is essential is that the voltage supply matches the rating of the equipment to be plugged in.

Virtually all power supplies and chargers for portable video equipment are capable of working on either voltage range. Some require adjustment of a voltage selector on the rear panel – but *unplug first*. Remember also that mains-driven video lights are not adaptable between high- and low-voltage supplies.

An increasing trend is toward 'universal' designs which work over the range 100–240V without adjustment. Before plugging in, be sure – check the rating plate. Incorrect operating voltage can irreparably damage video equipment.

Mains plugs differ between countries. The UK and Ireland use a 3 rectangular-pin system, whereas 2-pin connectors are common elsewhere. In Europe, mains plugs take the form of 2 round pins and, in the USA and Canada, they are a pair of flat blades. Suitable adaptors are available.

GLOSSARY

ACCESSORY SHOE: Metal slot on top of some camcorders to which you can attach a microphone or small video lamp.

AMBIENT SOUND: Prevailing atmospheric sounds of any location.

ANGLE OF VIEW: The angle seen by the lens. The zoom lens of most camcorders typically varies from 40–50° at the widest angle to 8–10° at the narrowest telephoto angle.

APERTURE: Adjustable opening (called the iris diaphragm) that controls the amount of light reaching the camcorder's image sensor. Calibrated in f-stops.

ASPECT RATIO: The fixed format of the TV screen: 4 parts wide to 3 parts high.

ASSEMBLE EDIT: Method of electronic editing that involves copying material from the recorded tape on to another, blank tape so that shots can be rearranged, or assembled, into coherent sequences. *See* insert editing, tape-to-tape editing.

AUDIO-DUB: Control that allows you to record or replace sounds on tape without disturbing the original pictures.

AUTOMATIC GAIN CONTROL (AGC): Electronic circuit that automatically controls the audio or video input levels during recording.

AUXILIARY MICROPHONE: Any separate mic that can be plugged into the camcorder to replace its built-in mic. *See* cardioid, clip-on, gun, omnidirectional mics.

BACKLIGHT: A lamp set slightly behind and above the subject to give a rim of light around the edges, creating depth by separating the subject from the background.

BACKLIGHT COMPENSATOR (BLC): A control to open up the aperture when shooting into the light, so as to give correct exposure to the foreground.

BACKSPACING: A feature present in most camcorders, whereby the tape is automatically rewound for a short section when the machine is paused and then wound on by the same amount when the machine is restarted. This ensures disturbance-free edits between recordings, but means that a second or two at the start of a recording is lost.

BATTERY BELT: High-capacity batteries worn as a belt to give extended shooting time.

BETAMAX: ½in video cassette format, developed by Sony.

'BLACKING' A TAPE: A method of laying a new control track on a tape to prepare it for insert editing. Shoot with the lens cap on to get a recording with no pictures.

BOOM: A long pole (also called a 'fishpole') to which a microphone can be attached to get as close as possible to the sound source. It should be held out of shot.

BOUNCED LIGHT: A form of indirect lighting, where a lamp's beam is directed toward a large reflective surface (eg pale walls or ceilings) to reflect light back on to the subject, creating soft even illumination.

BROAD-BEAMED LAMP: Produces a powerful flood of diffused light (3,200°K) from a linear, quartz-halogen bulb housed horizontally in front of diffusing reflectors.

'BURNT OUT': Describes an image that has been so overexposed that all detail is lost and colours are bleached out.

CAPTION GENERATOR: Can be built in to the camcorder or purchased as an optional extra. It produces lettering and numbers in different colours and sizes, which can be superimposed over the image on screen. May also have stopwatch and dating functions.

CARDIOID MICROPHONE: Auxiliary mic that picks up sound in a heart-shaped pattern (ie primarily from one direction).

'CLEAN' EDITS: Cutting or edit points where the synchronizing pulses are in step, so there is no electronic disturbance in the picture, ie the edits are 'invisible'.

CLIP-ON MICROPHONE: A small unobtrusive auxiliary mic that is clipped to the lapel or tie of the speaker. Ideal for recording speech at close quarters, but beware of clothes rustle.

CLOSE-UP LENS: A supplementary lens that magnifies the image and allows you to focus even closer than the minimum focus distance of the zoom lens.

COLOUR TEMPERATURE: Measures (in ° Kelvin) the colour of light emitted from a light source. Sources have different temperatures and hence different colours. Important when mixing natural and artificial light.

COMMENTARY: Narration that is specially written and timed to fit with the edited pictures to give additional information about the subject.

COMPATIBILITY: Relates to the playing back of video tapes and is dependent on, eg, a country's broadcast system and the tape format used.

CONTINUITY: Ensuring consistency of detail from shot to shot, including lighting, clothes, make-up and props. *See* eyeline, line of action, screen direction.

CONTRAST RANGE: Ratio between the brightest and darkest parts of a subject. Video operates best over a low-contrast range.

CONTROL TRACK: Made up of synchronizing pulses that are laid down during recording on a track, usually along the edge of the tape. This controls the accuracy of playback speed.

'CRABBING': Moving sideways in an arc around a stationary subject or across the action. The smoothest crabbing (also called 'trucking') shots are obtained with a dolly.

CUT-AWAY SHOT: Additional shot of some subsidiary action related to the main subject and used to link 2 separate shots of the main action. Can also be inserted between shots to avoid a jump cut.

CUT-IN SHOT: Additional shot showing a detail of main subject and used as an insert between 2 related shots to draw attention or maintain continuity.

DEPTH OF FIELD: The range of distances over which a scene is in sharp focus. This will vary with the aperture and focal length (eg the wider the aperture, the greater the depth of field; the longer the focal length, the shallower the depth of field).

DEW LIGHT: A warning light signalling condensation inside the camcorder.

DIFFUSED LIGHT: A form of direct lighting created by scattering light from a lamp with a diffuser (wire gauze, tracing paper) to give a gentle even effect, with reduced contrast and soft shadows.

DOLLY: A mobile shooting platform or set of wheels on which the camera and tripod are mounted to get smooth shots of moving subjects or stationary objects. 'Crabbing' and 'tracking' are types of dolly shots.

DUBBING: Part of the editing process, which involves copying various sounds (including original track) on to a tape via a sound mixer to form the finished track.

'DUTCH TILT' SHOT: Composition where the subject is set at a deliberate angle to the horizon to give the shot a dynamic framing.

8MM: *See* Video 8.

EDITING: The arranging of pictures and sound into meaningful sequences that have visual sense and flow. *See* assemble, in-camera, insert, tape-to-tape editing.

EDIT CONTROLLER: Machine placed between the camcorder and edit VCR that allows you to control both machines to fix edit points with precision. Edits can also be previewed before recording.

EDIT RECORDER: The VCR used to record the edited version of the original tape. Called the 'master' machine.

EYELINE: Describes the direction in which a person is looking across screen. To retain continuity, successive shots of people talking to each other should have matching eyelines, ie one person looking off-screen left, the other off-screen right.

f-STOPS: Numbers that refer to the size of the aperture.

FADE: Progressive increase or decrease in picture brightness or sound volume. Used creatively to change scenes or indicate time passing.

FILL LIGHT: Any lamp placed on the opposite side to the main light source (key light) to fill in shadows and lift the lighting level.

FILTER: Transparent material (glass, plastic or gelatin) used to change or modify light passing through it. Can be used to correct or balance colour, and for special effects.

FLAG: Lighting accessory of opaque material (wood or card) used to control a light beam.

FLUORESCENT LIGHTING: Has a high colour temperature and gives a bluish-green cast, which can be overcome with appropriate filters (eg violet). Can also pulse or flicker on screen.

FOCAL LENGTH: The distance from the optical centre of the lens to the surface of the image sensor, with the lens focused on infinity. In practice, a lens with short focal length is a wide angle; a long focal length is a telephoto; a variable focal length is a zoom.

FOLLOW FOCUS: Adjusting focus manually to keep a subject in sharp focus as it moves toward or away from camera.

FORMAT: Design of the video cassette and its tape. *See* Betamax, VHS, Video 8.

GELS: Filters, made of gelatin, that are placed over lamps to adjust their colour temperature (also called 'blues') or to give special effects.

GENLOCK FACILITY: Electronic circuitry that generates 'master' synchronizing pulses and locks or enslaves other video sources (eg 2 cameras) to it, to ensure disturbance-free recordings. Useful for multi-camera coverage.

GOBO: Lighting accessory of opaque material with cut-out sections, used to cast shadow patterns on a subject or background.

GUN MICROPHONE: Auxiliary mic with highly directional pickup area and narrow angle of receptivity. Also known as a 'rifle' mic.

HEAD DRUM: A rapidly rotating drum, set at an angle, around which the tape is wound. The recording heads are mounted on it.

'HEADROOM': Space left between the top of a person's head and the upper frame.

HELICAL SCAN: Diagonal laying down of video signals on tape during recording.

HIGHLIGHTS: Brightest parts of image.

'HOWL ROUND': Loud high-pitched sound that occurs when, eg, a camcorder is recording while connected to a nearby TV whose volume is not turned down.

IMAGE SENSOR: Electronic device on to which the image seen by the lens is focused. It converts light into electronic signals to produce the picture information. Can be a photoconductive tube or solid-state chip (CCD or MOS).

IN-CAMERA EDITING: Shooting shots and sequences in the order you want them to appear in the final programme, ie editing as you shoot.

INSERT EDITING: Adding new pictures into an already edited tape without disturbing the control track, using a camcorder or VCR with insert edit facilities. Greater precision is got with an edit controller.

IRIS: A ring of overlapping metal leaves that controls the amount of light entering the lens through the aperture and hence controls exposure.

JUMP CUT: An edit between 2 successive shots that causes an unaccountable break in continuity, usually of action, position or time. To avoid, change the camera angle or size of the second shot, or insert a cut-away between similar shots.

KEY EFFECTS: Cutting one image into another on screen, especially lettering, using a special effects generator.

KEY LIGHT: Lamp providing the main directional source of lighting, placed in front and to one side of the subject.

'KEYSTONING': Visual distortion of perspective caused by the camcorder not being positioned at 90° to the subject (eg a transparency projected on a screen).

LINE OF ACTION: An imaginary line representing the direction of a moving subject. For visual continuity, successive shots must be taken from one side only of this line, allowing 180° coverage, otherwise screen direction is reversed. *See* neutral shot, screen direction.

LOGGING A TAPE: Listing the pictures and sounds of a recorded tape prior to editing, by noting the contents of each shot and its number on the tape counter.

'LOOKING SPACE': Space left in front of a subject who is looking or pointing off-screen, to aid composition and screen direction. Always position subject to one side of frame, with space ahead, in direction of look.

LOW-LIGHT CONTROL: Used in poor lighting conditions to boost the video signal electronically. Gives 'acceptable' results.

LUMINANCE: The brightness or intensity of a light source. Also, part of the video signal carrying data about image brightness.

LUX: Measure of illumination at a surface. Used to indicate the sensitivity of a camcorder's system to light.

MACRO SETTING: A setting on most zoom lenses for very close range shooting of details and small-scale objects.

MASTER SHOT: The widest shot of a sequence that establishes the whole scene and captures all the action in one continuous recording. A 'safety' shot, useful for editing purposes.

MONITOR: The TV is used as a viewing monitor. A small, portable, battery-run monitor is useful on location for instant checking of colour and exposure.

MONOPOD: A collapsible, one-legged support useful for steadying a hand-held camcorder in, eg, tight corners and crowded places.

NEUTRAL DENSITY (ND) FILTER: Grey filter that reduces the intensity of light in an overbright scene, without changing colour balance. Also reduces depth of field.

NEUTRAL SHOT: A head-on shot of a subject, with no evident screen direction. By inserting it between 2 successive shots taken from opposite sides of the line of action, you can change screen direction and retain continuity.

'NODDIES': Cut-away shots of an interviewer's visual responses (nodding, smiling); useful for inserting during editing for continuity.

'NOISE': Any interference to the video signals, manifested as, eg, hiss or hum on sound track, or snow or graininess on pictures.

NTSC: The TV colour system, laid down by the National Television Standards Committee, used in the USA, Canada and Japan, and in parts of South America and Asia.

OMNIDIRECTIONAL MICROPHONE: Auxiliary mic with the widest angle of receptivity, picking up sounds from all directions.

PAL: Phase Alternate Line, the TV colour system used in western Europe (except for France) and other parts of the world including Australia, India, China, Argentina, Brazil and most of Africa.

PANNING: Moving the camcorder through a horizontal arc. With a moving subject, pan ahead to leave 'walking room'.

PHOTOFLOOD LAMP: Produces diffused light (3,400°K) over a wide area and softens the edges of shadows.

PICKUP RANGE: Distance over which a microphone is receptive to sound. The more directional the mic, the greater its pickup range.

POLARIZING FILTER: Light-grey filter that eliminates reflections in glass and water, and reduces glare from shiny surfaces. Also intensifies sky colours and clouds.

PRE-FOCUS: To ensure sharp focus of a subject (including during zooming), zoom in first and focus on a detail, then pull back and the subject will remain in focus. Also describes setting up focus in advance on an area before the action occurs.

PULL FOCUS: *See* throw focus.

QUARTZ LAMP: Produces a concentrated light (3,200°K) that can be flooded or spotted by moving the bulb in relation to the lamp's housing.

RF LEAD: Radio frequency connection that carries the video and audio signals from the camcorder to the aerial socket of the TV receiver.

'RECCE': Short for reconnaissance, a detailed survey of a shooting location.

RECORDING HEADS: Pictures are recorded by heads mounted on the head drum. They convert the electronic signals from the image sensor into magnetic pulses and 'write' these helically on the tape to give the video data. Sound is recorded in a linear strip by a fixed head, or in hi-fi models, by heads mounted on the drum so that the audio signals are encoded within the video track.

REMOTE CONTROL UNIT: A connection lead or infra-red control that allows you to operate the camcorder's main functions from some distance away.

REVERBERATION: The time taken for a sound to die away. Indoor locations especially, with many reflective surfaces, can be acoustically 'live' and produce multiple short echoes that reduce audibility.

REVERSE ANGLE SHOT: Often used in dialogue scenes, where one shot is followed by its complementary view so the two form a natural pair (eg speaker, then listener).

RIM LIGHTING: Placing a lamp behind a subject to give a rim of light around the edge.

ROSTRUM CAMERA: Set-up of camcorder/tripod for shooting stills material (eg photos, captions) on a wall or table, lit with an even flood of light from 2 lamps at 45° to the subject.

RULE OF THIRDS: A guide for composing shots, with strong vertical and horizontal elements balanced in an imaginary grid.

SCREEN DIRECTION: General direction of movement within the frame. For continuity, it must be consistent from shot to shot.

SCRIPT: Written formulation of a video's planned contents. Different formats used for documentaries and dramas.

SCROLL: Movement of a title or caption up or down the screen. Can be done with a caption generator or a computer.

SECAM: *Séquential Couleur à Mémoire*, 'Sequential Colour with Memory', the French TV colour system, also used in the USSR, eastern Europe, most of the Middle East and parts of Africa.

SEQUENCE: Autonomous series of shots, linked thematically or temporally.

SPECIAL EFFECTS GENERATOR (SEG): Electronic device that processes video signals to produce a variety of effects (eg wipes, superimpositions, key effects).

SHOT: Individual recording of a single subject. Can be of various sizes (eg long, mid or close-up shots) and types (eg low angle, top shot).

SHOT PLAN: Graphic representation of camera positions and order of shooting for a scene in a drama video.

SNOOT: Metal cone used to restrict the light beam from a lamp.

SOLARIZATION: Visual effect produced by deliberate overexposure of an image.

SOUND MIXER: Unit that enables audio signals from more than one source to be blended together on to a single recording.

SPLIT SCREEN: A shot with 2 separate images combined in the frame; done with a special effects generator.

STANDARDS, INTERNATIONAL VIDEO: Various forms of signal encoding used by different TV systems. Material recorded on one system cannot be played back on another without conversion. *See* NTSC, PAL, SECAM.

'STOP-START' SHOTS: Technique for creating simple live action animation (pixillation) by moving subjects within the frame between each recording of the same shot.

STORYBOARD: Graphic representation of the planned sequence of shooting, with a brief written description of each shot's action, size and type.

SUPERIMPOSITION: Overlaying one image on another (eg caption or title on a background scene).

SUPPLEMENTARY LENSES: Auxiliary lenses that can be screwed on to the front of the camcorder's lens. *See* close-up lens, tele-converter, wide-converter.

TAKE: A single recording of a shot; sometimes a shot needs several 'takes' to get it right.

TAPE-TO-TAPE EDITING: System of assembling shots in desired order by copying them from the original tape in the camcorder on to a blank tape in a VCR (the edit recorder).

TELECINE TRANSFER: The copying of projected ciné film or transparencies on to video tape.

TELE-CONVERTER: Supplementary lens that can be attached to the camcorder's lens to increase magnification (by about 40%) for shooting distant subjects.

TELEPHOTO: Position of the zoom lens that gives the longest focal length, narrowest angle of view and shallowest depth of field.

THROW FOCUS: Changing focus from one subject to another within a scene. Also called 'pull' focus.

'TIGHTEN UP': Zoom in on a subject to change shot size or improve composition.

TILTING: Moving the camcorder through a vertical arc.

'TOP' SHOT: Shot taken from a high angle to show the subject from above.

TRACKING SHOT: Smooth dolly shot that follows a moving subject or moves toward or away from a stationary subject.

TRIGGER VIDEOS: Short programmes made to stimulate or promote discussion within small interest-groups.

TRIPOD HEAD: Top of the tripod on which the camcorder is mounted and which enables it to be swivelled for panning and tilting movements. A 'fluid' head gives the smoothest operation.

TUNGSTEN LIGHTING: Generic term for various forms of artificial lighting (including domestic) with a colour temperature of 3,200°K.

TWO-SHOT: Shot showing 2 people only, often used to isolate them from a group.

ULTRAVIOLET (UV) FILTER: Transparent filter that absorbs UV wavelengths to give clear shots on hazy days and for distant views.

UNIDIRECTIONAL MICROPHONE: *See* cardioid microphone.

VHS: Video Home System, developed by JVC, is the most popular video cassette format, using ½in tape. VHS-C is a compact version, developed for use in camcorders and which can be played back on standard VHS-format machines with an adaptor.

VIDEO 8: Video cassette format, developed by Sony, that uses 8mm tape in a small cassette. Capable of recording hi-fi sound and both standard and long play.

VIDEO LAMP: Portable, low-voltage, battery-powered lamp (3,200°K) that can be hand-held or clipped on to the camcorder. Also known as a 'sun gun'.

VIEWFINDER: Viewing screen built into the camcorder that allows you to view the image being recorded. An electronic viewfinder also functions as a monitor and allows playback (in black and white only) of the recorded material.

VIGNETTE: A black mask with an aperture cut into it to create a variety of shapes within the conventional screen format. The vignette is mounted in a holder attached to the front of the lens.

VISION MIXER: An electronic device that can receive signals from 2 or more sources and either combine the images or switch between them. Used with multi-camera shooting and for electronic effects.

VOICE-OVER (V/O): Part of an interviewee's speech heard over images on screen, without the person being in shot.

VOX POPS: From the Latin *vox populi*, 'voice of the people'. Short informal interviews of people's opinions that can be edited into a sequence of statements.

'WALKING ROOM': Space left ahead of a moving subject in a panning shot, to aid composition and screen direction.

WHITE BALANCE: Electronic circuitry in the camcorder that ensures the correct reproduction of colours under various lighting conditions. White balance can be set for 'daylight' or 'tungsten', or the function may be automated.

WHIP PAN: Rapid panning movement in which the subject is deliberately blurred. Used to link shots or sequences. Also known as a 'zip' or 'swish' pan.

WIDE ANGLE: Position of the zoom lens that gives the shortest focal length, the widest angle of view and the greatest depth of field.

WIDE-CONVERTER: Supplementary lens that can be attached to the camcorder's lens to increase the angle of view (by about 40%).

WIND GAG: A foam-rubber sleeve placed over a microphone's head to prevent wind noise.

WIPE: An electronic effect in which one scene progressively replaces another by moving from one edge of the frame. A 'wipe to black' involves the progressive blacking out of the screen.

'YO-YO' SHOTS: Repeated zooming in and out on a subject; to be avoided because of the discomforting effect on the viewer.

ZOOM LENS: Standard lens for most camcorders that allows focal length to be varied during a zooming shot.

ZOOMING: Varying the focal length of the zoom lens during a shot.

INDEX

Bold figures indicate principal entries.

A
accessory shoe 95, 114
acoustics 32, 78, 186, 200
action: anticipating 45, 68, 104; compressed **94**; continuity of, **48–9**, 51, 92–3, 96, 100; continuous 91, **95**, 97; following 22, 28, 144–5; high-speed 57, **94–5**; line of **48–9**, 50, 162; matched 123; parallel 122; pattern of, 90, 94
adaptor: car 14, 88, 207, 212; cigar-lighter 212; mains 88, 89; slide-copying 120, 121
aerial videos **107**
angle of view 18, 26
animals **100–5**
animation 31, 121, 146, 147
aperture **16–17**, 18, 36, 38, 116, 119, 206
architecture, *see* buildings
archive material **160–1**, 166, **170–1**
artwork: production of **112–13**; shooting of **112–14**
audience: assumptions by 51, 122; expectations 52, 123, 148, 181; needs of 56, 78, 168, 176, 192
audio-dub 15, 124, **126–7**
automatic functions, limitations of: exposure 16, 107, 120; focus 20, 105
automatic gain control (AGC) 32, 126, 209
auxiliary microphone, *see* microphone

B
background, choice of 98, 110–11, 119
backlight, *see* lighting
backlight compensator 14, **17**, 85, 94, 101, 105
backlit subject 14, 16, 59, 85, 121
backspacing 15, **57**, 93, 95
barn doors 37, 132, 133, 135
batteries 14, 201, 207, 209, 211
battery belt 88, 93, 94, 102, 207, 211
battery charger 88, 89
Betamax 15, 62
birds 101, 102
birth of child **200–1**
'blacked' tape 123
bounced light, *see* lighting,

reflected
brace, camera 28
broad-beamed lamp, *see* lamps
budget, production **187**
buffer, visual 27, 49
buildings 26, **89, 171**
bulbs: care of 37, 211; types 36–7
business presentations 146, **172–181**

C
camcorder: functions **12–15**, 202; specifications 206–7
camera movements, *see* panning, tilting, zooming
camera positions 49, 57, 67, 76–7, 79–81, 83, 92–3, 96–7, 126, 136, 156, 162
camera steadiness 28–9, 30, 66, 92, 94, 145, 161
candlelight 36, 74, 198, 206
'candid camera' shooting 68, 78, 82, 90
captions 110, 113, 114, 169, 181
caption generator 13, 66, 89, 96, **110–11**, 117, 136, 153, 162, 169, 174, 178, 189, 197, 201
car 'advertisement' 192
cassette recorder, 88, 91, 126
casting, drama 188
CCD, *see* image sensor
ceremonies **78–83**, 136–7
children **66–7**, 113, 115, 192, 202–3
ciné, *see* film
close-up lens 114, 115, 121, 192
clothing, choice of 28, 93, 160
colour: balance, *see* white balance; cast 34, 39, 118, 201, 208; nature of 34; temperature **34–5**, 36–9, 132, 206
commentary: adding **125**, 126, 127, 158, 164, 175, 176, 193; linking 158, 166, 168; running 97, 162, 179; writing **158–9**, 162
communications, business **178–9**
compatibility of tapes 212–13
composition 22, 27, **44–7**, 58–9, 60, 72, 90, 117
computer graphics **146–7**, 176
condensation 84, 208
conferences 179
confusion, visual 46, 49, 50
continuity: of action **48–9**, 60, 92–3, 96, 100; of appearances **51**, 60, 100; of eyelines **50–1**;

of screen direction **48–51**, 97, 136, 162, 188
contrast, coping with 16, 17, 34, 38–9, 84–5, 105, 121, 130, 138
control track 15, 57, 122, **123**
conversations, recording of **68–9**, 82, 193
cookie, *see* gobo
copying, problems with 62, 120, 209
copyright 124, 127, 140, 148, 184
correction filters, lamps, *see* gels
counter, tape 15, 62, 127, 141, 158, 209
'crabbing' 29, 144
credits 110, **112–13**, 114, 147, 169
crew, video **152–3**, 154, 166, 186–7; camera person 153, 189; director 152, 153, **188–9**; editor 153; interviewer 152, **154–7**; lighting person 153; production manager 152, 153, 166, 187; sound recordist 68, 92, 126, 153
cross-polarization 160
cut-aways **52–3**, 66, 122, 136, 137, 156, 162, 163, 196
cut-ins **52–3**, 54, 122, 162
cutting, *see* editing

D
dating, video **196–7**
daylight 36, **84–5**, 131
'daylight' mode 34, 35, 38–9, 131, 199
demonstration videos **162–3**, 181
depth, creating **46–7**, 58, 73, 89, 130, 156
depth of field **18–19**, 21, 26, 84, 85, 94, 101, 102, 117, 118
dew 84, 208, 209
diffusers 132, 135, 160
direction, screen 44, 45, 47, **48–51**, 55, 72, 90, 95, 148, 198; reversal of 49, 50
Disneyland 86–7
distortion, visual 26, 44, 112, 120, 160, 171
documentaries **150–71**; crew 152
dolly **144–5**
drama 51, 123, 152, **182–9**; crew 186–9
dubbing **126–7**, 160
Dutch tilt 47

E

8mm, *see* Video 8
edit controller 62, **122**, 123,
  167
editing: assemble 62; backspace
  57, 62, 95, 101, 208; creative
  122–3; in-camera **56–7**, 60,
  68, 70–3, 88, 110, 113, 116,
  121, 126, 140, 162, 163;
  insert 15, 57, 62, 73, 110,
  114, **122**, 123, 127, 136, 137,
  142, 146, 163, 208; pace of
  56, 72, **123**, 169; tape-to-tape
  56, 60, **62–3**, 88, 122, 123,
  126, 136, 141, 154, 163, 167,
  209
edit points 15, 62, 122, 141,
  209
edit recorder **62**, 122, 127, 138,
  147, 208
edits, 'clean' 15, **57**, 62, 122,
  207
electronic effects **138–9**
equipment **10–39**; care of
  210–11; faults 208–9;
  protecting 84, 89, 102,
  210–11; specifications 206–7
erotica **198–9**
eyelines **50–1**, 148, 156, 198
exposure 14, **16–17**, 24, 38, 51,
  84–5, 91, 94, 101, 105, 107,
  120, 138

F

4mm 15
f-stops 17, 206
fades 14, 76, **116**, 119, 138, 147,
  162
family occasions **70–7**
feedback **138**, 140
fill light, *see* lighting
film, transfer of **120–1**
filters: camcorder's balancing
  34; lamp, *see* gels; lens 74,
  88, **118–19**, 138, 140, 192,
  198, 201, 206, 208
filter holder 116, 117, 118
fireworks display 90, 91
flag 133, 135
flicker problems 121, 201
flow, visual **52–5**
fluid head 30, 102
fluorescent light, *see* lighting
focal length **18**, 26, 102, 144,
  206
focus: automatic 14, **20**, 105,
  145, 207, 209, 210; follow
  94, 145; manual 14, **20–1**,
  94, 95, 101, 105, 145; soft 82,
  119, 198; throw 21, 112; *see
  also* pre-focus

focus differentials 46–7
foreground 19, **46**, 82, 89
format, *see* tapes
framing **44–5**, 59, 72, 76, 104,
  115, 117, 121, 156, 160; *see
  also* composition
freeze-frame 98
friction head 30

G

gels 38–9, 69, 74, 132, 199
genlock facility 137, 147,
  206–7
glass, shots through 85, 103,
  105, 118, 160–1
gobo 131, 133
graphics tablet 147

H

hand-held camerawork **28–9**,
  30, 68, 207
haze, reducing 85, 89, 102, 107,
  118
headphones 12, 32, 58, 68, 94
headroom 27, 45
hide, shooting from a 102
hi-fi recording 15, 207
high-angle shots 31, 42, 51, 68,
  148
highlights, coping with 75, 84,
  119, 160, 208
horizontals 22, 24, 25, 31, 44,
  171
house sales **174–5**, 192
housing, camcorder **106**
'howl round' 125, 209

I

image sensor 13, 16, 20, 36, 37,
  118, 206, 210; solid-state
  chip (CCD, MOS) 13, 206,
  207, 210; tube 13, 206, 208,
  210
impressionistic shooting 87, 97,
  141
insert edit, *see* editing
insurance 89, 187, 211
intercutting shots 51, 93, 105,
  122, 123, 148, 160, 169, 170
intermittent controller 178
interviews 33, 148, 152, **154–7**,
  158, 164, 166, 168, 169, 170,
  178, 194, 196–7, 202; *see also*
  voice-over
iris 14, **16–17**, 24, 84, 90, 94;
  see also aperture, exposure

J

jump cuts **52–3**, 123, 142, 156,
  162
juxtaposition **123**, 127, 148

K

key effects 138, 139
key light, *see* lighting
keystoning 120

L

lamps **36–7**, 38, 130–5, 160,
  198, 211; broad-beamed 37,
  78, 135; photoflood 36, 82,
  114; quartz 37, 78, 82, 83;
  small video 36, 69, 78, 88,
  114; *see also* lighting
'leapfrog' ahead of action 73,
  136
lens: cap 34, 58, 84, 91, 210;
  care 210; cleaning 88, 210;
  height 31; specifications 206;
  see also angle of view
lenses, supplementary 26, 44,
  102, 115
lettering, types of 110–13
letter, video **192–3**
light, intensity of 36, 114, 206;
  nature of 34, 107
lighting, artificial **36–9**, 74–5,
  130–5, 188, 208; back 74, 77,
  82, 101, 130–1, 133, 134,
  135, 194; background 130–1;
  bounced, *see* reflected; depth
  with 47; diffused 66, 69, 83,
  130, 132, 134, 161, 170, 199;
  direct 132; domestic 37, 130,
  134–5, 198; fill 38, 75,
  130–1, 134, 135, 161;
  fluorescent 118, 201, 208;
  front 98, 134; high key 119,
  134; indirect 69, 101, 132;
  key 75, 130–1, 134, 135; low
  key 134–5, 198; mixed 38–9,
  131, 132; reflected 38–9, 66,
  74, 83, 107, 121, 130, 132,
  134–5, 162, 165; rim 131,
  135, 198; rostrum 114; safety
  37, 74, 132, 135, 198; set-ups
  74–5, 114, 130–5, 160, 194,
  198–9; silhouette 135, 198;
  top 134; *see also* daylight,
  flag, gobo, lamps, snoot
line of action, *see* action
linking shots **52–3**, 54–5, 60,
  69, 70, 72–3, 88–9, 91, 116
locations 153, 166, **186**, 188,
  200
logging a tape 62
'looking space' 44, 69
low-angle shots 42, 51, 54, **94**,
  97, 100, 148
low-level shooting 31, 66, **100**,
  193
low-light control 14, **17**, 36,
  105, 198

lux **36**, 206, 208

M

macro shooting 12, **101**, 121, 192
mains power 74, 89, 170, 179, 186, 198, 200, 207, 212–13
manual operation: focus 14, 94, 95, 101, 103, 105, 145; iris 14, 17, 24, 116, 120; white balance 14; zoom 26–7
maps 115
marker board 153, 189
markets 90, 91
master shot 76, 142, 188
microphones **32–3**, 74; boom 153; built-in 12, 32, 57, 68, 73, 124, 209; clip-on 33, 156, 163; cardioid 33, 68, 78, 83, 92, 125, 156; gun 33, 92; omnidirectional 32, 33, 75, 156; superdirectional, *see* gun; telescopic 32; unidirectional, *see* cardioid; zoom 32
mirrors, shooting in 46, 67
mixed lighting, *see* lighting
mixing sound **127**
monitor, portable 98, 102, 135, 206
monopod 31, 102
MOS, *see* image sensor
multi-camera coverage 80, **136–7**, 166, 196, 206–7
music: dubbing 126, 127, 141; playback of 140, 142; use of 87, **124**, 127, 140, 160, 164, 168, 169, 175, 176–7, 181, 192, 196, 198

N

narrative, camera 115, 161
nature studies 100–5, 113, 192
negatives, transfer of 120, 121
neg/pos facility 121, 138, 139, 198, 207
netting, shots through 105
newspapers 115
night shooting 91, 96, 135
neutral density filter 36, **85**, 94, 118, 119
neutral shot 49, 50, 72
'noise': picture 14, 17, 62, 206, 208; sound 62, 207, 208
NTSC 212–13

O

optical effects **116–17**; *see also* electronic effects, special effects
over-the-shoulder shot 42, 156

P

pace 72, **123**
'paintbox', electronic 142
paintings 115, 160–1
PAL 212–13
panning **22–3**, 27, 31, 45, 58–9, 92, 95, 107, 135; timing of 22–3, 56, 95, 115
parades 90, 91
parallel play 126
parallel action **122**, 148
parties 68–9, 74–7
'pause' mode 15, 57
performance, analysis of **194–5**
perspective 20, 26, 44, 46, 94, 144, 160, 161, 171
persuasive documentary **168–9**
photoflood, *see* lamps
photographs 115, 161, 170, 196
picture quality: loss of 36, 146, 208; variations in 136, 167
planning and preparations 30, 56, 68, 74, 76, 78, 82, 88, 92, 136, 154, 174, 200
playback: camcorder, *see* music, review facility; VCR 98, 142, 177
point-of-view shot 52, 70, 73, 198
polarizing filter **85**, 89, 105, 107, 115, 118, 119, 160
pop videos 138, **140–3**
portrait, video **164–5**, 166, 196
pre-focusing **20**, 26, 94, 100, 201
presentation 108–125, 130–5, 138–9, 146–7, 172–181
preview facility 122
product sales **176–7**
production team, *see* crew
profile shot 42, 44
programme length **56**, 62, 66, 166, 168, 174, 176, 177
projection system, video 177
promotional videos: business 142, 164, 174–7; causes 168–9; personal 196–7
props and costumes 51, 143, **187**, 195

Q

quartz lamp, *see* lamps
quartz bulb, *see* bulbs

R

RF leads 88, 208
reading time 56, 114, 158
recce, *see* locations
recording principles **15**
recurring shot 69, 76
reflected light, *see* lighting

reflections, eliminating 79, 103, 105, 115, 118, 160
reflectors **38–9**, 88, 132, 161
reflective surfaces 32, 36, 39, 85, 94, 200
remote control 102, 207
research, documentary 154, 162, 164, 166, 170
resolution 146, 147, 206
reverberation 32, 78, 186, 200
reverse angle shots **53**, 54–5, 68, 71, 73, 81, 156, 188
review facility 15, 57
rise-and-fall shots 31
rostrum shooting 79, **114–15**, 140, 160, 166, 170, 171, 196
rule of thirds **44**
rule, 180° **48–9**, 50, 162

S

safari, on 102–3, 107
safety: with lighting 37, 153; personal 103, 106; training 180–1
scheduling, production 186
scratch videos **148–9**
screen direction, *see* direction
screen shape 44, 47, 112, 115; creating new 46, 47, 117
script, documentary 163, 164, 166, 167, 168, 174, 176; drama **184–5**, 188, 189
scrolling 110, 113
SECAM 212–13
self-analysis 98–9, **194–5**, 200
self-promotion **196–7**
sense, visual **48–51**; *see also* continuity
sequences, closing, 26, 69, 73, 76, 87, 116, 164, 166, 169, 201; linking 53, 88–9, 122, 158, 166, 168, 192–3; opening 26, 72, 116, 164, 168, 185
shadows, coping with 38, 74–5, 85, 118, 130–1, 162, 165; creating 133, 135
'shooting blind' **67**, 90–1
shot lengths 22–3, 24, 27, 53, **56–7**, 63, 73, 83, 90, 114, 121, 122, 141, 158, 162, *see also* reading time; list 56, 70, 79; plan 188; sizes **42–3**, 52–3, 115, 148, 156, 162, 194; types **42**, 52, 162
signalling system 93, 94, 95
silhouette effect 85; *see also* lighting
skills analysis 181
slides, *see* transparencies
snoot 133

snow, shooting in 93, 94
solarization 138, **139**
sound **32–3**, 57, **124–7**, 179;
    computer-generated 147;
    dubbing 126–7; effects **125**,
    126, 127, 160; levels 12, 32,
    124, 125, 126, 154; live 57,
    58, 73, 86–7, 91, 94, 124,
    125, **126**, 162, 164, 166, 198;
    mixing 86, **127**; monitoring
    12, 32; separate audio
    recordings 79, 80, 82, 91,
    126, 196; test 74, 125, 154,
    179
sound baffles 186
sound mixer 124, 127, 156
special effects 36, **118–19**, 120,
    132–3, **138–9**, 140, 192, 207
special effects generator (SEG)
    137, **138**, 140, 142
spectacles, coping with 75
splicing video tape 211
sports **92–9**, 136, 137; aerial
    107; field 97; team 96–7;
    track 92–3, 97, 136, 146;
    water 97, 106–7
standards, international video
    89, 193, 207, **212–13**
statues 88
stills material: choice of 115;
    shooting of 79, **114–15**, 140,
    160–1, 171
stop-start shots 31
stopwatch captions 96, 136,
    201
storyboarding **60–1**, 79, 140–1,
    162, 163, 164, 168, 175, 176,
    188, 196
subject, choice of 58, 70, 164
superimposition 138, **139**, 147
supplementary lenses, *see* lenses
supports, camera **28–9**, 66, 68,
    103, 145

T
tapes: care 211; faults 209;
    formats 15, 62, 88, 136, 193,
    207; specifications 207;
    storage 171, 211
tape-to-tape editing, *see* editing
technical references **204–219**
teleciné transfer **120–1**
tele-converter 26, 94, 101, 102,
    103
telephoto, shooting in: depth
    of field 19, 21, 85, 94; distant
    subjects 101, 102, 103; focus
    problems 21, 25, 94; to
    isolate subject 19, 82, 94;
    panning 95; perspective 26,
    44, 94, 120, 160; steadiness

28; surreptitious shots 67, 68,
    81, 90, 100; through wire
    netting 105
three-quarters-on shot 42, 44
tilting **24–5**, 27, 31, 97, 107;
    timing of 24–5, 56
'time-lapse' video 178
time of day for shooting 89,
    107, 166, 171, 186
titles 57, 89, **110–13**, 114, 116,
    117, 138, 147, 162, 169
top shot 97
towns 89, **166–7**
tracking **144–5**, 161, 174
training videos 162, **180–1**
transcript 155
transparencies, transfer of
    120–1
travel: equipment 88, 89;
    security 89, 211; subjects
    84–91, 146
travelling shots 88, 145
tripod **30–1**, 92, 94, 100, 102,
    144
'tungsten' mode 34, 35, 39, 120

U
ultraviolet filter 84, 85, 102,
    107, 118, 210
underwater videos **106–7**

V
vehicles, shooting from 88–9,
    102–3, 145
verticals 22, 24, 44
VHS 15, 62, 207
Video 8 15, 62, 207
viewfinder 12, 34, 44, 210;
    adjustable 13, 24, 91, 178;
    electronic 13, 15, 17, 57,
    202, 206; optical 12
vignettes **117**
vision mixer **136**, 137, 138, 147
voice-over 164, 165, 166, 170,
    176, 196, 197; *see also*
    commentary
voltage transformer 89
vox pops 148, 154, 155, 168

W
'walking room' 22, 45, 58
warning lights, camcorder's 13,
    16
water, shots through 85, 118
weddings 57, **78–82**, 136, 148
whip pan 25
white balance 14, **34–5**, 38–9,
    58, 135, 206, 208; 'wrong'
    effects 34, 35, 38, 138, 199
wide angle, shooting in: to
    accentuate speed 26, 94;

camera shake 28, 107, 144;
    to dramatize 26; focus
    problems 95; groups 82, 193;
    to accommodate movements
    194, 198; surreptitious shots
    67, 90
wide angle lens 44, 69
wide-converter 26
wildlife **102–5**
wind noise 126, 209
wipes **116**, 117, 138, 139, 147
wire, shots through **105**
written material 52; *see also*
    reading time, shot length

X
X-rays 89, 193, 211

Y
'yo-yo' shots 26

Z
zip pan, *see* whip pan
zoom lens 12, **26–7**, 32, 103;
    motor 26, 210; ratio 206
zooming 18, **26–7**, 28, 144,
    156, 209; timing of 26–7, 56
zoos **104–5**

ACKNOWLEDGMENTS

Picture Credits
l = left; *r* = right; *t* = top; *c* = centre; *b* = bottom

16/17 John Foley; 19*t* John Cleare/Mountain Camera; 19*c* John Bulmer/Susan Griggs Agency; 19*b* John Bulmer; 20/24 Roland Lewis; 27 John Bulmer; 35*t* Rosenfeld/Zefa Picture Library; 35*b* Spike Powell; 38/39 Spike Powell; 43/44*t* John Bulmer; 44*b* Jonathan Bigg; 45/47 John Bulmer; 48/49 Tony Stone Associates; 50/55 John Bulmer; 56/57*l* J. Alex Langley/Aspect Picture Library; 57*r* John Gilbert/Aspect Picture Library; 58/59 John Bulmer; 63 Roland Lewis; 66 Spike Powell; 68 Peter Rauter; 69 Teasy/Zefa Picture Library; 70/71 John Bulmer; 74/76 Camera Press; 78/79 Ian Bradshaw; 82 Ted Spiegel/The John Hillelson Agency; 83*l* University of Kent; 83*r* Anthea Sieveking/Vision International; 84 Peter Miller/The Image Bank; 85*t* P. Steel/ Stockmarket-Zefa Picture Library; 85*bl* G & J Fotoservice/The Image Bank; 85*br* Camilla Jessel; 86*t* Spectrum Colour Library; 86*bl* L. Rhodes/ Daily Telegraph Colour Library; 86*br* Tony Stone Associates; 87*tl* J. Alex Langley/Aspect Picture Library; 87*tr* Robert Harding Picture Library; 87*b* Spectrum Colour Library; 88/89 Jon Hoffmann; 90 Tony Stone Associates; 90/91 B. McAllister/ The Image Bank; 91 Zefa Picture Library; 94*l* Bezard/Zefa Picture Library; 94*r* Havlicek/Zefa Picture Library; 95*l* John Kelly/The Image Bank; 95*r* Braennhage/Zefa Picture Library; 98/99*t* Peter Underwood; 99*c* Peter Frey/The Image Bank; 99*b* Ian Bradshaw; 101 Robert Harding Picture Library; 103*l* Franz J. Camenzind/Planet Earth Pictures; 103*r* Jonathan Scott/Planet Earth Pictures; 104*t* Guido Alberto Rossi/The Image Bank; 104*b*/105 John Bulmer; 106 Sony/PCL; 107/110*t* Kalt/Zefa Picture Library; 110*b* Roger Phillips; 113*t* John Bigg; 113 *c* & *b* Roger Phillips; 115 The Bridgeman Art Library; 117 John Bulmer; 118/119*l* Tony Stone Associates; 119*r* J. Alex Langley/Aspect Picture Library; 122/123 *l* to *r* John Bulmer, Jon Hoffmann, John Bulmer, Jon Hoffmann, John Bulmer, Jon Hoffmann, John Bulmer; 130/135 John Bulmer; 136 Colorsport; 136/137 Tony Stone Associates; 137 Steve Powell/All Sport; 139*t* Robert Ellis; 139*cl* P. Steel/Stockmarket-Zefa Picture Library; 139*cr* John Bulmer; 139*bl* Peter Underwood, *inset* John Bulmer; 139*br* John Bulmer, *inset* Spike Powell; 142/143 Robert Ellis; 146*t* The Communication Studio; 146*c* T.B.S. Colour Slides, Brighton; 146*b* The Communication Studio; 148*t* John Bulmer; 148*ct* Camilla Jessel; 148*cb* Robert Ellis; 148*b* John Bulmer; 149*t* John Bulmer; 149*ct* Franz J. Camenzind/Planet Earth Pictures; 149 *cb* & *b*/157 John Bulmer; 159 *t* to *b* The British Tourist Authority, Spectrum Colour Library, J. Allan Cash, Spectrum Colour Library, J. Allan Cash; 160/161 Roger Phillips; 165 Chris Jones; 169*t* Syndication International; 169*c* Dominique Gutekunst/Gamma/Frank Spooner Pictures; 169*b* Rex Features; 170 Homer Sykes; 171*l* Tony Latham;

171*r* John Cole/Network; 180 John Sturrock/ Network; 192*t* John Bulmer; 192 *c* & *b* Spike Powell; 193*t* The British Tourist Authority; 193*c* Roland Lewis; 193*b* Spike Powell; 195*tl* Sarah Ainslie; 195*tr* Alice Fursdon; 195*b* Sarah Ainslie; 199 Robert McFarlane/Susan Griggs Agency; 200/201*l* Syndication International; 200/201*r* Daisy Hayes; 202 Barbara Kreye/The Image Bank; 203 John Bulmer.

Suppliers Credits:
We would like to thank the following suppliers for the loan of these items:
p. 19: Tracksuits by Olympus Sport.
p. 110: Caption generator by JVC.
pp. 130–1: Clothes from Simpson, Piccadilly; microphone from Lion Audio.
pp. 134–5: Clothes from Simpson, Piccadilly.
p. 203: Handycam by Sony.

'Tips from the Top'
We gratefully acknowledge the following individuals, publishers and organizations for permission granted to use these quotes:
p. 28: By courtesy of Charles Stewart.
pp. 45, 60, 132: Excerpts from *A Man with a Camera* by Nestor Almendros. English translation copyright © 1984 by Nestor Almendros. Reprinted by permission of Farrar, Straus and Giroux, Inc, New York. Published in UK in 1985 by Faber & Faber, London. First published in Switzerland in 1980 by FOMA, © Nestor Almendros 1980, 1982.
p. 103: By courtesy of Maurice R. Tibbles..
p. 122: Alfred Hitchcock quote from *The Filmgoer's Book of Quotes*, by Leslie Halliwell, Grafton Books, A Division of the Collins Publishing Group, London, 1973.
p. 124: David Lynch quote from *The Elephant Man: The Book of the Film*, by Joy Kuhn, Virgin Books, W. H. Allen, London, 1980.
p. 142: Lol Creme quote from *Telegraph Sunday Magazine*, 9 July 1983.
p. 154: Ed Murrow quote from the British Broadcasting Corporation, 1955. By permission of the Ed Murrow Estate.
p. 180: By courtesy of Antony Jay, Video Arts Ltd.
p. 185: William Goldman quote from *The Craft of the Screenwriter*, by John Brady, Simon and Schuster (Touchstone Edition), New York, 1982. By courtesy of William Goldman.
p. 189: Rod Steiger quote from *The Moving Picture Book*, Copyright © 1975 by William Kuhns, Pflaum, Dayton, Ohio, 1975.
p. 189: Alan Parker quote from *Observer Magazine*, by Ray Connolly, 30 May 1982.